Masculinities, modernist fiction and the urban public sphere

Manchester University Press

Masculinities, modernist fiction and the urban public sphere

Scott McCracken

Manchester University Press
Manchester and New York

distributed exclusively in the USA by Palgrave

Copyright © Scott McCracken 2007

The right of Scott McCracken to be identified as the author of this work has been asserted by him in accordance with the Copyright, Designs and Patents Act 1988.

Published by Manchester University Press
Oxford Road, Manchester M13 9NR, UK
and Room 400, 175 Fifth Avenue, New York, NY 10010, USA
www.manchesteruniversitypress.co.uk

Distributed in the United States exclusively by
Palgrave Macmillan, 175 Fifth Avenue,
New York, NY 10010, USA

Distributed in Canada exclusively by
UBC Press, University of British Columbia, 2029 West Mall,
Vancouver, BC, Canada V6T 1Z2

British Library Cataloguing-in-Publication Data is available

Library of Congress Cataloging-in-Publication Data is available

ISBN 978 0 7190 4484 7 paperback

First published by Manchester University Press in hardback 2007

This paperback edition first published 2013

The publisher has no responsibility for the persistence or accuracy of URLs for any external or third-party internet websites referred to in this book, and does not guarantee that any content on such websites is, or will remain, accurate or appropriate.

Printed by Lightning Source

Contents

List of illustrations vii
Preface ix
Acknowledgements xiii

Introduction: masculinities and the urban public sphere 1

Part I New Women, New Men
1 George Gissing, urban modernity and modernism 13
2 Dorothy Richardson and New Woman fiction 21
3 Going up in smoke: Mr Richardson 26
4 Fathers and cities 30
5 On the threshold: Franz Kafka 35
6 Journeys through the city: James Joyce 40

Part II Bodies
7 Bodily innervation: food, eating and the everyday 49
8 George Gissing and the cultural politics of food 54
9 Smoking and consumption 61
10 Dietetics and aesthetics 68
11 'Lestrygonians': a place to eat 80

Part III Cities
12 Phantasmagoria and the public sphere 89
13 Teashop dreams 95
14 Gissing and eating out 105
15 Modernism's ABC 120
16 Miriam, teashops and the industrialised public sphere 132
17 Kafka, masculinity and the public sphere 145

Notes 151
Bibliography 184
Index 197

List of illustrations

1 Adrian Allison, Portrait of Alan Odle and Dorothy
   Richardson at table. Reproduced by permission from the
   Beinecke Library, Yale University   72
2 ABC teashops in central London, 1890   102
3 Lyons teashops in central London, 1902   102

Preface

This book's basic argument is relatively simple. Modernist literature's primary subject is the experience of urban modernity. In so far as it is concerned with masculinity, its interest is in the new urban masculinities that emerged in the late nineteenth and early twentieth centuries. The industrialised, technological city transformed gender relations, changing the experience of being or (more properly, to adapt, de Beauvoir's phrase) becoming a man in the city. This means that, in order to understand modernist masculinities, we need to examine the urban public cultures that produced them.

The logic of this argument led me to an interest in teashops, an interest that dominates approximately a third of this study. London's new chain teashops, I argue, were exemplary products of the new industrialised public sphere, in which new urban subjectivities emerged. In London, the ABCs and Lyons teashops appeared almost simultaneously, on London's streets and in English fiction, at the turn of the century. A focus on teashops allows a development of three strands of this book's argument: first, the importance of the new urban public sphere; second, a materialist understanding of gender as an embodied experience; and third, the importance of the intersubjective situation in which the experience of becoming a man or a woman takes place. London's new chain teashops were new urban spaces in which men and women worked, consumed and interacted. The study of their treatment in modernist literature lends itself to the critical methodology I pursue: a cultural materialist approach.

However, this project has been troubled (I hope productively) by dialogues between a cultural materialist approach and other critical methodologies, such as psychoanalysis, feminist criticism, lesbian and gay studies, and queer theory, each of which has contributed to political as well as academic debates. Feminism, lesbian and gay history and queer theory all provide essential perspectives for the analysis of masculinity. The relationship with psychoanalysis has been more difficult. Freud's Oedipus complex and the psychoanalytic concept of the 'law of the father' have extended a long shadow over this study. In the end however, I found psychoanalysis too much of a closed system and I stress the importance of the intersubjectivity of city life over the oppressive influence of the father on the gendered subject. I see what Christopher Lane calls 'identificatory failure' as a result of wider social and historical processes than the family.[1] While a ghostly father continues to haunt modernist texts, notably those written by male modernists, I argue that it still makes more sense to read those texts in relation to the urban public cultures in which they were produced. This approach, I maintain, gives a better account of the subject in process that modernist fiction attempts to represent.

My stress on the material conditions that gave rise to modernist masculinities mean that much of this book involves a detailed historical study of London in the late nineteenth and early twentieth centuries. My key authors are George Gissing and Dorothy Richardson, both unparalleled observers of London's public culture in this period. Both writers found their material in the everyday. As described in Part I, each was acutely aware of changing gender relations; and, as Part II will show, each was concerned to represent, however differently, an embodied subjectivity produced by an interaction between the intimate and personal, and the industrial and technological systems that make up the modern city. As Part III will demonstrate, both make eating out in London's new public spaces a key focus of their work. However, my focus on those spaces involves reference to a range of texts, including both formally modernist and non-modernist prose, and 'literary' and 'non-literary' texts: thus not only Baudelaire, Kafka, Joyce, Richardson but also Gissing, Maugham, Wells and New Woman writing; not only fiction and literary letters, but journalism, autobiography and historical material on turn-of-the-century London. I also make several excursions to other European cities: Paris, Berlin, Dublin and Prague. Originally, I wanted to provide as much information about the public cultures of these other modernist cities as I do about London. While that proved unfeasible in one study, reading the work of Charles Baudelaire, Franz Kafka, James Joyce and Walter Benjamin has strongly influenced the way I read English modernism. Modernism was an international movement and modernist texts (and their authors) circulated between cities. Walter Benjamin, who made studies of Berlin, Moscow, Naples and Paris, wrote 'all cities are beautiful to me'.[2] I would argue that the international character of modernism justifies, indeed demands, the inclusion of an international range of cities and texts. The weight I give to Benjamin's conception of the modernist city and the readings I give of Joyce and Kafka are designed to deepen the analysis of London's public culture and to extend the argument made for London modernisms to other European cities.

In this book, I adhere to a more positive view of modernism than is fashionable. In recent years, critical discussion of modernism has dismissed it as outdated, elitist or, more recently, as irredeemably complicit with market capitalism. For example, in the essays he wrote towards the end of his life, posthumously collected in *The Politics of Modernism*, Raymond Williams argued that modernist innovations were quickly incorporated into mass culture.[3] But this was hardly a new observation. The origins of modernism had long been recognised in Victorian commodity culture. In the 1920s, Siegfried Gideon argued that the arrangement of commodities in the nineteenth-century Great Exhibitions anticipated the total work of art;[4] and indeed the exhibitions might also be seen to anticipate modernism's use of *objets trouvés*, torn from their context and reassembled for public display. Franco Moretti, for example, sees modernism in the composition of the department store window, where dissimilar objects are juxtaposed to create new relations of meaning, 'a commonplace object transformed into something unexpected and strange', can be compared with 'the de-automatization of everyday perception advocated by that crucial Modernist principle – the "*ostranenie*" [estrangement] of Russian Formalism'.[5] And, according to Andreas Huyssen, Madison Avenue's advertising industry consciously exploited 'modernist pictorial strategies'.[6]

In recent years, critical debates about the relationship between modernism and mass culture have become, if anything, more intense.[7] John Carey takes a populist stance, arguing that the English literary intelligentsia between in the first half of the twentieth century were unremittingly hostile to the mass of the population and unapologetic in their elitism: 'the principle around which modernist literature and culture fashioned themselves was the exclusion of the masses, the defeat of their power, the removal of their literacy, the denial of their humanity'.[8] Michael Tratner takes an alternative view: modernist writers were not so much opposed to mass society as opposed to the mass culture on offer. Writers such as Joyce, Woolf and Eliot were not against but rather proposed an alternative mass culture.[9] Eric Hobsbawm is less charitable. Taking a historian's perspective that what affects the majority is more important than the tastes of the few, he argues that it was the new technologies of mechanical reproduction, above all cinema, that revolutionised the arts.[10]

Hobsbawm, at least, holds on to the concept of revolution, even if he does not accord modernism much of a role in its achievement. Overall, the critical emphasis on mass culture and the market has revised the work of earlier radical critics, such as Marshall Berman and Perry Anderson, who saw what Anderson calls the 'imaginative proximity of social revolution' as an important element in the 'modernist conjuncture'.[11] Thus, for example, John Xiros Cooper in *Modernism and Mass Market Culture* revises his earlier investment in modernism's revolutionary potential to argue that, from the perspective of the early twenty-first century, modernism can now be seen as not an alternative to but in the vanguard of consumer capitalism: 'modernism readies us, via a new aesthetics, for a regime of exchange, and, as a result, for the Wonderland of disembodied consumption of things'.[12] In effect, Cooper's thesis stakes out a position of which modernist studies long fought shy. An unambiguous statement of modernism's complicity with market culture marks a painful conclusion to the argument. But is it right to finish there?

A counterargument might be that this new emphasis is itself as a product of the time in which it was written, a time when the possibility of social revolution seems further away than it has for over a century.[13] We are living at a historical moment when it is easy to lose sight of the alternative paths that looked to many as not just possible but probable futures at the beginning of the twentieth century: futures that ranged between feminist, anarchist, communist, Fabian, liberal and Fascist. To fix too hard on modernism's relationship to the market at a time when the market reigns supreme smacks of the preoccupations of the present, as if all roads led to this moment in history. A historical view of modernism must also look at the roads not taken. So in this study, I am more hopeful than the strange and dismal beginning of the twenty first century might otherwise allow. The turn-of-the-century city, capitalist and saturated by the market as it was, did offer alternatives, alternatives that modernist fiction registered. Some of my selected examples emphasise the possibilities offered by the city. And even writers such as Gissing and Kafka operate a negative dialectic that allows the reader to posit a different way of becoming masculine in urban modernity.

The book's structure is conditioned by these arguments. In the Introduction, I make the argument for a conception of modernist masculinities as the lived experience of becoming a man in urban modernity. In Part I, 'New Woman, New Men', I defend the inclusion of George Gissing as a pre- or proto-London modernist, whose keen observation of the city offers valuable insights into the genesis of modernist form. Part I continues with a discussion of Richardson's work in the context of New Woman fiction. Miriam, the protagonist of *Pilgrimage*, is a complex figure: a response to older incarnations of masculine authority, to urban masculinities, and herself an exploration of a new emergent subjectivity, neither masculine nor feminine by Victorian conventions. Miriam's symbolic destruction of her father (discussed in Chapter 3) is, I argue, just the beginning of her engagement with the urban public sphere. Similarly, the entanglements charted in the fiction of Joyce and Kafka (discussed in Chapters 5 and 6) are best read through that engagement. The city provides an escape from rather than a reinvention of the father.

Part II, 'Bodies', attempts to materialise the analysis in Part I by examining the embodied forms of subjectivity that emerged in late nineteenth- and early twentieth-century fiction. It includes extended discussions of Gissing's fiction and Richardson's early journalism on diet and concludes with a reading of the 'Lestrygonians' chapter from *Ulysses*. Where the focus of Part I is on the texts, Part II explores the embodied experience of new urban subjectivities. It focuses on the material embodiment of city life as represented by the consuming, eating, drinking and smoking body in modernist fiction. Adapting Walter Benjamin's concept of 'bodily innervation', it argues that corporeal experience is constituted by a sedimented complex of social relations, which are mediated through the technical apparatus of the industrialised city. The natural, diurnal and learned rhythms of the body come into conflict with its the city's own rhythms: its networks of production, distribution and consumption. But modernist texts were as interested in alternative responses to the negative aspects of modernity. Both Richardson and Joyce are examples of modernist writers who were fascinated by the body as a threshold between the quotidian and the 'systems-world' of the city. Part II's focus on the eating body offers it as a metonymic figure for the totality of conditions that make up Marx's 'sensuous human activity',[14] even if that totality cannot, ultimately, be fully represented and many of its routes, paths and passages are destined to remain lost to conscious thought.

In that context, Part III, 'Cities', argues for an awareness of the stage on which the performance of embodied subjectivities takes place as the precondition for an analysis of the transformation of the economy of London's city streets at the turn of the century. This requires a somewhat broader focus than that provided by textual criticism or even the most rigorously materialist account of the body. Part III makes that the argument that those embodied subjectivities can come into being only in the context of an enabling public sphere: the streets, cafés, restaurants, clubs and teashops that are the venues in which the modernist city's public culture takes place. This involves an investigation of the importance of public spaces in modernist fiction as the spaces of intersubjectivity in which masculinities are produced. Hence the extended discussion of the chain teashop in English modernism that takes up the bulk of this section.

Acknowledgements

If I had to trace the origins of this book, I would probably start in Stoke Newington in 1983, when I first visited a socialist-feminist shared house.

That visit was the first of many and culminated in a new household in Dalston, in which I lived from 1986 to 1989. My encounter with the urban, having been brought up, comfortably and happily, in a small village in Oxfordshire, was personal, political and intellectual. I was confronted with new ideas that challenged my sense of myself at a time when my own sexuality was still being formed. Socialism, feminism, anti-imperialism and the ideas generated by lesbian and gay liberation were part of everyday discourse. I made free use of the book shelves that were laden with literature, history and political theory. This reading set up numerous dialogues with my mother's well-stocked shelves of English fiction at home and the reading lists dealt out at university.

But talk and reading were only part of it. There was also London itself. Hackney then, as now, was in a state of permanent revolution, with one of the most rapid demographic turnovers of any part of Britain. At that time public sector professionals were moving in, Kurdish refugees were arriving from eastern Turkey and the battle against Thatcherism was taking place on the streets. A participant in any protest going, I was also a frequenter of the local pubs, cafés and curry houses and then later, while doing graduate research in the (old) British Library, an aficionado of every espresso bar in the surrounding streets of Bloomsbury. My own pleasure in the public life the city offers partly explains the importance I assign to it in modernist texts. But, I hope will come clear, it is more important than that.

This book has thus been taking shape over a long period and the list of those who contributed is necessarily long. I'd like to thank my parents, Pamela and Garry McCracken, for their help and support. Alison Lee, Sue Lee, the late Kate Poulton and Daniel Poulton started me thinking about masculinity. Anita Roy at Manchester University Press encouraged the initial proposal. Her successor, Matthew Frost, has waited patiently and cheerily for the result.

The earliest research was done on a Fulbright Scholarship spent at Stanford University and University of the Pacific. Joel Beinin, Elliott Colla, Bob Cox and Camille Norton helped to make it a year to remember. Over the years my colleagues at Salford University and Sheffield Hallam University, Peter Buse, Paul Callick, Rachel Connor, Angus Easson, Avril Horner, Angela Keane, Antony Rowland, Ian Baker, Steven Earnshaw, Chris Hopkins, Barbara MacMahon, Archie Markham, Sean O'Brien, Jane Rogers and Matt Steggle have all contributed with ideas and advice. Along the way, Tim Bewes, Ted Bishop, Marlene Briggs, Peter Brooker, Laura Chrisman, Paul Delany, Laura Doan, Philip Holden, Tamar Katz, Neil Lazarus, Sally Ledger, Laura Marcus, Benita Parry, Marco Pustianaz, Martin Ryle, Alan Sinfield, John Spiers,

Bertrand Taithe, Jenny Bourne Taylor, Luisa Villa, Jo-Ann Wallace and Steve Watts have given encouragement, suggestions and material help. Over the last eight years, I have benefited immeasurably from working with all the members of the *new formations* editorial board.

Particular thanks go to David Glover, whose help has been incalculable, to Regenia Gagnier, whose support and encouragment has never failed, and to Mandy Merck for telling me to be bold. Thanks also to Miles Ogborn for years of debate and for telling me to map the teashops because it would tell me things I didn't know. It did. The maps themselves could not have been done without the technical expertise of Steve Xerri. Ken Hirschkop, Ben Highmore, Lisa Hopkins, Mary Peace, Andrew Thacker all read parts of the manuscript in draft. All gave me invaluable feedback.

The book was finished at the University of British Columbia in the first half of 2005 and I am grateful to the English Department there and to Keele University who honoured a long overdue sabbatical, allowing me to find the time to write in what must be one of the most beautiful urban spaces on earth. Special thanks to John Xiros Cooper, who faciliated my visit, gave me an office and was a true friend who took the time to read and comment on the whole manuscript. In Vancouver, Miguel and Fergus Mota, Margaret Linley, Patsy Badir, Mary Chapman, Jake and Kate Fry, Beth Seaton, Mary Chapman and Susan O'Reilly helped to make our stay productive and enjoyable. I'd also like to thank the anonymous reader for Manchester University Press, whose perceptive critique helped enormously with the final redrafting. I only wish I were able to answer all the questions it wanted answered.

Earlier versions of sections were published in *Textual Practice* and the collections: *Body Matters; Maschilità decadenti: La lunga fin de siècle; Voices of the Unclassed; The Geographies of Modernism*; and *Gissing and the City*. I am grateful to the staff at the Green Library, Stanford University; the University of Salford Library; the John Rylands University Library of Manchester; the London Metropolitan Library; the Berg Library New York; the Koerner Library, University of British Columbia; and the Beinicke Library, Yale University.

Final thanks and much love go to Georgina and Jessica Waylen, one an established, the other an apprentice critic of masculinity. Both have treated this book with as little respect as it deserves.

Introduction: masculinities and the urban public sphere

Chapter IV of George Gissing's *The Nether World* (1889) can be read as an allegory for the emergence of new urban masculinities at the end of the nineteenth century. It describes a walk taken by Sidney Kirkwood and Clara Hewett from Clara's family home in the densely packed streets of working-class Clerkenwell to the public space of the Angel Islington, where Upper Street offers 'the promenade of a great district on account of its spacious pavement'.[1] Gissing describes London's public sphere as one in which gender relations are in transition. Sidney has known Clara since she was a child, when, we are told, 'his bright manly face did everyone good to look at' and he 'still took little Clara on his knee'.[2] But by the opening of the novel, men have lost power in the family home. As Clara's father remarks: 'there's not much heed paid to fathers nowadays'.[3]

Sidney Kirkwood's early relationship with Clara had been framed in terms of her subordination to his age and gender and his future hopes of marriage.[4] He has long desired the ideal of femininity his phantasy imagined she would become. But their urban journey marks the end of the masculine ideal their marriage would confirm: an ideal rooted in paternal power and filial subservience. Sidney quickly discovers that Clara has grown up to be a woman with a mind of her own. His offer to escort her is endured rather than welcomed. For Clara, the walk is a journey away from the authority of her father, towards economic independence; and, equally, an escape from Sidney's plans to make her his wife. She is going to confirm a job as a barmaid in Mrs Tubbs 'Imperial Restaurant and Luncheon Bar', an opportunity deeply resented by both Sidney and her father. They recognise the part London's new public sphere plays in her empowerment.

Clara was far from unique. She is one of the 'New Women' that were an icon of the period.[5] More prosaically, her experience was typical of thousands of young women who were looking for jobs in London's expanding service sector in the late 1880s. If her new femininity is a performance – her job as a barmaid requires good looks and new clothes and is a rehearsal for her later career as an actress – it is a performance conditioned by the stage on which it is set: *fin-de-siècle* London.[6] But the city of possibility now opening up to Clara offers only bleak and diminishing prospects to Sidney. Her obvious delight in London's new public culture contrasts with his lack of place.[7] His desolation emerges from the impression of Upper Street itself:

> Here was the wonted crowd of loiterers and the press of people waiting for tramcar or omnibus – east, west, south, or north; newboys, eager to get rid of their last batch, were crying as usual . . . and a brass band was blaring out its saddest strain of merry dance music. The lights gleamed dismally in rain puddles and on the wet pavement. With the wind came whiffs of tobacco and odours of the drinking bar.[8]

The passage conveys both the modernist city of Clara's dreams and Sidney's despair. The tram, mass communication, popular music, entertainment and the effects of street lighting indicate the possibilities that fuel her hopes and, at the same time, and as a consequence, signify the loss of his, phantasmal, object of desire. With every step towards the Angel, Sidney loses power over Clara so that he is forced to confront his own situation, alone on London's streets: 'irritated by the conversation and laughter that fell on his ears, irritated by the distant strains of the band, irritated above all by the fume of frying that pervaded the air from many yards about Mrs Tubb's precincts'.[9] After she completes a successful interview, he insists on walking Clara back to Clerkenwell, where, in the shadow of the prison, he attempts to summon up some patriarchal authority and remind her of her duty to her parents. But for Clara the 'lecture' is 'new proof of the power she had over him'. Sidney's capacity for speech diminishes in the face of her defiance: 'his voice all but failed him at the last'.[10]

In fact, Clara's moment of freedom is short lived. *The Nether World* ends with Clara married to Sidney and confined to her bedroom. She has been exiled for ever from the public world that was to have been her salvation by the burns that scar her face, inflicted by acid thrown by a jealous rival. Characteristically, Gissing the 'modernist' opens up his text to London's public culture, only to close it down again with a depressingly 'realist' narrative resolution. None the less, Clara's brief moment of hope inaugurates the urban scene in which modernist masculinities were made. In that scene, Sidney's and Clara's stories cannot be disentangled. The entry of new women workers and consumers into the public sphere transformed the terms on which the city was negotiated.[11] Nor were the city's streets necessarily as depressing as *The Nether World* would have us believe. The new public cultures emerging in Europe's urban centres gave new opportunities, including new opportunities for disappointment, to men and women.

In the period in which modernist fiction emerged, new masculinities and femininities, and new subjectivities not previously recognisable as either, were produced at the interstices between private and public spheres: between the family home and new spaces like Upper Street that allowed new forms of gendered intersubjectivity. These everyday city spaces produced the ordinary 'vernacular' modernisms on which literary modernisms drew.[12] It is no accident that, in *The Nether World*, it is a 'Restaurant and Luncheon Bar' that is the scene of Clara's brief liberation and the beginning of Sidney's long disappointment. Mrs Tubb's establishment gives the first clue as to why a study that sets out to analyse the relationship between masculinity and modernist fiction is devoted in large part to a discussion of representations of eating and eating out in the city. There is no shortage of such examples in modernist fiction. The two authors who are the main focus of the study, George Gissing (whose claim to be a modernist I argue in Chapter 1) and Dorothy Richardson, were both keen observers of London's public culture. Gissing, like Sidney, was both horrified and fascinated by its impact. Richardson's *Pilgrimage* is not only one of the great achievements of modernist prose, it is also a philosophical reflection on urban modernity. The importance of London's teashops, cafés and restaurants to its heroine, Miriam Henderson, is therefore significant not just as part of her ordinary, everyday environment but because the teashop seems to offer to Miriam, like the bar to Clara, a new way of becoming a woman in the city. But neither Gissing nor Richardson is alone in these observations. Teashops, the subject of Chapters 13–16, and particularly the two largest chains in turn-of-the-century London, the ABCs and Lyons teashops, were a major preoccupation of early twentieth-century literature, mentioned by, amongst others, Bram Stoker, H. G. Wells, Arnold Bennett, Somerset Maugham, Dorothy Richardson, Ezra Pound, Bertha Ruck, Katherine Mansfield, Jean Rhys, T. S. Eliot and Virginia Woolf.

Often the new chain teashops appear as signifiers of a new mass culture, but, almost as often, as examples of women's assertive presence in London's new public sphere. Unfriendly and threatening to some, they also appear as places of refuge, a space in which it is possible stop, look, think, read and write, even if, in the busy city, the time, money and opportunity for intellectual activity is always limited. In Virginia Woolf's *Night and Day* (1919), Katherine Hilberry goes into an ABC to write a letter to Ralph Denham and 'by ordering a cup of coffee . . . secured an empty table', but she quickly becomes 'aware of a waitress, whose expression intimated that it was closing time, and, looking round, Katherine saw herself almost the last person left in the shop'.[13] In Richardson's *Interim*, published in the same year as *Night and Day*, Miriam gets carried away reading Ibsen in an ABC and is late for an appointment with her sister, Eve.[14] Later in *Revolving Lights* (1923), she remembers extending her lunch hour to read Conrad: 'and afterwards, joyful strength to face the disgrace of being an hour or more late for afternoon work'.[15] The teashop could provide a brief opportunity to become something or someone other than a person pressured by the demands of family and work. However, perhaps their most important function was as places of meeting and encounter. Teashops provided a space in the city, in which new forms of social relations and new forms of intersubjectivity could come into being.[16] As such, they were part of the city's new public culture, the culture in which modernism was born.[17]

As stated in the Preface, this study aims to give a cultural materialist account of the relationship between masculinities and modernist fiction. Cultural materialism, a methodology originally developed by Raymond Williams, is concerned to situate texts in the historical and social context in which they are produced. It understands society as conflictual, as characterised by struggle between social groups. As a consequence, it focuses on contested, rather than pre-given, ideas and identities.[18] A study of the relationship between modernist fiction and the urban public cultures in which that fiction emerged thus requires accounts of the broader literary and cultural contexts, the city's economy, the social and political conflicts that took place, and the kinds of contested gendered identities that emerged.

In this respect, it is close to what Rita Felski describes as the methodology used by cultural studies, which relies on the concept of 'articulation': a 'forged connection' between different aspects of the aesthetic, the social, the political and the economic. Felski writes that, in cultural studies, the 'political import of a text cannot be inferred from its internal form or logic, but derives from its position in a constellation of texts, practices, and interests'.[19] The discovery, in the course of my research, that teashops proliferated in texts as well as in London's streets suggested a distinctive way to explore the relationship between the production of literary masculinities and new material spaces of the city. A focus on eating out in a particular city in the late nineteenth and early twentieth century offers the possibility of a historically situated study.

This, I want to suggest, might then be extrapolated to suggest that the modernisms of Walter Benjamin, James Joyce and Franz Kafka work in a similar way in relation to Berlin, Paris, Dublin and Prague. A comparative approach is warranted because the international character of modernism justifies, indeed demands, the inclusion of an international range of texts. But a cultural materialist methodology requires that, even if the reception of modernist texts was international, each should be situated in relation to the location of its production. Prague, Dublin, Paris, Berlin and London operate here as comparable examples urban modernity, but each city called up different, local, and indeed individual, responses. If Virginia Woolf's *Mrs Dalloway* offers the best example of a fiction about a single spatial and temporal zone, even in that novel central London is experienced in a multitude of different ways on a single day. Modernism's international character requires a dialectic between locality and an internationalising modernity that was practised by all literary modern*isms*.

The chain teashop was a notable feature of London's public sphere from the late nineteenth century to after the Second World War. The chain teashops that multiplied on London's streets at the end of the nineteenth century were places to have a cup of tea and a muffin. But they were also part of a much larger economic transformation that included: increasing competition to Britain's position as leading industrial power and a greater dependence on its colonies as protected markets for its products; changes in London's labour force, which included the rapid expansion of women's employment; the construction of a new transport infrastructure of suburban and underground railways; and the concomitant expansion of a culture of consumption, from West End shopping to music hall and theatre. Having a cup of tea in an ABC teashop was made possible by the new economy. The tea and wheat were imported from the colonies. The muffin was industrially produced. The new workforce provided the customers and the reasonable prices were aimed primarily at the new workforce as well as shoppers and theatregoers. The teashop was thus not just a meeting point for the city's inhabitants, it was also a point at which the contradictory demands of work and leisure, production and consumption, met.

As a consequence, the teashop was a site of struggle, although a struggle usually fought out through symbolic or verbal, rather than physical, means.[20] The stage upon which these conflicts were fought was enabling and limiting, productive of new subjectivities and socially restricting at the same time. Questions of class and status were to the fore. The notorious audacity and disdain of the ABC waitresses struck terror into many a bourgeois heart. They also made the teashop an assertively female zone. For some men this was attractive, and either instructive or an opportunity for voyeurism. Arnold Bennett wrote that 'the waitresses offered an inexhaustible field for the study of character . . . unveiling the secrets of their natures in every trifling action'.[21] For other writers, Ezra Pound and Somerset Maugham as discussed in Chapter 13, for example, the attraction was tempered with a sense of unease.

Masculinity in this context is best understood not in relation to a mythical father figure but in relation to situated experiences in which gendered subjectivities were made through social interaction in a particular place. In a society that, then as now, was structured by inequality between the sexes, such interactions did not take place on a level playing field, but women's increasing presence in the public sphere had altered the balance. In Part I, 'New Women, New Men', I argue that industrial modernity means that the power of fathers in this period is more (to borrow Raymond Williams's terms) residual than dominant.[22] Industrialisation had periodically favoured women and children over men as workers, in order to undercut wages. As the century progressed, the power of fathers was further challenged by the impact of a new, socially dynamic urban public sphere, in which women's intervention into the public life set the scene for new forms of masculinity.[23] It is, as I argue in Chapter 3, too easy to read Joyce or Kafka's fiction in terms of an Oedipal battle for a full masculine identity, when the real struggle for self-definition is against a much more complex urban social scene.

Peter Dews suggests that in modernity 'moral self-control is no longer seen as simply the internalized continuation of the social compulsion required for the control of nature, but is rather acquired through a process of interactive identification with a variety of other subjects in the immediate environment, a process which has an independent dynamic'.[24] Arguing for a theory of intersubjectivity rather than the primacy of the subject, Dews takes up Jessica Benjamin's suggestion that: 'the Oedipal model of individuation can be seen as merely *one* model, which institutionalizes an isolating and manipulative independence, at the cost of the values of co-operation and reciprocity'.[25] For Jessica Benjamin:

> Men's loss of absolute control over women and children . . . exposed the vulnerable core of male individuality, the failure of recognition which previously wore the cloak of power, responsibility and family honor' . . .
>
> . . . The three pillars of oedipal theory – the primacy of the wish for oneness, the mother's embodiment of this regressive force, and the necessity of paternal intervention – all combine to create the paradox that the only liberation is paternal domination. Oedipal theory thus denies the necessity of mutual recognition between man and woman. Construing the struggle for recognition in terms of the father-son rivalry, the theory reduces woman to a contested point on the triangle, never an other whose different and equal subjectivity need be confronted.[26]

While it is true that Clara and Sidney's walk in *The Nether World* can be read, quite legitimately, as dramatising a decline in the power of fathers, it is the city or, more precisely, city spaces like Upper Street in *The Nether World*, that create the possibility of different kinds of social interaction and therefore different kinds of gendered intersubjectivity. Modernist fictions are still concerned with the shadow of the symbolic father, but they use the city both as an escape and as the conditions for new forms of consciousness.[27] London's new public culture was sufficiently fluid to mean that the power of fathers had to be continually reinvented and remobilised because it was constantly being questioned. This does not mean, of course, that there was no gender bias, enshrined in law and social institutions. But, as I argue below, this was not the same thing as a 'law of the father'.[28] Indeed, both the law and the all-male institutions that dominated Victorian society were being challenged in the period.

In this context, masculinity is best understood using what Toril Moi (following Simone de Beauvoir) calls the 'lived experience' of becoming a man or a woman. Moi describes 'lived experience' as 'a central existentialist concept', comparing it with the subject's 'situation':

> The situation is not coextensive with lived experience, nor reducible to it. In many ways 'lived experience' designates the whole of person's subjectivity. More particularly the term describes the way an individual makes sense of her situation and actions. Because the concept also comprises my freedom, my lived experience is not wholly determined by the various situations I may be a part of. Rather lived experience is, as it were, sedimented over time through my interactions with the world, and thus itself becomes part of my situatedness.[29]

Eating and eating out, the subject of Part II, 'Bodies', are examples of embodied subjectivity, where the 'body both is a situation *and* is placed within other situations'.[30] Moi illustrates her point with an example from de Beauvoir about sitting, talking in a café, where the 'actual physical female body sitting there at the café table discussing philosophy is both a situation for the woman who is talking and a background to her words for the man who is talking to her'.[31] This lived experience, through which both man and woman become their gender, is, in one sense, unrepresentable in literature. No literary work can fully account for it. One of the characteristics of modernist fiction, however, is its project to represent experience in modernity as simultaneously, intimate, bodily and also part of a larger background or situation, in which subjectivity is shaped by vast systems beyond the subject's immediate control. This sedimentation, to borrow Moi's term, incorporates earlier experiences and, importantly, historical experiences that may precede the modern situation by centuries. Masculinity, in this respect, incorporates a residual history of male domination, as well as a current masculine hegemony. The present experience of becoming a man involves a dynamic relationship between the sedimented layers of gender oppression and a process, in which what it means to be a man is challenged, subverted and changed through social interaction. Masculinity as lived process is always part of an intersubjective formation rather than an individualised subjectivity. Café masculinities, in other words, always depend on who else is in the café.

Masculinity then is not the same thing as patriarchy, the traditional respect for and authority of older men. In Victorian modernity, traditions, including the traditions that privileged men, had to be continually reinvented.[32] As Eve Kosofsky Sedgwick's 1985 monograph *Between Men: English Literature and Homosocial Desire* demonstrated, the reproduction of a gendered ideology was shaped by the homosocial institutions – the public schools, the Church, the Army, Parliament, the civil service, the legal and medical professions – that governed Victorian society.[33] Homosocial bonds are predicated on the exclusion of same-sex desire, which none the less acts as a subterranean force between men, both consolidating the group and making homophobia part of its identity. Women are also excluded and the taint of the feminine associates male homosexual desire with women's subordinate position.[34]

In the nineteenth century, male hegemony depended on the insulation of power from the more anarchic culture of the streets. The teashop, as a point somewhere between the respectability of bourgeois society and the street, is helpful in gaining an understanding of the ideologies of masculinity that found their material embodiment in Victorian homosocial institutions, because it enables us to see gendered subjectivity in process. If we differentiate between *subjectivity* as becoming, and *identity* as an ideological concept that artificially fixes the limits of subjectivity, then the teashop is a space in which ideological gendered identities come into conflict with lived experience. This lived experience is necessarily complex, but it might be understood on a number of sedimented levels. The first is as embodiment, but Moi, I think, underestimates the extent to which the experience of embodiment is mediated. While lived experience is always at a deep level about living in a sexed body, the cultural meanings that constitute 'sex' are highly contested.

The conceptual distinction between sex and gender does not always help to define the lived experience of becoming a man. As both poststructuralist and socialist feminists have pointed out, the differentiation between sex (male/female) as biology and gender (masculinity/femininity) as social role, while useful in combating biological determinism, creates an opposition between body and consciousness that cannot account for the embodied experience of being a man or a woman.[35] Eating out offers a concrete example of how we become masculine or feminine in a specific (and contested) social situation. It helps us to define a modernist maculinity as the lived experience of becoming masculine in urban modernity.

Walter Benjamin's distinction between two kinds of modern experience is useful here. His concept of shock experience, *Erlebnis*, describes a widely noted phenomenon in the period: the overstimulation or sensory overload that produced a kind of numbness or anomie common to all modern cities.[36] But Benjamin differentiates between *Erlebnis*, which can be translated as 'shock experience' and *Erfahrung*, long, reflective or considered experience, to describe the impact of industrial modernity on the body. *Erlebnis* describes both the alienated experience of the worker, bound to routine attendance on a machine, and the anaesthestic effects of the city's constant stimulation.[37] *Erfahrung*, a reflection upon and a reconfiguration of *Erlebnis*, is a necessary philosophical response to the shock effects of modernity. Benjamin's understanding of modern experience draws on modernist literature. Baudelaire's poetry transforms *Erlebnis* into *Erfahrung*.[38] In Part II, I argue that modernist fiction was acutely sensitive to the impact of urban modernity on the body and the strategies through which that impact can be parried, countered or transformed into something else. Eating, as basic a bodily function as sex, is represented as much more than a necessity by writers who take urban modernity as their subject matter. Eating in the city requires the eater to become part of extended systems of production and consumption, systems that make the chain teashop possible. In that context, eating can become an instrumental act, the consumption of the fuel that drives the city's new work force: *Erlebnis*. But the meal is also a symbolic act. Where we eat, when we eat, what we eat and how we eat depends upon a matrix of signifying practices. Modernist fiction takes the meal as an opportunity to reflect upon the social relations the 'food event' brings into existence: *Erfahrung*.

To return to the passage with which I started: Clara and Sidney's urban walk, at once pragmatic and performative, furnishes examples of the three key aspects of this book's argument. First, Clara's refusal of patriarchal authority bears witness to a decline in the cultural power of fathers in the late nineteenth century. Despite the fact that Freud's Oedipal theory (which should perhaps be understood as a symptom and response to that decline) emerges from this period, the symbolic power of the father is weakened by the opportunities offered by the public culture of the city. In that context new urban masculinities arise. Second, Clara's employment, the economic basis of her relative freedom, and its corollary, Sidney's exclusion, are examples of the production of new gendered subjectivities in the urban public sphere that embody the new relations of production, distribution and consumption that characterised European imperial economies. These are defined not only through discourses of sexuality but through every aspect of everyday life. Clara and Sidney's walk from Clerkenwell to the Angel, for example, might be understood not just as the lost supplement that forms a subjectivity in excess of the relations of work but also as a difficult mediation between the social and historical conditions that constrain identity and the possibility of new and pleasurable performances. Finally, such performances need an enabling space to act as a stage on which they might be performed. The journey taken by Sidney and Clara demonstrates the importance of location for the production of these new subjectivities, which occur at the city's thresholds and boundaries. In that context, urban spaces, like Upper Street and the Angel, but also the new urban public sphere constituted by cafés, teashops and restaurants, such as Mrs Tubb's Imperial Restaurant and Luncheon Bar, provided the new spaces of intersubjectivity that permitted an alternative to Oedipal domination. Clara and Sidney's walk takes the reader from the closed worlds of Victorian fiction to the possibilities of that new sphere. Modernist texts in the period battle against the re-emergence of antiquated and archaic fathers, but the coherence of the paternal edict is constantly disrupted by the boundaries, crossing points and thresholds of the city. In Walter Benjamin's words: 'As threshold, the boundary stretches across streets: a new precinct [*Rayon*] begins like a step into the void – as though one had unexpectedly cleared a low step on a flight of stairs.'[39] This void, or emptiness [*Leere*] opens up the possibility of new masculinities.

Part I
New Women, New Men

1

George Gissing, urban modernity and modernism

Part I looks at the relationship between modernist fiction and the new gendered subjectivities that emerged in Europe's new urban public cultures. In this chapter, I make the case for one of the key authors of this study, George Gissing, as a modernist. Gissing criticism has often focused on the relationship between his fiction and the city, but, with a few recent exceptions, the important relationship of his work to modernism has not been discussed. Both Gissing's fiction and New Woman fiction, discussed in Chapter 2, can be understood as responses to London's new public sphere. My second key author, Dorothy Richardon, discussion of whom begins in Chapter 3, can be read in relation to New Woman fiction. As an experimental work that takes London as its subject matter, *Pilgrimage* offers the perfect counterpoint to the modernist masculinities found in Franz Kafka and James Joyce. Chapters 4–6 move beyond London to argue the importance of a European public sphere that included the metropolitan city spaces of Paris, Berlin, Prague and Dublin. The new masculinities that emerged in these spaces exceeded the father–son dyad and are best read in relation to the new complexity of the urban social scene.

One of the formal characteristics of modernist prose is its attempt to represent subjectivity in a way that refuses clear identification.[1] The city offered transformative possibilities to modernist artists and writers. In this respect, modernist form was a response to the revolutionary transformations set in train by capitalism. But modernisms reconfigured the shock effects of capitalism (Benjamin's *Erlebnis*) into *Erfahrung*, a reconfiguration that suggested that the world contained the possibility of being something new forms of social organisation. The alternatives included different forms of gendered subjectivity. Men and women took up new positions that challenged older identities, even if they do not always manage to overcome them. But necessarily, these positions were not easy to conceptualise. Nineteenth-century realism, a complex response to modernity in itself,[2] had privileged the domestic sphere even although it often made urban modernity its subject. The street represented a dangerous space. As critics such as Sally Ledger, Ann Ardis and Ann Heilmann have shown, New Woman fiction, which emerged in the 1880s, anticipated modernism in crossing the dividing line between private and public spheres.[3] New Woman fiction reconfigured the ideological co-ordinates of the mid-nineteenth-century English novel by deploying a range of new forms from naturalism to impressionism in texts that ranged in style from the sensationalist to aestheticist.

Gissing's work responds to the same cultural contradictions as New Woman fiction and, like that fiction, he makes for a, perhaps unlikely, precursor to modernist writers such as Walter Benjamin, James Joyce and Dorothy Richardson.[4] But modernisms' refusal of a full and complete identity takes different forms. Gissing's fiction operates a kind of negative dialectic. Raymond Williams wrote of Gissing: 'he is . . . the spokeman of . . . despair: the despair born of social and political disillusion. In this he is a figure exactly like Orwell in our own day, and for much the same reasons. Whether one calls this honesty or not will depend on experience.'[5] Later in the same work, Williams argues that 'Gissing found the London poor repulsive, in the mass; his descriptions have all the generalising squalor of a Dickens or an Orwell'.[6] Historically, he places him in the transition between the nineteenth and the twentieth centuries he calls the 'interregnum'. Politically, he marks him out with Orwell (with whom *Culture and Society* concludes) as an exile. Orwell was 'one of a significant number of men who, deprived of a settled way of living, or of a faith, or having rejected those which were inherited, find virtue in a kind of improvised living and an assertion of independence'.[7] His self-imposed isolation echoes Gissing's 'proper study' which was 'the condition of exile and loneliness'.[8] With this definition, Williams sets the terms for later left-wing criticism of Gissing: he was a maverick, not particularly sympathetic to the Left, yet his novels offer the opportunity for a reading against the grain. The refusal in his fiction to accept the morality or the social palliatives offered by Victorian society allows us to see its truth.

Williams's conclusions about his subject seem at first to be marked by the tendency to biography that is the bane of so much Gissing criticism. He was, Williams remarks, a 'deeply sensitive, deeply lonely man'.[9] Yet a comparison with his Orwell essay makes it clear that, for Williams in the proper mode of the cultural materialist, the politics of both men were a reaction to what each, in his own way, saw as the impossible contradictions of urban modernity – rather than, on the one hand, the trauma of Gissing's expulsion and imprisonment, and, on the other, Orwell's deep-seated psychological complexes. For Williams the lesson to be drawn is that:

> We have to understand, in the detail of experience, how the instincts of humanity can break down under pressure into an inhuman paradox; how a great and humane tradition can seem at times, to all of us, to disintegrate into a caustic dust.[10]

The reference to dust is, of course, an allusion to the opening of *Nineteen Eighty-four*, where it signifies, as so often in realist fiction, the urban in all its material grittiness.[11] But the image of the city as caustic dust also indicates the objection Williams has to both authors' representations of the urban masses. He sees their novels as dismissive, condescending, belittling, as putting the working class in their place. Their texts cap or limit the potential of the new industrial cities. This view became orthodox in Gissing criticism and yet, despite its limitations, the period between the publication of *Culture and Society* in 1958 and the publication of Fredric Jameson's *The Political Unconscious* in 1981 constituted, one of the most fruitful periods both of cultural Marxism and of Gissing criticism. It is one of the many paradoxes in a century of literary criticism that, while Gissing's politics, whether of class or gender, lack easy definition, it has been, by and large, left-wing critics who have kept his reputation alive and latterly, and perhaps more surprisingly, feminist critics, who have continued to find him of interest.[12]

A key figure in this process was John Goode, who wrote some of his key essays in the 1960s, but whose monograph, *Ideology and Fiction*, now recognised as amongst the best works on Gissing, wasn't published until 1978. Goode claims two of the most fashionable Marxists of the 1970s as key influences: Antonio Gramsci and Walter Benjamin. Reading *Ideology and Fiction* now, it is also clear that his acknowledgement of their 'pervasive influence'[13] is partly an attempt to distance the book from two other currents, the older influence of Georg Lukács's treatment of nineteenth-century realism and the iron grip of Althusser's theory of ideology on literary studies at the time.

Goode specifically compares Gissing to Lukács's, broadly following Lukács', periodisation of European realism to the extent that he sees Gissing as 'having a place in the large aesthetic disruption which takes place in European literature from the late 'fifties on'.[14] But he attributes to Gissing a better grasp of ideology than Lukács. Gissing is able to see that 'classic realism' was 'a product of the particular possibilities released not by a general historical situation but by the specific determinations of the relationship between the writer and his public'.[15] It was the change in that relationship at the end of the century that propelled Gissing into a new mode of realism, a realism that had limitations, but ones of which he was highly conscious.

In fact, Goode argues, it was a consciousness of limitations that makes his work so significant.[16] Gissing was aware of the ideological boundaries of both the forms of middle-class culture of earlier realists, such as Dickens, and, his own selection of a particular form of prose. Goode, and, as we shall see, this is also true of Fredric Jameson, finds Gissing's value as a writer in the reading strategies his texts offer to see through the late nineteenth century's ideologies of class. The theory of ideology here is developed within a broadly Althusserian framework, more, one suspects, because Goode was in a dialogic relationship with the theoretical debates of the time than because he espouses a fully fledged Althusserianism. This is apparent not just in terms of his understanding of ideology as an imaginative relationship to the real but also in the pessimism he articulates about the ideological function of literature itself. The conclusion to *Ideology and Fiction* defines the most radical element of Gissing's texts as their refusal to conform to literature's ideological function. Instead, they operate a kind of negative dialectic against literature itself as bourgeois form.

The concept of the negative dialectic belongs properly to T. W. Adorno as a methodology for seeing through idealism: 'Insight into the constitutive character of the non-conceptual in the concept would end the compulsive identification which the concept brings unless halted by such reflection.'[17] Gissing's work resisted identification with a comfortable, middle-class view of Victorian society, even if his fall-back position was often reactionary – in Adorno's terms, a different kind of identity thinking. But Goode's analysis of this results in a kind of circular argument, in which literary criticism itself shores up the dominant ideology:

> The most important institutional function of literature is its making of ideology. In fact, most teachers of literature would claim that the close analysis of literary texts liberates the student from ideological conditioning – frees him from the stock response. It is this claim which precisely constitutes the ideological function of literature, because it creates the very important illusion that choice is still theoretically possible. . .The most revolutionary text can be immunised in this way, the conditions of its production are obscured by its canonisation; it becomes a kind of gospel ripe for commentary – it reflects, represents, mobilises itself as an object. What it ceases to do is to intervene in the world of social action. Reading is a private affair and literature calls into being a group, an élite, a specialised section of traditional intellectuals who can convince themselves that they are not conquered by the dominant ideology (which is an important condition of its conquest).[18]

Traditional intellectuals here are implicitly opposed to Gramsci's organic intellectuals, the agents of social and political change,[19] but, without them, this truly is a nether world, a circle of hell from which there is no escape. Gissing's success is in writing novels that cannot be recuperated by the institution. Not because they are bad novels, although the worst aspect of his work involves his weak attempts to reimpose a cultural hierarchy against the commercial age, but because Gissing insists on concentrating on what Goode calls the 'urbanisation of the unclassed'.[20] In effect, his texts operate an anti-aesthetic, where the poetic does not allow the reader-critic to be distracted from the real, class-based conditions of production: 'Gissing wrote novels to make a living, and he wrote them about the struggle to make a living in the remote respectable corners of urban society: the motive and the representation are at one, and because they are at one, we can never feel that we ignore the conditions of production.'[21]

As with Williams, Goode's theoretical conclusions stem from his understanding of Gissing's relationship with the city. Even his understanding of the ideological function of the institution of literature is arrived at via his reading of Gissing's London. In that reading, there is a close fit between Gissing's textual mapping of the city and Charles Booth's cartography in his *Inquiry into the Life and Labour of the People in London*.[22] Just as the colour coding of Booth's maps implies rigid boundaries between zones defined by class, so Gissing's characters inhabit particular zones which break up a conception of the city as a totality. In his analysis of Gissing's London, Goode returns to Lukács and his understanding of naturalism as part of an aesthetic disruption caused by a working-class threat to the bourgeois world-view, so that the representation of a social totality is no longer possible. Instead, Gissing's London is made up of distinct locations: 'not "the city" as a conceptualised response, as a totality', but 'delimited spaces that have to be lived in or crossed'.[23] Although Waymark in *The Unclassed* is described as a flâneur, moving at will through the city's different spaces, Goode argues that 'the hustle of the city streets with its random contingencies is London, but only part of Gissing's London. Mostly, the novel is based on areas with contained social structures which hold even the unclassed within them – the West End is a specific location within the city, not the city itself.'[24] The city's meaning is constructed from motifs that are attached to specific domains of these delimited spaces;[25] and Goode goes further to argue that working-class domains offer a privileged view of the city: 'Only London could create the unclassed, but only the unclassed can see London.'[26]

Goode, like Williams, favours the novels of urban deprivation over the later suburban novels. But, this is a dubious selection not just between novels but also within novels. Goode chooses to understand the city on only one level, on the level of what might be called 'real material processes', here class relations. He stands on one side of a dividing line in cultural studies: between those who hold to an understanding of modernity in terms of such processes, and who then perform an ideology critique to get at those processes (or real worlds); and those who argue that the saturation of modernity with images and symbols, that which Benjamin called the return of myth in the midst of modernity,[27] means that those dreamworlds offer quite different versions of the city. Thus, in his analysis of *In the Year of the Jubilee*, the novel which offers the most panoramic vision of the city and which, above all others, is concerned with the city streets, Goode limits that vision to the aspirations of suburbia, which appears as just another delimited zone of the city, the preoccupation of Gissing's later period.

If we turn to the other most influential Marxist critic on Gissing, Fredric Jameson, we find that Jameson also makes the city central to his understanding of Gissing's work. But Jameson's approach to the real is, as one might expect given the pages of mediations that constitute the theoretical first chapter of *The Political Unconscious*,[28] more complex than that of Goode – although that complexity leads to differerent rather than better readings of the novels. Of *The Nether World* he writes that it:

> is best read, not for its documentary information on the conditions of Victorian slum life, but as testimony about the narrative paradigms that organize middle-class fantasies about those slums and about 'solutions' that might resolve, manage, or repress the evident class anxieties aroused by the existence of an industrial working class and an urban lumpenproletariat.[29]

None the less, when it comes to the city, Lukács's theory of realism is again the reference point:

> In Gissing. . .the Dickensian city is little by little drained of its vitality and reduced to the empty grid of calls by one character to another, visits to oppressive rooms and apartments, and intervals of random strolls through the poorer quarters.

Interestingly, it would be easy to substitute Kafka's *The Trial* for *The Nether World* in Jameson's passage: comparison that can also be made between Kafka's three spheres of interiors, city streets and a utopian green space (see the discussion of 'The Judgement' in Chapter 17 of this book) and Gissing's urban trinity of the slums (in the novels of the 1880s), the suburbs (in the novels of the 1890s) and the rural (in *The Private Papers of Henry Ryecroft*). But such a comparison is not usually made because Gissing is thought of as a realist or, in Jameson's Lukácsian categorisation, a naturalist writer rather than a modernist.

Instead, Jameson, like Goode, chooses to focus on the scientific discourse of classification in Gissing's texts: 'a form of high naturalist specialization that seeks to pass itself off as a map of the social totality . . . the characters of the novel will be reduced to nothing more than illustrations of their preexistent presences'.[30] This analysis, which corresponds with Williams and Goode to the extent that it finds the core of Gissing's value in a negative aesthetic, is, however, supplemented with an account of how desire is dealt with in the novels, an account that offers Jameson's most influential contribution to critical discussions of Gissing: the concept of *ressentiment*, whereby the humiliation of the subaltern class is turned upon the ruling class through a morality that itself glorifies self-abasement. Desire in the novels is classified, as in the case of Richard Mutimer in *Demos*, as a kind of class envy. As will be discussed in Chapter 8, Jameson is alert to the later novels' wit, but he too commits the cardinal sin of Gissing criticism, the biographical impulse, referring us back to the youthful misdemeanour and imprisonment as 'an incurable wound'[31] in order to offer an original account of Gissing's use of language as that of a thwarted classicist who uses English as 'if it were a dead language like Latin' or:

> Better still Gissing's language offers perhaps an early example of what Roland Barthes has called *écriture blanche*, white or bleached writing. . . this linguistic practice seeks through radical depersonalization – as though a kind of preventive suicide – to neutralize the social conflicts immediately evoked and regenerated by any living use of speech.[32]

Thus, desire is neutralised: 'universal commodification of desire stamps any achieved desire or wish as inauthentic'.[33] If this appears, at last, to make Gissing into a modernist, a writer who is in many ways closer to Kafka or Beckett than to Balzac or Dickens, what it leaves out is the opportunity for play that such processes of defamiliarisation or strategic alienation allow. However, if Gissing is read as a modernist, then his relationship to the city becomes more not less important, because, as Williams reminds us, the city is the place where modernism is born. Jameson, however, follows earlier Marxist critics and leaves his subject in a cul de sac, imprisoned, this time as symbol of 'unhappy consciousness', when a different understanding of Gissing's city might lead us back to the streets.

In that context, Gissing's work can be read as a negative response to the new public culture was emerging in late nineteenth-century London. It responds both to the impact of industrial modernity on everyday bodily acts and to the new material contexts in which intersubjectivity is produced. Gendered subjectivity is the product of these interactions.

Gissing's fiction can properly be compared with that of Dorothy Richardson because her work is a response to the same public culture. *Pilgrimage* is a text that follows in the footsteps of the New Woman. As discussed in the following chapter, Miriam Henderson is a New Woman and *Pilgrimage* can be read as a response to the formal dilemmas of New Woman fiction. Where, in Gissing's texts, the lived experience of emergent subjectivities is circumscribed and fixed (albeit in such a way that suggests the lack that this creates) leaving them stranded and hopeless, Richardson develops a form that tracks subjectivity in process.

For example, one of the difficulties of this study has been finding definitions for subjectivities such as that embodied by Miriam Henderson, the heroine of Dorothy Richardson's *Pilgrimage*. Miriam reacts against conventional (Victorian) femininity and she has an ambivalent relationship to masculinity. This ambivalence begins with her relationship with her father, but this is worked through outside the family, amongst the new social possibilities offered by the city. Miriam reconfigures her relationships with both her parents in response to the material spaces in which London's public culture is made. As discussed in Chapter 16, she deals with the trauma of her mother's suicide, which haunts her through its association with a sign for 'Teetgen's Teas'. The strong father she experiences as a young girl quickly dissolves into more complex relationships with a number of male lovers, the experience of which finally brings Miriam to an analysis of a masculine modernity. One way of understanding Miriam's new gendered subjectivity might be, following Judith Halberstam,[34] as a kind of 'female masculinity'. Miriam undoubtedly does appropriate aspects of available masculine identities. But, charting her development over the whole of *Pilgrimage* it becomes clear that these acts of appropriation are part of a process, often of a response to her despair at the limited options for women available. Beginning with the chain cafés, London's new spaces enable her to develop a new gendered subjectivity that does not match earlier forms of femininity, but instead incorporates a feminist consciousness that is deeply critical of the dominant forms of masculinity.[35] One of the options Miriam explores is love between women. *Pilgrimage* as a text, however, refuses the fixity of secure boundaries for identity. The origins of this ambivalence, as I go on to discuss in Chapter 2, can be traced back to New Woman fiction.

2

Dorothy Richardson and New Woman fiction

In modernist fiction the urban scene is the site for the reconfiguration of gender relations. The streets and not the home supply the spaces through which a still dominant, albeit now more challenged and challengeable, male hegemony is produced. This is the case in Dorothy Richardson's *Pilgrimage*, but Richardson's heroine, Miriam Henderson, can be traced back to the New Woman fiction of the late nineteenth century. She is, like Clara in *The Nether World*, one of the new entrants who helped to transform London's public sphere.

New Woman fiction was characterised by three innovations:[1] first, the transgression of the public/private divide constructed by high Victorian fiction; second, the innovations in style that preceded modernism; and, finally, the representation of new gendered subjectivities. All three of these developments had implications for Victorian constructions of masculinity. The proliferation of new kinds of femininity fragmented the hegemonic forms of homosociality that structured Victorian institutions such as the public school, the Army, the Church and Parliament. One of the New Woman's most successful strategies was to put masculine authority into doubt so that, even if the difficulty of constructing a coherent feminine subject in the public sphere was never fully resolved, the period saw a comparable proliferation in masculinities each of which is fully represented in the literature of the *fin de siècle*: from Haggard's imperial heroes to Wilde's effeminate wits; from Edward Carpenter's Uranian to Gissing's embittered subjects; and which only slightly later would include the lonely masculine subjects that populate Conrad's modernist tales.[2]

The transgression of the public/private divide was perhaps the most significant material incursion made by *fin-de-siècle* women into traditional masculine domains. However, New Woman fiction was characterised by an uncertainty about the position of the new feminine subject: whether she was inside (private/domestic) or outside (public/political). Despite the heterogeneity of form found in New Woman writing, a common trope was the threshold which must be crossed, or which, if not actually transgressed, is hovered on uncertainly. One such example was the cover of George Egerton's *Keynotes* (1893), which had a racy illustration by Aubrey Beardsley.[3] The relatively reserved short stories between the covers contrasted sharply with the uncorseted, flirtatious figure that adorned them, impaled on a pierrot's pole. Instead, the stories play with metaphors of limitation, and the possibility of a new kind of subjectivity that will exceed women's allotted social role. At the end of one story, 'The Empty Frame', the protagonist dreams

> that she is sitting on a fiery globe rolling away into space. That her head is wedged in a huge frame, the top of her head touches its top, the sides its sides, and it keeps growing larger and larger and her head with it, until she seems to be sitting inside her own head, and the inside is one vast hollow.[4]

New Woman fiction often pushed at the formal boundaries of representation. In her only novel, *The Wheel of God* (1898), Egerton wrote of the new experience of urban space (here in New York) encountered by the New Woman, where the public position of the working woman transgressed the sanctity of the domestic sphere:

> Life seemed less concrete, less inside the houses and warehouses; it was everywhere, pounding like a gigantic steam-hammer, full of speed, in the air, in the streets – insistent, noisy, attention-compelling. Trains above one's head, one caught glimpses of domestic interiors, intimate bedroom scenes, as one whizzed past second stories in the early cars.[5]

Olive Schreiner's novels were also concerned with the limits of the domestic sphere. *The Story of an African Farm* tells of a failed attempt to break free. For all the cross-dressing and gender role reversal of the final pages, the heroine, Lyndall, dies having established her independence against the backdrop of the African karoo, but without finding a social formation that might give sustenance to the fragment of truth she has gleaned from her experience.[6] Schreiner's vision of existential despair was not, however, matched by the novel's reception in London's literary circles. Already, by 1883, the boundaries that defined women's public life had shifted significantly, ensuring Schreiner a rapturous welcome in the city.[7] A novel from the Empire's periphery found its audience in the imperial metropolis; and Schreiner's later collection of allegories, *Dreams*, published in 1890, became a kind of feminist manifesto.[8] In *Dreams* (1890) borders and limits are a recurrent theme. In 'The Sunlight Lay Across My Bed' the dreamer falls asleep to the noises that enter through her window from a city street. On the border between private and public the dream takes her to the threshold of a series of alternative realities each of which questions conventionally gendered roles.[9]

The innovations in form that emerged as a response to these contradictions are difficult to categorise except in their heterogeneity. The bestselling novel of 1893, Sarah Grand's *The Heavenly Twins*, was a manifesto for feminist social purity, in which decadence was blamed on the French: 'Their minds are hopelessly tainted with the exhalations of the literary sewer which streams from France throughout the world and their habits are not nicer than their books.'[10] It is possible to cite Egerton's impressionism (in her short stories), Schreiner's allegories or Sarah Grand's moralistic gothic in *The Heavenly Twins* as just three examples of the variety found in New Woman writing. Almost every form of realism, romance and sensation writing can be found in the upsurge that accompanies the rise of First Wave feminism. As Sally Ledger has argued, the various appropriations of New Woman writing as proto-modernist have to employ a selective eye that excludes 'the multiplicity of textual forms. . .deployed to articulate her [the New Woman's] complex presence in the cultural landscape of the *fin de siècle*'.[11] Ledger gives a subtle account of the vexed question of the New Woman's relationship to modernism, pointing to the paradox that, while New Woman writers did experiment with form, for the mass of readers 'realism offered a vehicle for feminist discussion which is almost unparalleled in literary history'.[12] Ledger's argument resists both the claims of Anglo-American criticism, which praises a primarily male canon for its opposition to a feminised mass culture and the claims of some French feminist critics for much the same canon as exemplifying *l'écriture feminine*. But realism also posed difficulties for New Woman writers, even when, as for Gissing, it was their chosen form. New Women's experiments with non-realist forms can perhaps be understood as a dialectical process where, on the one hand, Victorian society itself is fracturing, opening up new forms of social relations and, on the other hand, the formal innovations pioneered by New Women writers can be seen as part of the process in which new ways of seeing generate new forms of identification. New Woman texts of the late Victorian period exhibit what Rosie Miles has called a bi-textuality, where the necessity for public recognition via the codes of Victorian respectability that still govern gender relations clashes with the desire for new forms of subjectivity that articulate a rebellion against the confines of the domestic.[13] This explains the violent critical reaction to the representation of interiority in the work of Egerton and Schreiner and it goes some way to explaining their difficult engagement with the novel form.[14]

For example, an interesting aspect of Egerton's novel *The Wheel of God* is the disjunction between the impressionist moments from a young woman's psychological development and the harsh, normative tone of the realist narration that borrows from the new realist or naturalist writers of the 1890s, such as George Gissing, George Moore or Arthur Morrison. This strong opposition can be understood as the playing out of the contradictions between the negative, satirical and misogynist identities attributed to the New Woman in public 'realist' discourse and the emergent desiring subjects suggested by non-realist texts like Egerton's short stories or Schreiner's *Dreams*.

Even the bestselling novel of 1893, Sarah Grand's *The Heavenly Twins*, can be read in terms of this opposition. Grand reaches for two public discourses, one medical and therefore dangerous because it intrudes into both the public and the private, and one safe, the moral discourse of social purity deployed by suffragist women to claim the higher ground over their detractors. Against these public or offical discourses the novel produces an extraordinary number of gothic monsters (including syphilitic men, monstrous babies and cross-dressing girls). For those readers who still engage with the novel, this carnivalesque profusion of bizarre performances triumphs over the attempt to contain them within a moralising framework.

The New Woman's dilemma was, then, the difficulty of staging her performance in a way that would be admissible in the public sphere. In a broad sense this was a problem with masculine authority. But in so sense should the gendering of the public sphere as masculine be confused with an idea of a monolithic masculinity. While a New Woman identity proved a problematic concept, the idea of the New Woman had its greatest success in fragmenting any sense of public culture as an undifferentiated bloc. The proliferation of new masculinities both in New Woman fiction and in men's fiction of the period is testimony to this and formal innovation an important part of the cultural process. Egerton's impressionism, Schreiner's *Dreams* and even *The Heavenly Twins* are proto-modernist n their challenge to a public (Victorian) symbolic order as well as in their form.

Dorothy Richardson was then within a traceable tradition. As Ledger has argued, modernism should not be seen in some way a better alternative (either for elitist or for feminist reasons) to a realist tradition that is increasingly associated with mass culture.[15] The binary opposition of modernism and mass culture is a false one as well as too narrow an account of the development of prose from the late nineteenth century onwards. Rather, the cultural politics of modernism extends directly from the cultural politics of the *fin de siècle*. Modernist writers responded to the same sense of crisis. Much of the deliberate inaccessibility of modernist prose is a response to the public backlash against the decadent, aesthetic and New Woman movements of the 1890s. It is of course difficult to generalise. Modernism is a notoriously vague term for a broad set of cultural movements. With Richardson, however, it is easy to place her modernist project in relation to the New Woman. Richardson was herself a New Woman in the 1890s: not, at first, a New Woman intellectual like Schreiner or Egerton, but one of the army of new workers who moved to the capital seeking employment in the growing white collar sector that was opening up to women.[16] After a brief spell as a teacher in Germany and North London she took up a post as a dental receptionist in Harley Street, where she worked from 1896 until 1908, and it is this period that that forms the bulk of the years covered by the volumes of *Pilgrimage* published between 1915 and 1938 (one posthumous volume was published in 1967). In fact, the sections of *Pilgrimage* that cover the 1890s read like a deliberate performance of the public image of the New Woman, even while the text itself is an early and indeed pioneering example of stream of consciousness. Long passages are devoted to the joys of the cigarette and the bicycle.[17]

3

Going up in smoke: Mr Richardson

Detailing her break with the paternalism of nineteenth-century realism, in her Foreword to the four-volume edition of *Pilgrimage*, Richardson describes Balzac as the 'father of realism'.[1] In the opening 'chapter-novel' of the series, *Pointed Roofs*, the actual father is a domestic patriarch and tyrant. His reading is exactly that which the father of the heroine of Sarah Grand's *The Heavenly Twins* finds so horrifying in the hands of a woman, Victorian scientific materialism: William Lecky, Charles Darwin, Herbert Spencer, bound *Contemporary Reviews* and the *Proceedings of the British Association*.[2] But the break that Richardson's semi-autobiographical heroine, Miriam Henderson, makes with the father is neither immediate nor final. Miriam experiences a problematic identification with her father and his attitudes: 'Pater knew how hateful all the world of women were and despised them'.[3] Partly as a consequence, she has an ambivalent relationship with the version of femininity on offer to girls of her class. On leaving home, she is unable to 'give any answering embrace' to 'the unexpected convulsive force of her mother's arms'.[4] Instead, she embraces the public sphere and finds her father's importance exposed as masquerade. Embarking on a journey away from home for the first time, she overhears him lying about the trip to a Dutch traveller.

> 'Very good, very good,' she heard him say, 'fine education in German schools.'
> Both men were smoking cigars.
> She wanted to draw herself upright and shake out her clothes.
> 'Select,' she heard, 'excellent staff masters . . .daughters of gentleman.'
> Pater is trying to make the Dutchman think I am being taken to a finishing school in Germany.[5]

The cigars here are not just cigars, but offer the full Freudian symbolic, even as the actual, weak father is detached from the myth. The truth, that Miriam is going to work as a teacher because her father cannot provide for the family, is also the beginning of Miriam's 'lonely pilgrimage' towards an independent subjecthood – the realisation of her desire to draw herself 'upright' and 'to shake out' her familial bonds. The scene takes place just after she and her father have crossed the channel. On the border of continental Europe, a new world, her allegiance starts to shift. At this point, she still supports her father in his performance – 'she shared her father's satisfaction in impressing the Dutchman. She was at one with him in that.'[6] Later, she will explore and use London's urban spaces to gain a greater freedom. In place of her father's cigar, Miriam will adopt the more ambivalently gendered cigarette, beloved of Wildean decadents and New Women, as a symbol of her independence: 'a protection against suburban influence'.[7]

But the cigarette does not entirely eliminate the influence of the father, rather it operates in a way not dissimiliar to Judith Butler's theorisation of the phallus as 'fundamentally transferable'.[8] If Butler's argument does not make much of the new possibilities that open up in modern city, the shadow of the phallus can be seen as one (and only one) version of the ghostly presence of the father in modernism. As will be discussed further in Chapter 9, with the cigarette Miriam's sense of a gendered self is transferred from the familial – 'her own disappointing birth as the third girl' and consequent role as the 'boy' of the family – to the relations of production and consumption that operate in the city.[9]

In the early 'chapter-novels'[10] of *Pilgrimage*, smoking becomes one of the rituals of modernity that allows Miriam to perform her New Woman subjectivity.[11] In the next 'chapter-novel' in the series, *Backwater*, she moves from making cigarettes for her father to making them for herself. Her first cigarette is made with his hand-held machine. In a quasi-revolutionary act, seizing hold of the means of (cigarette) production is to grasp the opportunity to produce her own subjectivity.

> Slipping the paper evenly into the slot she shut the machine and turned the roller. As the sound of the loosely working cogs came up to her she revolted from her self-imposed task. She was too happy to make cigarettes. It would use up her happiness stupidly.
>
> She was surprised by a sudden suggestion that she should smoke the single cigarette herself. Why not? Why had she never smoked one? She glanced at the slowly swinging door. No one would come. She was alone on the top floor. Every one was downstairs and busy. The finished cigarette lay on her knee. Taking it between her fingers, she pressed a little hanging thread of tobacco into place. The cigarette felt pleasantly plump and firm. It was well made.[12]

As important as the analogy with sexual experimentation here is the way the passage acts as an allegory of a whole industrial process in an individual act. The invention of the Bonsack machine in 1883 had allowed industrialisation of cigarette production to provide for rapidly expanding numbers of cigarette smokers, many of them women.[13] In modernity, the individual pleasure is the product of industrial systems. The powerful forces that have to be engaged just to smoke a cigarette are signified by its equivalence to the efforts of a man she sees when she looks out of the window: the gardener, pushing a mowing machine 'with all his might'.[14] Miriam's new subjectivity will be made in relation not just to bodily pleasures but to the might of industrial modernity.

In contrast with the production of the cigarette, the experience of smoking itself is described as intoxicating. The language used – 'yellow cloud' and 'yellow haze' – recalls a Baudelairean decadence:

> A third of the whole length was consumed. Her nostrils breathed in smoke and, as she tasted the burnt flavour, the sweetness of the unpolluted air all around her was a new thing. The acrid tang in her nostrils intoxicated her. She drew more boldly. There was smoke in her mouth. She opened it quickly, sharply exhaling a yellow cloud oddly different from the grey spirals wreathing their way from the end of the cigarette. She went on drawing in mouthful after mouthful of smoke, expelling each quickly with widely-opened lips, turning to look at the well-known room through the yellow haze and again at the sky, which drew nearer as she puffed at it. The sight of the treetops scrolled with her little clouds brought her a sense of power. She had chosen to smoke and she was smoking and the morning world gleamed back at her.[15]

The passage participates in what Benjamin calls the 'dialectics of intoxication', where the world of 'humiliating sobriety' complements the world of 'ecstasy'.[16] Here the ordinariness of air itself is made a 'new thing' by the smoke. The return of the symbolic 'strong' father is now transferred to the strong tobacco:

> No one would believe she had not felt ill. She found it difficult to understand why any one should feel sick from smoking. Dizzy perhaps . . . a little drunk. Pater's tobacco was very strong, some people could not smoke it . . . She had smoked a whole cigarette of strong tobacco and liked it. Raising her arms above her head she worked them upwards, stretching every muscle of her body. No, she was anything but ill.[17]

The strong father is consumed by fire with the tobacco, becoming in the process an ethereal or phantasmal figure rather than one with immediate social power.[18] According to Richard Klein, 'smoking is a "sacrificial ceremony". In which the disappearance of something solid, tobacco, is infinitely compensated by the symbolic gain I acquire in appropriating to myself the world around me.'[19] In *Pilgrimage*, the father, and the patriarchal world that gives him his authority, have gone up in a cloud of smoke; and, in the process, the available points of identification (or correspondences) open to Miriam expand. Klein cites Jean Cocteau: 'One must not forget that the pack of cigarettes, the ceremony that extracts them, lights the lighter, and that strange cloud which penetrates us and which our nostrils puff, have with powerful charms seduced and conquered the world.'[20] Where for male modernists (including Baudelaire and Joyce in *A Portrait of the Artist as a Young Man*) the breakdown caused by modernity is responded to by the discovery of a new myth of masculinity in the modern (a myth the ritual elements of their art rehearse) for Richardson the dialectic of the modern world opens up the possibility of the father's combustion and out of the ashes (or ashtray) is born the possibility of a new public femininity.

The 'chapter-novels' *Pointed Roofs* and *Backwater* play out the *fort/da* of Miriam's identification with, and disassociation from, her father. *Pointed Roofs* ends with a symbolic departure as Miriam leaves the surrogate family of the school in Germany:

> The train was high above the platform. Politely smiling, Miriam scrambled to the window. The platform was moving, the large bright station moved away. Fräulein's wide smile was creasing and caverning under her hat from which the veil was thrown back.
> Standing by the window, Miriam smiled sharply. Fräulein's form flowed slowly away with the platform.
> Groups passed by smiling and waving.
> Miriam sat down.
> She leaped up, to lean from the window.
> The platform had disappeared.[21]

The moment marks a real and a figurative moment on her journey. Prosaically, she leaves Germany by train; but by now the 'platform' that underpinned her youthful identity has 'disappeared'. Her pilgrimage has taken her to the point where the father's role is not only seen as masquerade, but no longer holds any attraction. In *Backwater* she begins to develop her own form of ambivalently gendered subjectivity. In the later chapter novels, the idea of the father returns in her relationships with men she meets in the city, but this time as a kind of phantasmic presence, in which the act of recollecting the father represents an attempt to reconfigure the shock of the modern in a series of correspondences with an earlier history: the prehistory that haunts modern manifestations of masculine hegemony.

4

Fathers and cities

In one sense, modernism was fathered by an earlier cultural epoch. It marked a rebellion against and a resistance to nineteenth-century realism's complicity with the symbolic and actual social power of the Victorian patriarch. When modernist writers of the early twentieth century remembered the 1890s as the time of their cultural formation, fathering was represented as an uncanny process. Weak fathers return to haunt their orphans as they explore the possibilities of the city beyond the bourgeois home. This is the case across a number of European cultures. Modernist texts such as *Portrait of the Artist as a Young Man*, *Pilgrimage* and Kafka's writings make the process of disengagement from the family their subject matter. When the father returns in the context of the city, he returns as myth rather than universal law. Some modernist texts represent this as a crisis – the novels of Wyndham Lewis, for example, or D. H. Lawrence[1] – reacting ambivalently, or with the clear desire to set up more authoritarian structures in its place. In contrast, Charles Baudelaire, Franz Kafka, James Joyce and Dorothy Richardson resist what Pierre Bourdieu calls 'the historical labour of eternalisation': 'the history of the continuous (re)creation of the objective and subjective structures of masculine domination, which has gone on permanently so long as there have been men and women, and through which the masculine order has been continuously reproduced from age to age'.[2]

Writing of the impact of architecture on consciousness, one of the main themes of *The Arcades Project*, Walter Benjamin commented:

> The impression of the old-fashioned can arise only where, in a certain way, reference is made to the most topical. If the beginnings of modern architecture to some extent lie in the arcades, their antiquated effect on the present generation has exactly the same significance as the antiquated effect of a father on his son.[3]

Just as the older material structures of the city linger in the present, ready to be rescued and reinvigorated, the ghost of the father lingers in the modernist city as a kind of after-effect.⁴ As Franz Kafka demonstrates, that effect can still be terrifying, even when it takes a weak embodied form. In his short story 'The Judgement', Georg Bendemann's father returns from his dotage:

> 'Am I well covered up?' asked the father once more, seeming to be strangely intent upon the answer.
> 'Don't worry, you're well covered up.'
> 'No!' cried the father, cutting short the answer, threw the blankets back with a strength that sent them all flying in a moment and stood upright in the bed. Only one hand lightly touched the ceiling to steady him.⁵

The impact of the modern, the notion of shock that Walter Benjamin appends to the word *Erlebnis*, shatters the social configuration in which the Victorian patriarch held prime position. But the power of the paternal myth does not completely disappear, no matter how well covered up (*gut zugedeckt*),⁶ nor does its ability to affect the present. In fact, it is the return of myth in modernity that interests Benjamin in *The Arcades Project*.⁷ Rather than a return to the eternal – to archetypes or complexes rooted in a collective unconscious or the anatomical – Benjamin is concerned to establish the correspondences that will make for a new and redemptive historical consciousness. He found his early models amongst the German romantics, but later the aesthetic ideas of Baudelaire became central to his conception of modernity:

> What Baudelaire meant by *correspondances* may be described as an experience [*Erfahrung*] which seeks to establish itself in crisis-proof form. This is possible only within the realm of the ritual ... *Correspondances* are the data of remembrance [*Eingedenken*] – not historical data, but data of prehistory.⁸

Benjamin suggests that, Charles Baudelaire's *Les Fleurs du Mal*, seen by many as modernism's originary text, begins with the void left by the absent father. He argues that Poems 99 and 100 are the oldest parts of the book and that

> Both present the image of the fatherless family; the son, however, far from occupying the place of the father, leaves it empty [*leer*]. The distant sun that is setting in the first poem is the symbol of the father, of him whose gaze – 'Huge open eye in the curious sky' – lingers without jealousy, sympathetic and remote, on the meal shared by mother and son.⁹

The absent, phantasmal father watches:

> Qui, derrière la vitre où se brisait sa gerbe,
> Semblait, grand oeil ouvert dans le ciel curieux,
> Contempler nos dîners longs et silencieux

Poem 100, according to Benjamin, 'evokes the image of the fatherless family situated not around a table but around a grave. The sultriness of life pregnant with possibilities has entirely yielded to the cool night air of death.'[10] Baudelaire's imagery is bleak and soulful:

> Les morts, les pauvre morts, ont de grandes douleurs
> Et quand Octobre soufflé, émondeur des vieux arbres,
> Son vent mélancolique à l'entour de leur marbres,
> Certe, ils doivement trouver les vivants bien ingrats
> A dormir, commes ils font, chaudement dans leur draps

However, the absence that marks the beginning of Baudelaire's great work also creates a gap, 'pregnant with possibilities', into which new urban masculinities (such as those explored by Baudelaire in poems such as 'A Une Passante') can then move. None the less, these new urban masculinities are still haunted by the continuing presence of paternal power, an 'antiquated effect' that maintains its ability to spring into life. Masculine hegemony persists, but within modernity that persistence, like the changing technologies of the city, has to be made and remade. Its manifestations can be ferocious, but they need support, just as Georg Bendemann's father requires a steadying hand on the more secure structure of the ceiling. Benjamin writes of 'The Judgement' that: 'As the father throws off the burden of the blanket, he also throws off a cosmic burden. He has to set cosmic ages in motion in order to turn the age-old father-son relationship into a living and consequential thing.'[11] For Benjamin the relationship between father and son is no more direct than his view of history is linear. Both familial, the social, the aesthetic and the historical need to be represented as a constellation of relationships;[12] and, as in *The Arcades Project*, it is the city that provides both context and metaphor for such constellations.

Benjamin's work suggests that an understanding of the paternal in modernist prose can be achieved only in terms of its 'remembrance' in the context of the city. To do so is not to deny the role of the family or the psyche, but it does reintroduce into debates about modernism the importance of urban public culture, which is necessarily constructed in relation to familial, intimate, private and psychic spheres. Modernist masculinities were produced at the thresholds between all these spheres. Thus, in his memoir, 'Berlin Chronicle', Benjamin describes his autobiography in spatial terms: first as 'arranging the space of my life – Bios – graphically in a map [den Raum des Lebens – Bios – graphisch in einer Karte zu gliedern]';[13] then as 'a diagram of my life [ein graphisches Schema meines Lebens]'.[14] The possibility of such a diagram was enabled by the context of what was, in the early part of the twentieth century, the world's foremost modernist city:

> it had to be in Paris, where the walls and quays, the asphalt surfaces, the collections and the rubbish, the railings and the squares, the arcades and the kiosks, teach a language so singular that our relations to people attain, in the solitude encompassing us in our immersion in that world of things, the depth of a sleep in which the dream image waits to show the people their true faces. I wish to write of this afternoon because it made so apparent what kind of regimen cities keep over the imagination, and why the city – where people make the most ruthless demands on one another, where appointments and telephone calls, sessions and visits, flirtations and the struggle for existence grant the individual not a single moment of contemplation – indemnifies itself in memory, and why the veil it has covertly woven out of our lives shows the images of people less than those of the sites of our encounters with others or ourselves.[15]

Here, as for Toril Moi (see the Introduction), Benjamin's situation is significant. The idea of the diagram or map comes to Benjamin while sitting in a café. Coffee houses and cafés were key loci for the development of the bourgeois public sphere. For transient intellectuals such as Benjamin or Joyce, we might start to talk here of a European public sphere, where, in each city, places to eat and drink become points from which the city can be mapped. Thus, even the actual café is important: 'I was sitting inside the Café des deux Magots at St.-Germaine-des-Prés.' Now a tourist trap selling the most expensive coffee in Paris, the Café des deux Magots was, before and after the Second World War, a meeting point for modernist artists and intellectuals such as Simone de Beauvoir and Jean-Paul Sartre. At the centre of intellectual life between the wars, Benjamin was waiting – 'I forget for whom':

> I knew at the same moment exactly how it was to be done. With a very simple question I interrogated my past life, and the answers were inscribed, as if of their own accord, on a sheet of paper that I had with me. A year or two later, when I lost the sheet, I was inconsolable. I have never since been able to restore it as it arose before me then, resembling a series of family trees. Now, however, reconstructing its outline in thought without directly reproducing it, I would instead speak of a labyrinth. I am not concerned here not with what is installed in the chamber at its enigmatic centre, ego or fate, but all the more with the many entrances leading into the interior. These entrances I call 'primal acquaintances'; each of them is a graphic symbol of my acquaintance with a person whom I met not through other people, but through neighbourhood, family relationships, school comradeship, mistaken identity, companionship on travels, or other such – hardly numerous – situations. So many primal relationships, so many entrances to the labyrinth.[16]

As much of interest here as the modernism of Benjamin's urban situation is the surrealist moment that occurs as a flash of 'illumination' and is followed by a form of automatic writing in which the insights flow 'as if of their own accord'. The ability of the city to produce surrealist moments is a theme of modernism that runs from Baudelaire through to Mass Observation.[17] The multiplicity of relationships produced by urban living overwhelm paternal authority: 'so many primal relationships, so many entrances to the labyrinth'. Benjamin does not go as far as contemporary queer theorists who argue for a multiplicity of genders. His division is still binary, despite the network of corridors he describes, 'the male may be drawn to the right, female to the left';[18] but his own middle-class masculinity is produced through such intersections, particularly the threshold between interior and exterior, for example in a later passage from 'Berlin Chronicle', which describes the threshold between family and street:

> There is no doubt, at any rate, that the feeling of crossing for the first time the threshold of one's own class had a part in the almost unequalled fascination of publicly accosting a whore on the street. At the beginning, however, this was a crossing of frontiers not only social but topographic, in the sense that whole networks of streets [*ganze Straßenzüge*] were opened up under the auspices of prostitution.[19]

If the gendered perspective of the passage is unambiguously masculine, the class position unambiguously bourgeois, Benjamin's larger insight is striking: the family is now only one node in the city spaces formed by the 'networks of streets'.[20]

5

On the threshold: Franz Kafka

Comparable moments at which an urban masculine subjectivity is produced can be found in other European modernists. A key incident in Franz Kafka's 'Letter to His Father' – a text in which the narrator's relationship to his family is represented in excruciating detail – occurs when the young Franz makes a clumsy attempt to cross the borderline between familial relations and public sexuality and confronts his parents about their responsibility for his sexual ignorance:

> I remember going for a walk one evening with you and Mother; it was on Josefsplatz near where the Länderbank is today; and I began talking about these interesting things, in a stupidly boastful, superior, proud, detached (that was spurious), cold (that was genuine), and stammering manner, as indeed I usually talked to you, reproaching the two of you with having left me uninstructed; with the fact that it was my schoolmates who first had to take me in hand, that I had been close to great dangers (here I was brazenly lying, as was my way, in order to show myself brave, for as a consequence of my timidity I had, except for the usual sexual misdemeanours of city children, no very exact knowledge of these 'great dangers'); but I finally hinted that now, fortunately, I knew everything, no longer needed any advice, and that everything was all right.[1]

His father's advice, not given to the reader, but 'uninhibited in a very modern way' Franz finds the 'filthiest thing possible'.[2] It is usually interpreted as advice to go to prostitutes, considered at the time as a more healthy option than masturbation.[3] But more significant than the advice itself is where the exchange takes place, on a family walk through the streets of Prague, between a father and a son who can never quite break away. Franz's masculinity is produced on the threshold between public and private, here between family circle and public square.

Even taken as biographical evidence, the 'Letter' complicates rather than illuminates Kafka's fiction. However, the best critics of Kafka's work have warned against reading his non-fiction as a master text. In *Prosa der Moderne*, Peter Bürger points out that 'diaries are also literary texts'.[4] Bürger echoes the earlier judgement of Walter Benjamin, who wrote: 'It is easier to draw speculative conclusions from Kafka's posthumous collection of notes than to explore even one of the motifs that appear in his stories and novels.'[5] Elizabeth Boa argues that it was in his fiction that Kafka developed the conceptual framework that allowed him to understand his relationship with his father, rather than in the 'Letter' itself, which was not written until 1919, only five years before the author's death: 'the famous *Letter to His Father* could scarcely have been written without the earlier work on *The Trial*'.[6] As a late text, the 'I' of the 'Letter to His Father' is no less complex a representation of subjectivity than Kafka's novels and short stories.

Taken as a 'literary text', the 'Letter' demonstrates the dialectic within modernist fiction between mythical archetypes that depict a lingering patriarchal power and a critical uncoupling of the power of the father and modern masculinities. Thresholds are always central to Kafka's fiction. In his short story 'The Cares of a Family Man', the strange inhuman being, Odradek, who 'looks like a flat star-shaped spool of thread', inhabits transitional, threshold areas.

> He lurks by turns in the garret, the stairway, the lobbies, the entrance hall. Often for months he is not to be seen; then he has presumably moved into other houses; but he always comes faithfully back to our house again. Many a time when you go out of a door. . .he happens just to be leaning directly beneath you against the banisters.[7]

Even the origin of his name exists between languages: 'Some say the word Odradek is of Slavonic origin. . . Others again believe it to be of German origin and only influenced by Slavonic.'[8] Odradek's persistence troubles the 'family man' who narrates the story. Whereas he, the paterfamilias, will die, this creature who can escape the confines of the family home will, he fears, live on:

> Can he possibly die? Anything that dies has had some kind of aim in life, some kind of activity, which has worn out; but that does not apply to Odradek. Am I to suppose, then, that he will always be rolling down the stairs, with ends of thread trailing after him, right before the feet of my children, and my children's children? He does no harm to anyone that one can see; but the idea that he is likely to survive me I find almost painful.[9]

In his book *Kafka's Clothes* Mark Anderson identifies the importance in Kafka's work of the word 'Verkehr', which he translates as 'traffic, trade, commerce, exchange, social and sexual intercourse'.[10] For Anderson, the term *Verkehr* evokes the mobile, transient nature of the modern city in the tradition of the Baudelairean Dandy. In a refreshing contrast to the representation of self found in the 'Letter to His Father', he reports that

Kafka was himself something of a dandy: in the words of the Austrian writer Felix Stössenger, 'the "best-dressed man" he had ever seen'.[11] *Kafka's Clothes* suggests that, for Franz, Hermann's fancy goods business was paradigmatic of the circulation in people and commodities that constitutes urban *Verkehr*.[12] In the 'Letter', the business is, for the young Franz, an object of both fascination and repulsion:

> I fled everything that even remotely reminded me of you. First, the business. In itself, especially in my childhood, so long as it was in the shop, I ought to have liked it very much, it was so full of life, lit up in the evening, there was so much to see and hear; one was able to help now and then, to distinguish oneself, and, above all, to admire you for your magnificent commercial talents, for the way you sold things, managed people, made jokes, were untiring, in case of doubt knew how to make the right decision immediately, and so forth; even the way you wrapped a parcel or opened a crate was a spectacle worth watching; all this was certainly not the worst school for a child.[13]

For Anderson the key relationship is between the 'traffic in clothes and paternal authority'.[14] This suggests a view of modernism in which transactions between the urban connections described by Benjamin as much as primal family relationships produce modernist subjectivities. The key then is the new public cultures that emerge in European cities at the turn of the century. It is these public cultures that are the context in which the relationship with the father develops, as part of a transaction that is not just a closed relationship, but includes, amongst other things: commerce and the circulation of commodities; the city streets; and Prague's café culture. The last two are, of course, places in which Hermann's fancy goods would have been paraded.

In Kafka's fiction, masculine subjectivity is produced at the interstices of such transactions. While a key dimension of Kafka's work is his examination of the interior, enclosed spaces of home, business and law,[15] only a partial reading of his fiction could argue these constitute its limits. In *The Trial*, staircases, passages and suffocating rooms are metaphors for Joseph K.'s entrapment, but these interior spaces only exist in relation to exterior space; and the thresholds between these two spheres mark key moments in the text. In one of K.'s temporary escapes from the legal process, Leni, a maidservant, is guardian of the door that lets K. out on to the street. As in 'Before the Law', to have power over the threshold is to have social power: ' "Here is the key of the door, come whenever you like", were her last words.'[16] On leaving, K.'s aim is 'the middle of the street so as perhaps to catch a last glance of Leni at her window', a position that would give him a vantage point over both exterior and interior spaces.[17] It is at that moment that the law intervenes, in the form of his

Uncle. Uncles figure in Kafka's work as displaced father figures, taking up provisional positions of authority in the city. This Uncle moves to confine Joseph K. to one place: he 'seized him by the arms and banged him against the house door as if he wanted to nail him there'.[18] But, for however brief a moment, the city street stands for sexual and social freedom beyond patriarchal law.

In 'The Stoker', which became the first chapter of the unfinished novel *Der Verschollene*,[19] Karl Rossman finds himself unable to leave the ship and gain access to the streets of New York. Instead, he is drawn back into its labyrinthine interior by his unwillingness to give up a possession, an umbrella, which provides an emotional link to his homeland. Rossman experiences numerous different forms of incarceration – on board ship, in his Uncle's house, in the hotel with Delamarche and Robinson; but all are set against the vibrant public life of Kafka's imaginary new world, a public culture that includes striking workers, street fights between the followers of rival candidates for the position of judge, and the freedom of the 'Nature Theatre of Oklahoma', in which all, including Karl, are allowed to participate.

Kafka's interiors are negative forms, which define the possibility of a different kind of public sphere.[20] Karl Rossman for much of the novel stands at the border between public and private worlds, gazing into Mack's or later Brunelda's bedroom, working as a lift boy or watching the street fights from Brunelda's balcony. His final emancipation is unusual for Kafka's characters, but Kafka's depiction of closed, interior spaces always implies its alternative. They are an example of what Adorno calls the 'negativity' of Kafka's work: 'it expresses itself not through expression but by its repudiation, by breaking off';[21] 'Far more than for most writers, it may be said of Kafka that not *verum* but *falsum* is *index sui*.'[22] As with Gissing, the interpretation that Adorno argues 'each sentence demands'[23] forces the reader to make the connections between private and the public spheres that produce a modern subjectivity.

It is, however, through the transactions across the thresholds between private and public spheres that masculine subjectivities are produced. Walter Benjamin argues that 'the world of fathers and the world of officials are the same for Kafka',[24] an idea that interposes the idea of modernity between father and son; and which opens up his fiction as an engagement with the contradictory pressures on subjectivities caught between a powerful familial ideology and the alternative possibilities opened up by the modern(ist) city. Benjamin records Brecht as saying that *The Trial* conveys the 'fear of the inexorable and never-ending growth of big cities. From his own intimate experience, [Kafka] knows of the nightmare force with which this idea weighs on mankind. The incalculable mediations, dependencies, and complications that human beings find themselves in, thanks to modern forms of life find expression in these cities'.[25] Kafka's Prague is one of the 'big cities' that illuminates the international character of modernism.

6

Journeys through the city: James Joyce

Stephen Dedalus, in James Joyce's *A Portrait of the Artist as a Young Man*, like the young Franz on the threshold of a public persona, also finds his father's example an embarrassment. On a trip from Dublin to Cork, an episode in his father's gradual financial ruin, Stephen refuses to perform the role offered by his father's youth:

> Another, a brisk old man, whom Mr Dedalus called Johnny Cashman, had covered him with confusion by asking him to say which were prettier, the Dublin girls or the Cork girls.
> – He's not that way built, said Mr Dedalus. Leave him alone. He's a levelheaded thinking boy who doesn't bother his head about that kind of nonsense.
> – Then he's not his father's son, said the little old man.
> – I don't know I'm sure, said Mr Dedalus, smiling complacently.
> – Your father, said the little old man to Stephen, was the boldest flirt in the city of Cork in his day. Do you know that?
> Stephen looked down and studied the tiled floor of the bar into which they had drifted.[1]

Stephen rejects both the model of his father's provincial masculinity and the authority of earlier generations of Cork men. But the 'little old man' who provokes his disavowal also foreshadows a different kind of social order. Johnny Cashman's name is significant, a premonition of Stephen's later encounter with the commerce of the city, when the money from the family effects sold off in Cork has long gone. Virtually penniless, Stephen has to make his own subjectivity in the streets, without the dubious benefits of an influential father. When Simon Dedalus reappears in *Ulysses* it is as just another Dublin character, shorn of his old power over his son. In modernist literature, it is the mythicisation of the father that takes centre stage rather than the reinforcement of the paternal myth. In his essay, 'Reconciliation under Duress', Adorno wrote:

> All such categories as decadence, formalism and aestheticism can be traced back to Baudelaire, and Baudelaire shows no interest in an unchanging

essence of man, his loneliness or his derelict existence [*Geworfenheit*], but rather in the essence of modernity. 'Essence' itself in this poetry is no abstract thing in itself; it is a social phenomenon. The objectively dominant idea in Baudelaire's work is that the new, products of historical progress are what has to be conjured up in his verse. To use Benjamin's expression, we find not an archaic, but a 'dialectical' image in his work. Hence the *Tableaux Parisiens*. Even in Joyce's case we do not find the timeless image of man. . .but man as a product of history. . .Joyce does not invoke a mythology beyond the world he depicts, but instead strives to mythologise it, i.e. to create its essence, whether benign or maleficent, by applying the techniques of stylization. . .One is almost tempted to measure the achievements of modernist writing by inquiring whether historical moments are given substance within their works, or whether they are diluted into some sort of timelessness.[2]

In Joyce's *A Portrait of the Artist as a Young Man*, as in *Ulysses*, the organising aesthetic of the text is myth: the father–son relationship between Icarus and Dedalus. But, as Adorno suggests, Joyce's use of myth is to establish not the myth's essential truth but rather the dialectic of modernity. *A Portrait of the Artist as a Young Man* charts the decline of the father, his loss of power, in what might be taken as an allegory of the loss of symbolic paternal power during the nineteenth century. This loss is contrasted in a kind of reverse reflection by the son's encounter with the public culture of *fin-de-siècle* Dublin.

Dublin in this context is a modernist city: 'a new and complex sensation'.[3] Its effect is a Copernican revolution that resituates the family not as centre but as just one node in the network of streets:

> the disorder in settling in the new house left Stephen freer than he had been in Blackrock. In the beginning he contented himself with circling timidly round the neighbouring square or, at most, going half way down one of the side streets: but when he had made a skeleton map of the city in his mind he followed boldly one of its central lines until he reached the customhouse.[4]

As for Kafka, commerce or traffic is one of the defining characteristics of the city's public life and this traffic provokes in Stephen an, as yet undirected, desire:[5]

> He passed unchallenged among the docks and along the quays wondering at the multitude of corks that lay bobbing on the surface of the water in a thick yellow scum, at the crowds of quay porters and the rumbling carts and the ill-dressed bearded policeman. The vastness and strangeness of the life suggested to him by the bales of merchandise stocked along the walls or swung aloft out of the holds of steamers wakened again in him the unrest which had sent him wandering in the evening from garden to garden in search of Mercedes.[6]

The attraction of the city vies with the power of the father; although, here, the relationship is less complex, for where the young Franz Kafka was attracted by the spectacle of the business and yet repelled by its association with his father, for Stephen the docks figure an escape towards new possibilities. His new masculinity is defined against a consumer economy beyond his means: 'though they passed a jovial array of shops lit up and adorned for Christmas, his mood of embittered silence did not leave him'.[7] *A Portrait of the Artist as a Young Man* offers a distinctive mixing of city life, impressionism and the naturalism more characteristic of *Dubliners*. In the passage above, the image of the 'multitude of corks' calls up the, to Stephen as yet unknown, world of Dublin's public bars. The 'thick yellow scum' recalls the decadent imagery of the 1890s (like the 'yellow haze' in Richardson's *Backwater* discussed in Chapter 3) and the exploration of the senses Joyce takes from Joris-Karl Huysmans's *A Rebours* (1884) and Wilde's rewriting of that process in *The Picture of Dorian Gray*.[8]

Joyce's use of what Benjamin called 'the collections and the rubbish' of the city's public culture,[9] already offers the outlines of the more fully fledged project of *Ulysses*. It is against that public culture that Stephen's thoroughly modern individuality is developed. If we are told that 'His soul was still disquieted and cast down by the dull phenomenon of Dublin', that phenomenon is still the social context for the production of his masculinity. In the face of the power of the city, the authority of the father fades to ghostly whispers, haunting the young Stephen through the city streets as 'the constant voices of his father and his masters, urging him to be a gentleman above all things and urging him to be a good catholic above all things'.[10]

The conversion of the paternal law into a modern myth – to be connected later in *Ulysses* with the ghost of the father in *Hamlet* – occurs in the midst of city life and it is the return of the father as part of the dialectic of modernity – as product of modernity – that is 'the essence' of Joyce's modernism, rather than the persistence of the mythic father Icarus. In *Ulysses*, Bloom is both father and son, his relationship to Rudolph, his dead father and Rudy his dead son constructed fleetingly through memory, or in their fantastic reappearance in Nighttown.[11] Outside the determinations of biology, the filial relationship of Stephen's Telemachus to Bloom's Odysseus is created in the moment – on the day, as it were – and in the flow of the city streets.

Stephen's own crossing of the threshold begins after a brief attempt to usurp his father as economic provider by spending the money from an academic prize on his family. The money and his position gone, he 'returned to his wanderings'.[12] Stephen's flâneries take him into the urban sphere brought to life by late Victorian writers like George Gissing. In a description of Hoxton in *Demos: A Story of English Socialism* (1886), Gissing writes of 'corners and lurking holes'.[13] Stephen too wanders 'up and down the dark slimy streets peering into the gloom of lanes and doorways, listening eagerly for any sound'.[14] The streets are themselves embodied, tactile and lubricated, as Stephen hovers on the threshold of penetration. But, in a moment of gothic inversion that produces a more polymorphous masculinity, Stephen is himself penetrated by the streets. Echoing another late nineteenth-century text, he metamorphoses from Jekyll to Hyde, moaning 'to himself like some baffled prowling beast':

> He felt some dark presence moving irresistibly upon him from the darkness, a presence subtle and murmurous as a flood filling him wholly with itself. Its murmur besieged his ears like the murmur of some multitude in sleep; its subtle streams penetrated his being. His hand clenched convulsively and his teeth set together as he suffered the agony of its penetration.[15]

If this gives a slightly different inflection to Benjamin's 'entrances' (*Eingänge*), its purpose is not just to represent Stephen's embodied sexuality as polymorphous but to situate it in relation to the entrances and exits of the back streets of Dublin. Here a modernist masculinity is produced through the imbrication of gothic perversion, bodily sensation and urban space. The totemic force of the law of the father does not of course disappear, but a critical account of that law is enabled by a recognition of the different configurations of the masculine now available. Such a recognition permits Joyce to write beyond the father–son relationship, so that every action no longer depends on either identification or resistance. Instead, the full complexity of the social is allowed to play its part and this includes the presence of women on the city's streets.

Each urban walk in the novel acts as a crossing of a threshold from one realm of experience to another;[16] and each new experience creates new forms of desire. For example, his adolescent desire for the idealised figure of Emma Clere competes with fragmented images of the young women he meets in the street:

> Rude brutal anger routed the last lingering instant of ecstasy from his soul. It broke up violently her fair image and flung the fragments on all sides. On all sides distorted reflections of her image started out from his memory: the flowergirl in the ragged dress with damp coarse hair and a hoyden's face who had called herself his own girl and begged his handsel, the kitchengirl in the next house who sang over the clatter of her plates with the drawl of a country singer the first bars of *By Killarney's Lakes and Fells*, a girl who had laughed gaily to see him stumble when the iron grating in the footpath near Cork Hill had caught the broken sole of his shoe, a girl he had glanced

at, attracted by her small ripe mouth as she passed out of Jacob's biscuit factory, who had cried at him over her shoulder:
– Do you like what you seen of me, straight hair and curly eyebrows?[17]

The bourgeois femininity embodied by Emma Clere becomes less desirable because it reflects the limitations of a vision defined by the family home, but Stephen is sufficiently self-aware to recognise that 'however he might revile and mock her image, his anger was also a form of homage'.[18] If Emma becomes an image of Irish womanhood,[19] defined by her lack of interest in him, the women of the street are less representative of a national than of a modern urban culture. These working-class women return Stephen's gaze (in contrast, Emma's remains 'averted'[20]) challenging and mocking his own presence on the street. Stephen's sense of his class position acts to shore up a sense of dominance where Emma's disdain undermines it, but the street initiates a dialogic relationship between male and female *passantes* that more private spaces inhibit.[21]

This social context provides the background to the 'Scylla and Charybdis' chapter of *Ulysses*, which subjects the lingering and compulsive power of the father–son relationship to an extended parody, rendering uncertain both theological and literary paternities. In the library, Stephen, himself portrayed as self-parody of the academic scholar, attempts to prove that Shakespeare is both Hamlet and Hamlet's father and then, finally, that fatherhood itself is a fiction:

> Fatherhood, in the sense of conscious begetting, is unknown to man. It is a mystical estate, an apostolic succession, from only begetter to only begotten. On that mystery and not on the Madonna which the cunning Italian intellect flung to the mob of Europe the church is founded and founded irremovably because founded, like the word, macro and microcosm, upon the void. Upon incertitude, upon unlikelihood. *Amor matris*, subjective and objective genitive may be the only true thing in life. Paternity may be a legal fiction. Who is the father of any son that any son should love him or he any son?[22]

The term 'void' here echoes Benjamin's *Leere*, the void encountered in the city's streets or the 'empty [*leer*]' place left by Baudelaire's absent father. In the face of emptiness, the father has to be recreated as a haunting fiction. Acting out Stephen's theory, Bloom believes he can remember the moment of Rudy's conception in 'Lotus Eaters', but this memory is rendered uncertain when he appears to remember the occasion quite differently several pages later in 'Lestrygonians'.[23] In *Ulysses*, the act of conception can be represented only in remembrance. Bloom cannot know that that *was* the moment. Fatherhood is a retrospective fiction.[24]

Similarly, Stephen's thesis is riddled with inconsistencies. Its form enacts a desperate, rearguard attempt, 'battling against hopelessness',[25] to shore up an authoritative position. Against, this the influence of his mother, repressed in the discourse of the father, returns to haunt Stephen even as he tries to make himself understood. His guilt about his mother's death, and his refusal to pray for her, pursues him throughout *Ulysses*, but in 'Scylla and Charybdis' she is ever present:

> Mother's deathbed. Candle. The sheeted mirror. Who brought me into this world lies there, bronzelidded, under few cheap flowers. Liliata rutilantium.
> I wept alone.[26]

The absence of an authorising father reveals the significance of mothers even while the theory of the 'phallic mother' would seek to relegate their importance. Baudelaire's mother shares his 'long and silent' suppers. The importance of Ann Hathaway as Gertrude, the mother of Shakespeare's sons as the mother of Hamlet, takes up much of the discussion in the library. In Richardson's *Pilgrimage*, Miriam's mother continues to haunt her movements through the city streets long after she has shaken off the influence of her father.[27] But it is Miriam's *embodied* presence on the streets, the entrance of the New Woman into the public sphere, not the phantasmal presences of the father or the mother, that opens up the possibility of a new kind of gendered intersubjectivity. Part II looks in detail at the question of embodied subjectivities. For Miriam, her father is just the first barrier to the public sphere. *Pilgrimage* begins where *A Portrait of the Artist as a Young Man* ends, with a cutting free of the fetters of home, 'fatherland' and church.[28] Stephen's exile involves a mythicisation of the self, and specifically the masculine self, as Dedalus, which, in the last sentence, recuperates the paternal as a supportive structure for this flight: 'Old father, old artificer, stand by me now and ever in good stead.' If irony is never far away, Dedalus burns first, then crashes, Stephen stands at that moment – on the brink of flight – as both a counterpoint and a response to Miriam's own passage into exile. The New Man and the New Woman are created at the same moment.

Part II
Bodies

7

Bodily innervation: food, eating and the everyday

> She passed on and entered the place of refreshment that was kept by Mrs. Tubbs. Till recently it had been an ordinary eating-house or coffee-shop; but having succeeded in obtaining a license to sell strong liquors, Mrs. Tubbs has converted the establishment into one of a more pretentious kind. She called it 'Imperial Restaurant and Luncheon Bar.' The front shone with vermilion paint; the interior was aflare with many gas-jets; in the window was disposed a tempting exhibition of 'snacks' of fish, cold roast fowls, ham-sandwiches, and the like; whilst further back stood a cooking-stove, whereon frizzled and vapoured a savoury mess of sausages and onions.[1]

In Gissing's *The Nether World*, Mrs Tubbs's establishment stands as a metonymic representation of London's commercial culture. The aptly named proprietor signifies abundance. Mrs Tubbs is an allegorical figure of plenty, a female John Bull. Her renamed establishment indicates a patriotic pride in the origins of England's wealth. As important as the excess is the display. In the thematics of the novel, her shopfront exhibits national prosperity. In its small way, it is a kind of Crystal Palace of food.[2]

Later modernist texts followed Gissing in figuring the experience of eating as paradigmatic of urban production and consumption. At a basic level, money earned is used to pay for food, but the experience of consumption in the city is always accompanied by a sense of what cannot be bought. The eating body figures the point at which production and consumption meet. In Dorothy Richardson's *Pilgrimage*, smoking, eating and drinking signify the extent to which a New Woman subjectivity can be performed on a basic wage. In Kafka's *The Trial*, the first indication that there is something abnormal about the day is the non-arrival of breakfast.[3] The sinister intrusion of hard-faced officials into Joseph K.'s life disturbs because of its disruption of the everyday. Sent to find his papers, K. returns to see the 'warders' 'devouring' the breakfast that never arrived.[4] The warder continues to insist that K. is under arrest while 'dipping a slice of bread and butter into the honey-pot'.[5] This display of power has resonances with Hermann Kafka's eating habits described in the 'Letter to His Father',[6] underlining Benjamin's insight about the connection between fathers and officials in Kafka's work.[7] In the whole opening scene, the appropriation of K.'s food, so that he has to fall back on an apple and brandy, marks his dislocation from an undefinable centre of power.

Ulysses begins with two breakfasts. The tea and 'fry' in the Martello tower and Bloom's famous meal of fried kidneys (he eats 'with relish the inner organs of beasts and fowls'[8]) begin Joyce's project to map an embodied consciousness that comes into being through ingestion, digestion and excretion. Breakfast, and the chapter, only end properly with a trip to the jakes and a, not entirely satisfactory, bowel movement: 'No, just right. So. Ah! Costive.'[9] Breakfast defines the day, or at least the morning, creating a sense of well-being until hunger pangs return in the Lestrygonians episode. Even the aftermath reverberates in that chapter when Bloom recalls: 'Did I pull the chain? Yes. The last act.'[10] The work of Dorothy Richardson is replete with images of smoking, drinking and eating. In *A La Recherche du Temps Perdu*, Marcel can be propelled into a new realm of consciousness or his life can take an new turn not just as a consequence of a bite on a madeleine but by taking one too many cups of coffee.[11]

Modernism extended its comprehension of the real to include the whole body, but not a body complete in itself.[12] The modernist body is 'innervated' by its interconnections with a social and technological totality. The term 'innervation' is the opposite of enervation, a weakening or decline in nervous energy.[13] Nervous energy increases when the body is innervated by the stimulation it experiences in the modern city. Walter Benjamin developed the concept of 'innervation' from its original use in medical and psychological discourses, using it alongside the related concept of *Erlebnis* or shock experience. According to Miriam Hansen, in Benjamin's work innervation 'came to function as an antidote – and counterconcept – to technologically multiplied shock and its anaesthetizing economy'.[14]

Technological modernity inflicts such shocks with unpredictable effects. Although anaesthesia is the most common example, in the worst case scenarios, for example the First World War or the catastrophe that is Fascism, the results can be total destruction. But, for Benjamin, the concept of innervation also suggested a counter process, an inkling of which can be discovered in surrealism, where a collective response to technological modernity might bring about a transformation of the human condition:

> The collective is a body, too. And the *physis* that is being organized for it in technology can, through all its political and factual reality, be produced

only in that image space to which profane illumination initiates us. Only when in technology body and image space so interpenetrate that all revolutionary tension becomes bodily collective innervation, and all bodily innervations of the collective become revolutionary discharge, has reality transcended itself to the extent demanded by the *Communist Manifesto*.[15]

Benjamin adds a historical dimension to surrealism's counter-shocks, suggesting that the utopian vision offered by modernist art is supplemented by other, earlier forms of innervation: for example, the 'creative innervation' of children at play; or the ritual innervation of the Buddhist prayer wheel, a 'first' technology that enables and empowers the one who meditates. The revolutionary process he describes as 'bodily collective innervation' redeems, but cannot return to these earlier states. Miriam Hansen argues that for 'Benjamin there is no beyond or outside of technology'.[16] It must incorporate both:

> Innervation as a mode of regulating the interplay between humans and (second [i.e. industrial]) technology can only succeed (that is escape the destructive vortex of defensive, numbing adaptation) if it reconnects with the discarded powers of the first, with the mimetic practices that involve the body, as the 'pre-eminent instrument' of sensory perception and (moral and political) differentiation.[17]

Hansen's own investigation of 'bodily innervation' is concerned primarily with the implication of the concept for the study of film, but her work illuminates Benjamin's theories of modernity as a whole. One of her examples of what she calls 'mimetic innervation' is highly suggestive for a theory of embodied subjectivities in modernity. She suggests that

> the process of mimetic innervation entails dynamics that move in opposite, yet complementary directions: (1) a decentering and extension of the human sensorium beyond the limits of the individual body/subject into the world that stimulates and attracts perception; and (2) an introjection, ingestion, or incorporation of the object or device, be it an external rhythm, a familiar madeleine, or an alien(ating) apparatus.[18]

The ideas of 'introjection' and 'ingestion' suggest (or in the example of Proust's madeleine directly point to) the eating body. Eating, the process of introjecting and ingesting, is a sedimented social practice that involves embodied rhythms encultured in childhood as well as participation in rituals preserved and remade over generations. But in the context of urban modernity food – what one puts in one's mouth – is also the end-product of a vast technical apparatus, of which introjection is only one part of an industrial cycle. As Leopold Bloom notes after lunch: 'And we stuffing food in one hole and out behind: food, chyle, blood, dung, earth, food: have to feed it like stoking an engine.'[19] In modernist texts, the taste of food provokes an act of remembrance that mediates between the taste sensation and the past experiences recalled, consciously and unconsciously, in the present moment. These include childhood memories, the rituals of family meals, but also the social and economic apparatus that lies behind the industrial production of food.

All such experiences contribute to bodily innervation. In modernist fictions those experiences are reconfigured in the manner of Benjamin's *Erfahrung* – considered or 'long' experience. The reorganisation of experience through remembrance opens up the possibility of 'bodily innervation' as a creative response to modernity. In most modernist texts, however, as with surrealism, the experience explored is not collective revolution, but anticipations or traces of what that might be. This is what Miriam Hansen, translating Benjamin's term, 'Spielraum', calls roomfor-play: the possibility of turning the determining forces of technological modernity for a moment to ones advantage.[20] Joyce talked of how Ulysses was 'the epic of the human body':

> In my book the body lives in and moves through space and is the home of a full human personality. The words I write are adapted to express first one of its functions then another. In *Lestrygonians* the stomach dominates and the rhythm of the episode is that of peristaltic movement.[21]

Another way of thinking about this is that modernist fiction's representation of eating as everyday event reconfigures it as a kind of threshold that mediates between immediate sensation and the network of social relations of which taste is the only the most obvious affect. For Benjamin, the everyday is not just *what is*, because what exists is made up of the complex social relations that constitute collective living. It is at the fractures and joins of the everyday that the possibilities of *what might be* emerge and these fractures and joins relate to space, time, and the relationship between dreamworlds and awakening.[22] Eating and the meal are always threshold events, marking a before and after, an entrance and an exit. For Benjamin (as discussed in Chapter 4), it is the city that creates the necessary labyrinth in relation to which an embodied subjectivity emerges. One of his aims in *The Arcades Project* was to establish a 'mythological topography' of Paris. In the twentieth century, he wrote, traditional 'threshold experiences', 'the ceremonies that attach to death and birth, to marriage, puberty, and so forth' are in abeyance.[23] Yet, while on the one hand he argues that 'we have grown very poor' in such traditional experiences, the Paris he describes produces innumerable new thresholds in space and time: points of transition, passages from reason to myth, moments of magic that exist at the interstices of modernity.

The eating body acts as a useful vehicle in tracking these connections in the city because what goes in and what come out can be sourced and followed.[24] In *The Trial*, it is K.'s initial difficulty in identifying where his breakfast has gone, then its withholding that marks the beginning of his isolation from his ordinary social world. In 'The Metamorphosis' also, it is Gregor and his family's different relationships to food that marks the distinction between what he was and what he has become. Yet, despite its centrality in cultural symbolism, cultural critics have, with a few exceptions, usually left the masticating, digesting and excreting body to the anthropologists. As Terry Eagleton has commented: 'there has been strikingly little concern with the physical stuff of which bodies are composed, as opposed to an excited interest in their genitalia'.[25] It can be plausibly argued that food is as central to social organisation as sexuality; although food and sex are rarely unrelated. As Mary Douglas and Claude Lévi-Strauss have pointed out, the moment of eating is one of both material and symbolic embodiment.[26] Deborah Lupton offers a neat summary of Douglas's argument:

> For Douglas, in western as well as non-western cultures, the consumption of food is a ritual activity. She argues that food categories constitute a social boundary system; the predictable structure of each meal creates order out of potential disorder. The meal is thus a microcosm of wider social structures and boundary definitions.[27]

In modernist fiction, food appears both as the most basic, everyday necessity and the most mediated of cultural forms. It can be used to represent life at its most simple and ordinary – daily bread, a bowl of rice, the humble potato – or at its most sophisticated – as *haute cuisine*. It can attract to the point where it becomes the object of our greatest desires, or repel and disgust. Where we eat and how we eat are as important as what we eat. The meal is often the point at which intimate, private and public relations are negotiated: gendered subjectivities are produced at just such moments, which is why fiction so often focuses on the meal.[28] After Dickens few nineteenth-century novelists were as interested in the symbolics of food as George Gissing. In the rest of Part II, Chapter 8 discusses the politics of food in Gissing's work. Chapter 9 returns to Richardson and smoking. Chapter 10 examines Richardson's engagement with the modern technologies of diet and nutrition in her non-fiction. And Chapter 11 concludes 'Bodies' with a reading of the 'Lestrygonians' chapter of *Ulysses*, a chapter that is replete with references to food and eating.

8

George Gissing and the cultural politics of food

Food plays a key role in Gissing's fiction, but always in relation to his observations about the changing urban scene. His proto-modernism emerges in his understanding of food and eating as part of a larger context – in Jürgen Habermas's terms, part of the systems-world which had begun to penetrate all aspects of the ordinary life-worlds of London's inhabitants.[1] The place of food in the culture of late nineteenth-century Britain was a long way from the early twenty-first century's obsession with public, journalistic and televisual preparation and consumption.[2] But some of the tendencies that have made food an integral part of commodity culture were not only apparent but well under way. While London had been the belly of the Empire for three hundred years, the building of railways into the interior of colonial territories (Asia and Africa, Canada, Australia), former colonies (the United States) and client states (such as Argentina) and the use of steam ships accelerated the supply and increased the quantities of foodstuffs available to the imperial metropolis. This shift from production to consumption was indicative of a change in the balance of power in the food economy. The abundance of supply of tobacco, tea and grain meant that retailers gained the upper hand, playing off producers against one another, then selling at cut prices through outlets that attracted consumers, now accustomed to an exhibition culture, using ostentatious shop windows.[3]

In *The Nether World*, Clara's job as a barmaid situates her as both worker and delicious commodity on display.[4] Both roles discomfort Sidney Kirkwood, who embodies the other side of the late nineteenth-century's culture of abundance, poverty and lack.[5] In the novel, nothing is given, nothing promised – whether the attractions of the stage, the hopes of marriage or the Bank Holiday illusion of prosperity – that is not then taken away. At the Angel, Clara's entrance onto the stage of commodity spectacle underlines Sidney Kirkwood's exclusion, just as the riches of the griddle mark his poverty. He reacts with repugnance to the 'savoury mess', a reaction which, according to David Trotter, is a response to 'the loss of self-respect entailed by what he regards as an immersion in matter'.[6] But food in Gissing's fiction represents more than the binary opposition of lack versus plenty and there is as much delight in immersion in matter as disgust. In fact, food and eating might be taken as paradigmatic elements of Gissing's realism: their necessity signifies the text's adherence to the real, but the basic needs they signify mask the performative aspect of an apparently determinist narrative. Politically unsympathetic to Clara's New Woman subjectivity and to Sidney's disempowerment, the text none the less recognises the production of new embodied subjectivities in the new public culture of the city.

In his novel of 1887, *Thyrza*, the most vibrant representation of working-class life is the description of Lambeth market:

> On the outer edges of the pavement, in front of the busy shops, were rows of booths, stalls, and barrows, whereon meat, vegetables, fish, and household requirements of indescribable variety were exposed for sale. The vendors vied with one another in uproarious advertisement of their goods. In vociferation the butchers doubtless excelled; their 'Lovely, lovely, lovely! and their reiterated 'Buy, buy, buy!' rang clangorous above the hoarse roaring of costermongers and the din of those who clattered pots and pans.[7]

Food, eating, and eating out operate within a rich matrix of meaning in Gissing's work, the co-ordinates of which include social Darwinism, notions of bodily pleasure, Bacchanalia or *jouissance*, manners, civility, the meal as socially symbolic act, the boundary between public and private spheres, the industrialisation and commercialisation of food and food culture. However, as will become clear below, a proper analysis of Gissing's prose means that it is not possible to separate these aspects artificially or to work through them systematically. Instead, it demonstrates, as has been ably argued by Simon James, that his novels can be read both for the determinations of plot and for a rich textuality that exhibits something closer to Bakhtin's dialogism than the scientific definitions one might expect from naturalism.[8] This amounts to a textual version of what Miriam Hansen calls 'room-for-play' (see Chapter 7).

An investigation into the culinary belies Gissing's reputation as a dour and serious writer. Focusing on food reveals one of the best-kept secrets of his work – its humour. In an earlier passage from *The Nether World*, social Darwinism gives scientific authority to social prejudice, but that authority is subverted by Clem Peckover's robust enjoyment of both food and power. In what David Trotter calls 'one of the finest moments not only in Gissing's writing, but in the totality of nineteenth-century representations of the nether world',[9] a 'blow-out' of sausages brings a double opportunity to torture the hapless Jane Snowdon – both through violence and the withholding of food:

> The Speaker was a girl of sixteen, tall, rather bony, rudely handsome; the hand with which she struck was large and coarse-fibred, the muscles that impelled it vigorous. . .
>
> . . . 'Ah!' exclaimed Miss Peckover (who was affectionately known to her intimates as Clem), as she watched Jane stagger back from the blow, and hide her face in silent endurance of pain. 'That's just a morsel to stay your appetite, my lady! . . . Ha ha! ho ho! – These sausages is done; now you clean out that fryin'-pan; an if I can find a speck of dirt on it as big as 'arlf a farthing, I'll take you by the 'air of the 'ed and clean it with your face, *that's* what I'll do!'[10]

A blow to the head and her control of the food supply confirm Clem's superiority in the social order. We are told that:

> Civilization could bring no charge against this young woman; it and she had no common criterion. Who knows but this lust of hers for sanguinary domination was the natural enough issue of the brutalising serfdom of her predecessors in the family line of Peckovers? A thrall suddenly endowed with authority will assuredly make bitter work for the luckless creature in the next degree of thraldom.[11]

Clem exists in a state of nature, in which, according to nineteenth-century evolutionist science (and, earlier, Malthusian economics), access to nutrition ensures and perpetuates dominance: the fed rule the unfed. In *The Evolution of Sex*, published in the same year as *The Nether World*, Patrick Geddes and Arthur Thomson put digestion at the centre of the life-process:

> On the one hand, more or less simple dead matter or food passes into life by a series of assimilative ascending changes, with each of which it becomes molecularly more complex and unstable. On the other hand, the resulting protoplasm is continually breaking down into more and more simple compounds, and finally into waste products. The ascending, synthetic, constructive series of changes are termed 'anabolic,' and the descending, disruptive series, 'katabolic'.[12]

According to Geddes and Thomson, even sexual difference can be understood in terms of metabolising food. The processes of anabolism (building up) and catabolism (breaking down) mark the difference between female and male biologies:

> Femaleness is anabolic preponderance in reproduction, hence the ovum has necessarily the general character which this 'diathesis' produces in non-reproductive cells; and, similarly, katabolic preponderance stamps its

character of active energy upon spermatazoa as naturally as upon the ciliated cell or the monad.[13]

The sperm is described as hungry, as looking for nutriment,[14] and Geddes and Thomson conclude: 'Historically, then, fertilisation is comparable to mutual digestion, and, though bound up with reproduction, has arisen from a nutritive want.'[15] So unchallengable was the Social Darwinist discourse of nutritional necessity in this period that feminist writers like Olive Schreiner and Charlotte Perkins Gilman developed their theories of women's subordination in relation to it. In *Woman and Labour*, Schreiner argued that bourgeois women's 'parasitism' was a consequence of their exclusion from productive labour.[16] Gilman was more explicit about the role of nutrition in the 'sexuo-economic' relationship between men and women: 'We are the only animal species in which the female depends on the man for food, and the only animal species in which the sex-relation is also an economic relation.'[17]

Feminist accounts of the relationship between nutrition and sex attempted to construct an ethical or political sphere beyond the natural, where women could act to establish more equal gender relations.[18] Gissing's own relationship with Darwinist science was similary fraught.[19] This was partly because he too disliked the reductionist impulse in much Social Darwinism, but also because Gissing the modernist could not resist the polyvalent meanings in language that strove to be objective and truthful.[20] Clem's description offers both a discourse of biological determinism and a delight ('rudely handsome', 'vigorous') in her natural bodily health and vitality. Once explained as the product of evolution, Clem almost attains the status of noble savage: 'The frankness of Clem's brutality went far towards redeeming her character.'[21] The reader is further discouraged from taking the passage as a serious social commentary by Clem Peckover's name, which, as so often in Gissing's texts, acts as a self-conscious reflection on the character's theatrical role, signifying performance rather than function. Clem is at the top of a pecking order, from where she preys on weaker victims such as Jane and another young woman whose nickname, Pennyloaf, indicates her poor economic circumstances.

Despite the enjoyment to be gained from such passages, it has been a commonplace of Gissing criticism that his work elicits few if any pleasures for the reader.[22] Yet Gissing's bleakest ethnographic gaze offers a morbid enjoyment of the darkest 'lurking holes'[23] (see Chapter 6) of London's poorest districts. The (albeit vicious) humour visible in Clem's slapstick assault on Jane is just one end of a comic spectrum that extends from the mocking, sardonic humour of the 'Io Saturnalia' chapter of *The*

Nether World (see Chapter 14) to the more subtle domestic dramas of the novels of the 1890s; and even a novel like *The Odd Women* contains some fairly crude sexual jokes. The virile hero is named Everard, the celibate heroine Nunn, while the dried up, failed husband, Widdowson, retires to live with a friend called Newdick. More often than not Gissing's humour is dependent upon a dialogic relationship between a concept of brute necessity and a comedy of manners, in which the rituals of food play a central role. Bodily need is a signifier for economic necessity in his tales of impoverishment and near starvation, whether he is writing about working-class families, such as the Hewetts in *The Nether World* or the inhabitants of Lambeth in *Thyrza*, surviving on a minimal diet, or struggling writers starving in their garrets. But while brute necessity haunts his texts as the reality of poverty in nineteenth-century London, he never neglects the symbolic role of food in the rituals of everyday life.

Maud Ellmann has argued that hunger, like sexuality, is a 'culturally constructed drive'.[24] Just as the detailed account of the place of a working-class character's collar in the hierarchy of manual, semi-skilled and skilled workers in *The Nether World* anticipates twentieth-century cultural anthropology,[25] Gissing's work also anticipates twentieth-century anthropology in its understanding of the meal, or what Mary Douglas calls the 'food event', as socially symbolic act.[26] If food deprivation is represented as a sign of evolutionary failure, and eating well a sign of success, this is just the starting point for his investigation of the rituals of food and eating, where the 'meal is. . .a microcosm of wider social structures and boundary definitions'.[27] In *New Grub Street*, for example, the history of Alfred Yule's marriage is presented initially in terms of an exact correlation between access to nutrition and the possibility of reproduction:

> Living in a garret, and supplying himself with the materials of his scanty meals, he was in the habit of making purchases at a little chandler's shop, where he was waited upon by a girl of no beauty, but, as it seemed to him, of amiable disposition. One holiday he met this girl as she was walking with a younger sister in the streets; he made her nearer acquaintance, and before long she consented to be his wife and share his garret. His brothers, John and Edmund, cried out that he had made an unpardonable fool of himself in marrying so much beneath him; that he might as well have waited until his income improved. This was all very well, but they might just as well have bidden him reject plain food because a few years hence he would be able to purchase luxuries; he could not do without nourishment of some sort, and the time had come when he could not do without a wife.[28]

New 'grub' indeed,[29] the closed economy of Yule's sexuality is neatly portrayed: a poor diet is determined by a low income, and thus limited purchasing power, in the growing culture of consumerism. Consequently he has restricted access to a wider public sphere and his narrow social and sexual opportunities are represented through the metaphor of food – 'plain food' versus 'luxuries'. To this extent, the passage invites a reductionist account of sexual desire as nothing more than brute instinct: a need that must be satisfied. But, while hunger and a Darwinian urge to reproduce function as the kernel of the real that authorises a social commentary, the passage comes almost immediately after a more directly satirical account of Yule's appetites in the context of a family meal. Arriving home in a 'mood of silent moroseness', he finds that dinner is not on the table:

> Even the average man of a certain age is an alarming creature when dinner delays itself; the literary man in such a moment goes beyond all parallel. If there be added the fact that he has just returned from a very unsatisfactory interview with a publisher, wife and daughter may indeed regard the situation as appalling.[30]

The silent, family meal, subdued by the bad-tempered patriarch, acts as a microcosm of the wider social structures of work, production (here literary production) and reproduction (the patriarchal family). Food and books perform a dialectic in Gissing's texts. According to Ellmann, scarcity of food is seen as a spur to literary production in his work.[31] But books can also replace food as a source of enjoyment.[32] In *Born in Exile*, Godwin Peak is 'compelled to contract his diet, that he might purchase books'.[33] In a passage in *The Private Papers of Henry Ryecroft*, the young Ryecroft forgoes food in order to buy the works of Tibullus.

> Many a time I have stood before a stall, or a bookseller's window torn by the conflict of intellectual desire and bodily need. At the very hour of dinner, when my stomach clamoured for food, I have been stopped by the sight of a volume so long coveted, and marked at so advantageous a price, that I *could* not let it go; yet to buy it meant pangs of famine.[34]

During the Yule family meal, Alfred's daughter tries, at first unsuccessfully, to distract him from his hunger with a book. He is only satisfied when she tells him of the prospect of an editorship, and family harmony is restored when Yule finds a glowing reference to his own work in the proffered book, which he then proceeds to read as he eats. Everyone finally gets their just desserts when Yule remarks 'casually that the custard was very well made today' (123).

Thus, the Social Darwinist account of Yule's courtship should be read as just one discourse in a dialogic narrative that also includes Yule's masculinity as embodied performance, and the place his eating body occupies in the symbolics of particular meals as 'food events'. At first he eats hurriedly, without enjoyment: 'He began his meal by drinking half a glass of ale; then ate a few mouthfuls in a quick hungry way, his head bent closely over his plate' (120). When Marian mentions the editorship, 'Yule stopped in the act of mastication. He fixed his eyes intently on the sirloin for half a minute; then, by way of the beer-jug and the salt cellar, turned them upon Marian's face' (121). On digesting the news, 'he continued eat more slowly, and as if in appreciation of the viands'. Finally, after reading the good notice, 'he took a draught of ale, like one who is reinvigorated in the battle for life' (122).

Bodily performance here is in dialogic relationship with the social situation of the family and the wider public sphere, in which Yule's literary reputation is made. In the home, Yule's brittle masculine authority is supported by his wife's culinary and his daughter's intellectual efforts. Outside the domestic sphere, the place of the male intellectual was far less secure. In London, new opportunities for consumption were opening up opportunities for new, dangerous subjectivities. In contrast to Yule's 'plain food', working-class Totty Nancarrow, in *Thyrza*, lives on luxuries:

> If she had not money enough for both bread and marmalade, she chose to have the marmalade alone; if she could not buy meat and pickles at the same time, she would have pickles and go without the meat. Marmalade and pickles she deemed the indispensables of life.[35]

Totty's taste for sweet and sour figures independent appetites that require a larger stage than the bourgeois home. In Gissing's early fiction that stage is the street, the market or the corner shop, urban spaces which give greater freedom to working-class women such as Totty, who represent, like Clara, different aspects of the New Woman. In his later work, eating out – in coffee shops, eating houses or 'dining' in restaurants – at a time when opportunities for public consumption in all senses were widening, becomes a symbolic act in which individual human needs are mediated through larger social forces (see Chapter 14). But for the emerging New Woman, acts of consumption could become an embodied performance that rattled the chains of earlier forms of gendered identity. Dorothy Richardson's protagonist, Miriam Henderson, is an extended exploration of the potential room for play in the city's new social formations. Surviving on a clerical wage of one pound a week, Miriam has to exist, for the most part, on plain food, but like Totty, she has luxuries, the most important of which are cigarettes.

9

Smoking and consumption

> A cigarette is the perfect kind of pleasure. It is exquisite, and it leaves one unsatisfied. What more can one want?[1]

While Wilde had the best epigram on the cigarette, Dorothy Richardson gives the best retrospective on the symbolic meaning of smoking for women in the 1890s. Whereas the consumption of food can be easily assimilated into the representation of a productive economy – the workers have to eat – smoking cannot. According to Fred Botting, 'smoking pertains to what Bataille calls a "general economy": outside the world of work, useful production and morally sanctioned consumption, smoking wastes time and expends resources without making a profitable return'.[2] As discussed in Chapter 3, Miriam's first smoke is a way of throwing off the father, but the father's absence opens up a difficult new terrain. For Botting, 'tobacco, poetically, symbolically, works within a restricted economy of difference as the remnant on which the paternal surplus is established, [but] it also drags with it an unassimilable aspect associated with vile and useless consumption'.[3] For Miriam, smoking in public produces an unstable gender identity partly because of the practice's association with the vile and the useless. And smoking is not an isolated example. *Pilgrimage* offers careful observations on a range of material practices, including smoking, eating and drinking, in relation to social and symbolic interaction. Richardson's modernism amounts to nothing less than a philosophical project to elaborate an aesthetics of everyday life – an aesthetics that seeks to find a place in the public sphere for Miriam and her habits. Gender politics are central to Miriam's aesthetic project. Its aim is to challenge the hegemonic public, realist aesthetic embodied in the figure of Hypo Wilson, the Wellsian novelist who is her lover and intellectual combatant.

Smoking in public was one of the key motifs of the New Woman.[4] In *Punch*'s parody of George Egerton's *Keynotes*, 'She-Notes' by Borgia Smudgerton, the cartoon New Woman is pictured lying in a bog and smoking a cigarette.[5] After Miriam's first experiment with the pleasures of tobacco in *Backwater*, the cigarette appears again in the third 'chapter-novel', *Honeycomb* (1917), which covers that key year of the *fin de siècle*, 1895, the year of the Wilde trials and his conviction.⁶ The scene of smoking exemplifies the gendering of the public/private divide outlined in Chapter 2, the context for Richardson's development of a new performative aesthetic through material practice: here the 'useless' leisure activities of billiards and smoking, although it is important to recognise that Miriam is taking part only in a subordinate role, as governess. She is an employee, not an equal in the house:

> 'Old Felix has secured himself the best partner,' Miriam heard someone mutter as she made her fluke, a resounding little cannon and pocket in one stroke. Wandering after her ball she fought against the suggesting voice. It had come from one of the men moving about in the gloom surrounding the radiance cast by the green-shaped lamps upon the long green table. Faces moving in the upper darkness were indistinguishable. The white patch of Mrs Corrie's face gleamed from the settee as she sat bent forward with her hands clasped in front of her knees. Beyond her, sitting back under the shadow of the mantelpiece and the marking board, was Mrs Craven, a faint mass of soft green and mealy white. All the other forms were standing or moving in the gloom; standing watchful and silent, the gleaming stems of their cues held in rest, shifting and moving and strolling with uncolliding ordered movements and little murmers of commentary after the little drama – the sudden snap of the stroke breaking the silence, the faint thundering roll of the single ball, the click of the concussion, the gentle angular explosion of pieces into a new relation and the breaking of the varying triangle as a ball rolled to its hidden destination, held by all eyes in the room until its rumbling pilgrimage ended out of sight in a soft thud. It was pure joy to Miriam to wander round the table after her ball, sheltering in the gloom, through an endless 'grand chain' of undifferentiated figures that passed and repassed without awkwardness or the need for forced exchange; held together and separated by the ceremony of the game. Comments came after each stroke, words and sentences, sped and smooth and polished by the gloom, like the easy talking of friends in deep twilight; but between each stroke were vast intervals of untroubled silent intercourse. The competition of the men, the sense of the desire to win, that rose and strained in the room could not spoil this communion. After a stroke, pondering the balls while the room and the radiance and the darkness moved and flowed and the dim figures settled to a fresh miracle of grouping, it was joy to lean along the board to her ball, keeping punctual appointment with her partner whose jaunty little figure would appear in supporting opposition under the bright light, drawing at his cigarette with a puckering half-smile, awaiting her suggestion and ready with counsel. Doing her best to measure angles and regulate the force of her blow she struck careless little lifting strokes that made her feel as if she danced, and managed three more cannons and a pocket before her little break came to an end.⁷

The passage is a good example of Richardson's 'feminine impressionism'.[8] The women characters fade back into the modernist canvas. They are a: 'white patch', 'soft green', 'mealy white'. The game itself marks a boundary between public and private. The men perform visibly on a public stage. Miriam's social position is, as always in the text, ambivalent, somewhere between the two. Having escaped the constraints of her family, she has not yet gained the freedom of London. *Honeycomb* describes a half-way house where she is outside her own home, but in somebody else's, having moved backwards into a subservient position in relation to her employers, Mr and Mrs Corrie. The male voice that emerges from the mass of colours 'in the gloom' articulates the ambiguity: 'the best partner' is double-edged, meaning both the most capable player and the most attractive young woman. Miriam, in the public eye, is 'fighting against' the latter suggestion in order to create a sense of autonomy.

This is achieved through the game, which is described both as a 'little drama' and as a 'ceremony'. As drama, the game gives Miriam a public role, as ceremony it provides a ritual through which she can create a sense of self despite the unsympathetic environment: an opportunity to (re)construct herself within the constraints of the situation. Typically for Miriam, the achievement of a sense of self through practice is joyous: 'it was pure joy for Miriam to wander round the table after her ball'; 'it was joy to lean along the board to her ball'. And this allows her to transcend the masculine stamp on the game itself: 'The competition of the men, the sense of the desire to win could not spoil this communion'. Whereas decadent poets such as Symons and Wilde represented the female dancer's delight in herself for the consumption of other men,[9] Miriam appropriates the role to establish what Miriam Hansen calls 'room-for-play' (see Chapter 7), a space that is for herself alone: 'Doing her best to measure angles and regulate the force of her blow she struck careless little lifting strokes that made her feel as if she danced.'

The possession of a cigarette distinguishes her male partner – 'drawing at his cigarette with a puckering half-smile' – by giving him a role to play when she is playing and he is not. His phallic objects are, in Butler's phrase, 'fundamentally transferable'.[10] He exchanges the cue for the cigarette. Where the desire to smoke in *Backwater* is part of a desire to usurp the father, here it is part of a wish to take up the public role occupied by men.[11] The cigarette allows the smoker to perform publicly even when otherwise unoccupied. The complex identification this sets up becomes the subject of the next section of the text.

Miriam's initial impulse is to identify with a masculine side of the gendered division she perceives in the room.

'It must be jolly to smoke in the in-between times,' said Miriam, standing about at a loss during a long break by one of her opponents.

'Yes, you ought to learn to smoke,' responded Mr Corrie judicially. The quiet smile – the serene offer of companionship, the whole room troubled with the sense of the two parties, the men with whom she was linked in the joyous forward-going strife of the game and the women on the sofa, suddenly grown monstrous in their opposition of clothes and kindliness and the fuss of distracting personal insincerities of voice and speech, attempting to judge and condemn the roomful of quiet players, shouting aloud to her that she was a fool to be drawn in to talking to men seriously on their own level, a fool to parade about as if she really enjoyed their silly game. (pp. 435–436)

'Companionship' was the word often used to describe an equal relationship between the sexes in the 1890s,[12] partly because it excluded the messy question of desire. It is conceived here in masculine terms – against both women and, specifically, female desire: 'I hate women and they've got to know it' (436). But it would be a mistake to see this as a permanent position. It is rather an expression of Miriam's gender confusion as she attempts to break free from a restrictive form of femininity. Earlier, considering Mrs Corrie, 'Dead because of something she had never known', Miriam thinks 'Nearly all women were like that, living in a gloom where there were no thoughts', only to worry: 'Perhaps I can't stand women because I'm a sort of horrid man' (404). At the end of the billiards chapter she reconsiders the middle-class wives in what is the beginning of a critique of masculinity that runs through the whole of *Pilgrimage*: 'She glanced at Mrs Corrie and Mrs Craven – bright beautiful coloured birds, fading slowly year by year in the stifling atmosphere, the hard brutal laughing complacent atmosphere of men's minds. . .men's minds, staring at things, ignorantly, knowing "everything" in an irritating way and yet *ignorant*.'

Smoking – 'I do smoke' (436) – then becomes a revolt against the dictates of femininity as passive display. The alternative, active role, is, almost inevitably, at first gendered as masculine and against femininity. The subsequent adoption of a 'New Woman' identity – 'I suppose I'm a new woman, I've said I am now, anyhow' (436) – is a provisional performance, which allows Miriam to participate in the masculine world, but which awkwardly cuts her off from feminine solidarity and is at odds with her position as feminised employee: 'wondering in the background of her determination how she would reconcile the role with her work as a children's governess' (436).

In this context, smoking, far from being useless, is a material practice that enables the public performance of a new gendered subjectivity. This practice offers an entry into the masculine symbolic, but the subjectivity produced is neither masculinity nor femininity as defined by the division between the (public) 'game' and the (private) 'sofa'. Judith Butler writes that the

> subject who would resist such norms is itself enabled, if not produced, by such norms. Although this constitutive restraint does not foreclose the possibility of agency, it does locate agency as a reiterative or rearticulatory practice, immanent to power, and not a relation of external opposition to power.[13]

Certainly Miriam's public persona, the New Woman, is constructed within such norms, but they are more than discursive and more than symbolic. While smoking is often represented as 'doing nothing', as useless, it is often paradigmatic of more general material conditions. Miriam's bold consumption does produce a new identity: she 'discharged a double stream of smoke violently through her nostrils breaking out at last a public defiance of the freemasonry of women' (436). However, the cigarette also locates Miriam within an economic system of production, consumption and exchange. While the cigarette is the means to an independent performance, it also reveals her dependence in terms of both gender and class. She aspires to a masculine role, but the role on offer comes ready made – like the cigarette itself, which (as noted in Chapter 3) had been manufactured industrially since 1883. If it is assumed that she obtains the cigarette from her male employer, her dependency is revealed not just in terms of cigarettes but in her class position, selling her labour power as a 'governess': a job for which, in English literary representations, gender and class cannot be divorced.

Smoking as a form of bodily innervation, no matter how sublime, cannot be read as free play even if it allows room-for-play. The mass consumption of cigarettes in the 1890s was facilitated both by new methods of industrial production and by new sales techniques. Before 1883, cigarettes were rolled by hand by women factory workers. In 1883, the British cigarette manufacturer Wills and Co. bought the Bonsack machine (see Chapter 3), which could produce hundreds of cigarettes in a minute.[14] The introduction of the Bonsack machine was preceded, by a few years, by the growth of cut-price outlets that catered to the rapidly increasing numbers of cigarette smokers. For example, the firm of Salmon and Gluckstein (whose owners were later to become part of the management of the firm J. Lyons and Co., discussed in Chapter 13) made its money by buying in bulk and selling cheaply. The firm expanded rapidly from 1873, and by 1897 had sixty-two branches. Such was their success that, despite manufacturers' attempts to fix prices, the firm's ability to move its stock meant that it could play one supplier off against another.[15] Salmon and Gluckstein was a good example of the new power of consumption in the economy. Britain led the world in adopting cigarettes as the favoured form of tobacco. Cigarettes amounted to 10 per cent of tobacco sales in 1900, rising to 50 per cent in 1920 and 84 per cent in 1950.[16] Identified with the 'New Woman', they were a signifier of a widening sphere (or room-for-play) for women in the positions of Clara, Totty or Miriam. That sphere enabled women to fashion a new public identity; but left them dependent upon their labour power (and the limited ability to consume which that allowed) even while it relieved them of some of the pressures of patriarchal surveillance.

Smoking a cigarette in 1895 was then both an aesthetic and an economic act. It allowed Miriam to perform, temporarily (as Wilde pointed out, it offers a notoriously short-lived fix), outside some of the constraints of class and gender. However, that very possibility also hints at a third position, neither masculine or feminine, employer or employee. Not yet articulated in this 'chapter-novel', a third space emerges through the unspeakable crime behind the Wilde trial, the great public event of 1895, which haunts the narrative of *Honeycomb*. Early in the text, Wilde is described as a genius (413), but then his name becomes tainted with something unspeakable, 'something dreadful that was happening in London', 'something that a human being had done that was worse than a murder or a divorce' (413).[17] Intriguingly, but unenlighteningly, Miriam is told by her employer, Mrs Corrie, that: 'It's the most awful thing there is. It's in the Bible', before Mrs Corrie 'fled into the house' (414). Bourgeois horror, far from putting Miriam off, creates a reverse discourse: her 'sympathies veered vaguely out towards the patch of disgrace in London' (429). What she despises is not Wilde's crime but the gendered conventions that keep it a secret. In fact, the 'patch of disgrace' provides Miriam with a possible solution to her own identity problems, 'some lonely solution of her difficulty that seemed to come shapelessly towards her' (437). She explores the possibility of another kind of subjectivity, a third term, which she later describes as a 'two natures, equally matched, mingle and fight', that resists the hegemonic norms and definitions of gender.[18]

While there is then evidence of both gendered subjectivity as performance and of a proliferation of gendered subjectivities in *Pilgrimage*, the example of the cigarette demonstrates that the production of such subjectivities is not just aesthetic, it is rooted in the material conditions in which the performance takes place. However, the cigarette is probably too aesthetic an object to fulfil that function effectively. A better example is the café, which was also a place of performance and consumption, but one for which the links can better be made between the production of new gendered subjectivities and the material spaces in which they were produced. Chapter 11 will examine Bloom's search for a space in which he can achieve a comfortable sense of self and Part III will look at the role of cafés in detail, but first the representation of diet and eating in Richardson's work deserves further attention.

10

Dietetics and aesthetics

Nutrition was a lifelong interest for Richardson. The scientific as well as the social and aesthetic aspects of food and eating pervaded all her writings, from her journalism to her correspondence, including *Pilgrimage* itself. Part of this chapter is devoted to her journalism, in particular the column she wrote between 1912 and 1922 in the *Dental Record*. But, surprisingly perhaps, for an author not usually noted for her poetry, her poem 'Afternoon Tea' acts as a useful starting point, because it makes an explicit connection between two key elements of Richardson's project: a gendered philosophy of everyday life (opposed to what she saw as masculinist, expert science) and modernist form. 'Afternoon Tea' was published in *Queen* magazine in 1932; but, according to a letter sent by Richardson to her friend Bryher (Annie Winifred Ellerman) in January 1933, it was one of two poems that had been sent to the magazine ten years earlier.[1] The year in which the poem was composed is significant, because 1923 saw the publication of the seventh 'chapter-novel' of *Pilgrimage*, *Revolving Lights*, in which Richardson further developed her theory of a feminine aesthetic. The date suggests that the poem and her theory were worked out in parallel. The aesthetic emerges through a Socratic dialogue between *Pilgrimage*'s female protagonist, Miriam, and the scientific world-view of her sometime lover, Hypo Wilson. Wilson is usually understood to represent H. G. Wells, and, even if that equation is too precise, Hypo certainly represents the Wellsian, scientific perspective that Richardson argued against in her journalism, and of which she wrote, in a review of Wells's *In the Days of the Comet*:

> One hopes for a book where womanhood shall be as well as manhood. So far he has not achieved the portrayal of a woman, with the one exception of Leadford's mother. His women are all of one specimen, carried away from some biological museum of his student days, dressed up in varying trappings, with different shades of hair and proportions of freckles, with neatly tabulated instincts and one vague smile between them all.

One hopes he may get rid of this rather irritating dummy and, along with her, of all his stage machinery – his men in towers, and men with voices, and men at writing-desks – and begin directly, without either apology or explanation, – laborious and altogether obstructive attempts to establish a rapport between himself and his readers.[2]

Richardson's critique here might at first appear as straightforward opposition between masculine rationality and feminine feeling, but the dialogue between Miriam and Wilson has a complex relationship to the narrative of *Revolving Lights*. It is represented in the novel through an act of remembrance, which takes some of its meaning from the context in which it is remembered. Miriam recalls their conversation in the course of a long nocturnal walk through London, during which she reconsiders various aspects of her identity, returning to some of the questions first raised in *Honeycomb* (see Chapter 9). The figure of Wilson/Wells can be seen as part of a continuing argument Miriam is having with herself, but whereas in *Backwater* and *Honeycomb* Miriam positions herself in relation to a father figure (first her actual father, then Mr Corrie as substitute), by *Revolving Lights* she is thinking about subjectivity in relation to an idea of scientific modernity. Not only has the figure of the father been absorbed into a more sophisticated understanding of state and society, but the binary of masculine and feminine that troubled Miriam at the Corries has given way to speculation about a third sex. Thus, it starts to make less and less sense to gender scientific rationality as purely masculine and Miriam's aesthetic as uniquely feminine.

In the key dialogue with Hypo, Miriam argues that women have a 'preeminence in an art. The art of making atmospheres. It is as big an art as any other. Most women can exercise it, for reasons, by fits and starts. The best women work at it the whole of the time. Not one man in a million is aware of it. It's like air within air.'[3] Searching for an example, Miriam uses the ritual of tea to illustrate her point, with infusion as the underlying metaphor: 'the thing I mean goes through everything. A woman's way of "being" can be discovered in the way she pours out tea' (257). It is an example that anticipates the paradox of the poem, where the context of art is in fact the art itself, 'air within air'. Written at same time as this passage, 'Afternoon Tea' can be read as an example of the aesthetic Miriam is devising, where form is found not in the overstated and underlined pronouncements of the novel (a genre Richardson usually dismissed as a 'guided tour') or in Wellsian science, but in the making and remaking of everyday life:

You,
    dry little bourgeoise
    not knowing it,

>   and so,
>   strong,
>   and
>   weak with ignoring what lies beyond the gates
> You, that afternoon when the overwrought man from Bicester,
>   wife-driven, child driven, was sinking glassy-eyed beneath
>   the tide of his preoccupations,
> You, sitting there, coldy shaping things for him in advance, accepting,
>   ignoring,
> You taught me form[4]

Tea flows, through the poem, as a dialectical image for the rejected forms of everyday life, which are the material of Richardson's modernism as much as they are for Walter Benjamin's *Arcades Project*. The distancing of the second person address 'You', a distancing emphasised by the form of the lines and by the apparent, high-modernist, contempt for the sterility of middle-class norms, is washed down by the familiar, ordinary, English discourse of tea, which the poem mimics, as in:

> – Fancy a cup of (Afternoon) tea?
> – Ooh, yes, I am a little dry (bourgeoise)
> – Do you like it strong or weak? (not knowing it)
> – I'll take it as it comes thank you (strong, / and / weak with ignoring what lies beyond the gates)

The middle-class woman (and mother) who in the elite, masculinist discourse of high modernism would be the antithesis of art is, it turns out, herself the artist, creating the atmosphere. As Miriam describes her concept of atmosphere to Hypo, 'It may be deadly. Cramping and awful, or simply destructive, so that no life is possible within it. So is the bad art of men. At its best it is absolutely life-giving. And not soft. Very hard and stern and austere in its beauty' (257). The bourgeoise woman is 'hard', 'stern and austere': 'coldly shaping things' of which her husband is unaware. The poem, which might, superficially, be taken to display some sympathy for the hen-pecked bourgeois, expresses the ambivalent sympathies towards both masculine and feminine positions that characterise Miriam's complex gendered identifications. Even the last and crucial word is double-edged: 'form' being the upper-middle-class word for etiquette – how things should be done – as well as an aesthetic term.[5]

The poem is thus an excellent example of Richardson's modernism as an aesthetic of everyday life, where the borderlines of art and the social, self and other, masculine and feminine are crossed and recrossed. Rita Felski writes of modern literature's paradoxical relationship to the everyday that it often seeks 'to both preserve and negate it'.⁶ The paradox of Richardson's form is that it situates itself outside the production of the atmosphere, looking in – hence the distance of the alienated 'You'. Yet, at the same time, the form of the poem reproduces the women's art of making atmospheres. Richardson seeks to both preserve and transform the everyday.

'Afternoon Tea' is also exemplary in that it underlines the central importance of eating and drinking to Richardson's aesthetic of the everyday. De Certeau might have been thinking of Richardson when he wrote that

> The wordless histories of walking, dress, housing, or cooking shape neighbourhoods on behalf of absences; they trace out memories that no longer have a place–childhoods, genealogical traditions, timeless events. Such is the 'work' of urban narratives as well. They insinuate different spaces into cafés, offices and buildings.⁷

Richardson's urban aesthetic has been recognised, but her tracing of the wordless history of eating and the importance of cafés for the production of new urban subjectivities and has been less commented upon. Diet was both a professional and an artistic preoccupation for Richardson. Accounts of her life suggest it was also a personal one. In a memoir her sister-in-law remembered:

> Tea was always beautifully set, a little ceremony. A white linen tablecloth, edged with fine drawn thread work and hand embroidered motifs of raised peacocks, (now in my possession) covered a trolley, under delicate eggshell china. So, I imagine, tea was served in the well servanted household of Dorothy's childhood, and the cloth and china may have been saved from earlier days. Tea from a golden brown Swedish teapot, given by an admirer, of a pattern I have seen nowhere else, with the lid on one side, not in the way of the handle, still admired by my visitors for its beautiful and practical shape.⁸

In Adrian Allison's painting of Dorothy and her husband, the artist Alan Odle, they sit at a fully laden table, set out for tea: cups, teapot and a large cake, both of them smoking furiously. Professionally, as a receptionist in a Harley Street dental practice, she worked at the sharp end of the eating body. Even in an interview with the musician George Antheil, published in *Vanity Fair*, she mentions tea, milk and many buns.⁹ An article about Upton Sinclair's *The Jungle* begins with an anecdote about a woman in Mudies who is looking for Horace Fletcher's book *Glutton or Epicure* (1899),¹⁰ the title of which she cannot remember, but which she describes as about '*Chewing*' (Horace recommended that each mouthful be chewed thirty-two times):

Figure 1 Adrian Allison, portrait of Alan Odle and Dorothy Richardson at table

'. . . you know the book I mean – *everybody's* reading it. I did not look up the name – about not really swallowing anything. I believe it's been out for years, but everyone's taken it up now. Mastication, you know – biting,' she finished incisively.

Unable to identify the book the woman asks, as an alternative, for Sinclair: '*Have* you a copy of that dreadful American book – that book about tinned meat!'[11]

The reason for the anecdote becomes clearer if you know that the review appeared in a vegetarian publication, *The Crank*; but the real reason is Richardson's interest in the politics of food, so that the industrialisation of food production is, for her, part and parcel of the socialist politics of *The Jungle* (which otherwise she doesn't think much of). Her very first published articles, all book reviews, were in *The Crank* and she translated three books on diet early on in her career: *Consumption Doomed* (1913), *Some Popular Foodstuffs Exposed* (1913), *Man's Best Food* (1914). Her preface to one of these, Paul Carton's *Consumption Doomed: A Lecture on the Cure of Tuberculosis* (which claimed that vegetarianism could cure tuberculosis), offers a critique of science that locates her within the ragbag group of vegetarians, anti-vivisectionists, feminists, socialists, and sexual freethinkers which Jo-Ann Wallace has characterised as the official Left's unconscious – that part of itself that it wishes to deny in order to present itself as credible.[12] Presenting the argument that diet is a crucial part of health Richardson wrote:

> The price paid for devotion to a set of facts torn from the context of reality is that we become in a measure their tool, we have grown to see all life through the narrow peep-hole of the specialist. Suffering humanity is learning that scientific knowledge does not 'explain' anything, that intellectual analysis kills that which it loves by the very process of detaching and observing it.[13]

This suspicion of scientific expertise is not dissimilar to that of Richardson's contemporary, the utopian socialist Edward Carpenter, a review of whose *Days with Walt Whitman* was Richardson's first publication. In his essay 'Modern Science: A Criticism', which was collected in *Civilisation: Its Cause and Its Cure*, Carpenter wrote: 'Placed in the face of the great unconstrained unit of Nature we can only deal with it by selecting certain details and isolating those (either wilfully or unconsciously) from the rest.'[14] More broadly, Richardson's critique of scientific specialism is drawn from the constellation of alternative world-views that flourished in the 1890s. These included vegetarianism, but also the example of Wilde, with whom the young Miriam Henderson identified in *Honeycomb* (see Chapter 9). In the review of Carpenter the reference to intellectual analysis killing 'that which it loves' alludes to 'The Ballad of Reading Gaol'. Other influences from the Bohemian Left included the sexologist Havelock Ellis, associated with the Fellowship of the New Life, a precursor of the Fabian Society.

Contemporary feminist thought was also an important reference point for Richardson's work. Olive Schreiner is mentioned in *Pilgrimage*, and in 1917 Richardson wrote an article about Charlotte Perkins Gilman's feminism in a pacifist publication, *The Ploughshare*, that also alludes to Schreiner's *Woman and Labour*.[15] Even as late as 1928, she was publishing in the alternative periodical *Focus*, which described itself as a 'Periodical to the Point in Matters of Health, Wealth, & Life' and advertised such wonders as 'Electric Bath, High Frequency, Radiant Heat, Ionization, Diathermy, Nauheim Bath, Sitz Bath, Phototherapy, Electric Light Bath, Bergonie Chair Artificial Sunlight Massage, X-Ray, [and] Baths of All kinds'.[16]

The influence of these dissident voices was evident in Richardson's most sustained journalistic endeavour, her column 'Comments by a Layman', published in the *The Dental Record*. In the column Richardson discussed an extraordinary range of topics, including diet and creativity, Balzac's appetites, Shelley's preference for figs and bread, and, the advantages of brown bread. The 'Layman' however, was not dogmatic in its criticisms of modern specialist or 'expert' opinion. The views expressed, in some cases explicitly disowned by the editor, draw equally on radical ideas and the more pragmatic, statist tradition associated with Fabianism.[17] The Fabians, whose founding members included Sidney and Beatrice Webb, Wells himself and Bernard Shaw, had rejected the communist tradition of William Morris and utopian socialists like Edward Carpenter in favour of top-down social reform by experts. Richardson attended Fabian meetings at the invitation of Wells. The influence of the movement, whose enthusiasm for technical solutions to social problems was part of a whole trend within early twentieth-century modernity,[18] is evident in the column's repeated calls for state intervention. A typical piece of social commentary on dietary reform incorporates familiar themes from the vegetarian movement, warning at the onset of the First World War against 'the return of white bread and the prospect of unlimited meat and alcohol and sugar!'; and yet couches that warning within a call for social reform in a statist framework: 'We cannot exclude the factor of Diet. Any plan of national reconstruction that ignores it is a plan built on a rotting foundation.'[19]

Fabianism is written into *Revolving Lights* as part of the dialogic context of Miriam's discussion with Hypo Wilson. Miriam attends a 'Lycurgan' (thinly disguised Fabian) meeting just before the urban walk in which she remembers the conversation with Wilson. In that context, Richardson's aesthetic can be seen to be working within and against various discourses of the state in the period. Her interest is in what Michel Foucault called biopolitics: the relationship between the disciplined body, medical technologies and state formation.[20] One of the extraordinary, quasi-surreal, things about reading Richardson's columns in the *Dental Record* is to see her comments juxtaposed with an article entitled 'A Reciprocating Guide for Deviation of the Mandible'.[21] However, rather than giving just a critique of expert science and thus constructing a kind of Habermasian confrontation between system and life-worlds,[22] Richardson's engagement is with the biopolitics of the disciplined bodies produced between the two.

This engagement has a gendered dimension, as is shown by a separate article published in the *Dental Record* under the title, 'Amateur Evidence in Dietetics'. Here she describes the responses to what she calls a ' "dental" dietary': 'a dietary properly balanced from the nutritional point of view, and at the same time necessitating the full exercise of the function of mastication and including stuffs, such as the juices of fruits, whose sole value from the dental standpoint is the cleansing of the mouth'.[23] This diet, she argues, 'stands convicted in the light of evidence coming from people who may be taken as fairly representative of the class that is mainly responsible for the feeding and rearing of children, *viz.*, their mothers'.[24] Against expert advice, the 'Layman' welcomes the contribution of subjective opinions to the debate, arguing that 'The child is, first and foremost, an individual human being with moral idiosyncrasies and only in the second place an assimilative mechanism'.[25] Elsewhere, in her letters, Richardson applauds children's diets which accept that the child may not want to eat, and may even fast for a few days. If few parents could tolerate such fasting, however common it may be, without suffering acute anxiety, Richardson's focus demonstrates a politically astute understanding of the relationship between diet and gender identity at a time when the state had begun to make strong links between good diet and good mothering.[26] In another of the 'Layman's' columns, she discusses the food handed out by the Women's League of Service for Motherhood to 'expectant and nursing mothers'.[27] In the context of the First World War, where soldiers' health (and the health of soldiers to be) was a priority and food shortages were common, Richardson does not argue specifically against what Habermas describes as those systems that 'have been consolidated into a monetary-administrative complex' and have 'been disconnected from the communicatively structured life-world (with private and public spheres)'.[28] Instead, she calls, as in her aesthetic, for a disruption of the subject–object distinction those systems set up and for an open and accountable state, in which working-class women and their children are not the objects but the subjects of a transformation in their own health. In this biopolitics, small resistances, of which the control of what we eat and drink is one, are, in part, structured by the disciplinary control of the state. Read not just contextually but as an intervention, Richardson's grasp of the biopolitics of early twentieth-century modernity can be seen to inform her modernist aesthetic – an aesthetic which, unlike that of Pound and Eliot, is not an anti-modern modernism[29] but one concerned to engage with the new possibilities opened up by modernity. This engagement performs a dialectical reversal in which Wellsian science and Fabian politics are faced with the modern subjectivities that are their other side. In both her journalism and in the aesthetic project that constitutes *Pilgrimage*, Richardson is concerned to site subjectivity within the constellation of material practices that combine to produce modern identities.

All expertise and specialism, the Layman claims, are inadequate on their own. Each part relates to a whole: 'good teeth are the alpha and omega of good health'; 'In Switzerland. . . the battle cry of dentists is "look after the diet and the teeth will look after themselves".' In the context of the First World War, Richardson's references to soldiers' health and Parliamentary committees reveal that her interest in the eating body was formed in relation to debates about the relationship between the self and the modern state. Her most extravagant claim (not entirely tongue in cheek) is in a review of a book by a Spanish dentist: 'civilization is based upon the stability of molars'.[30]

More seriously, the relationship between this holistic approach to health and Richardson's gendered aesthetic as exemplified by the 'atmosphere' can be found in one of the columns explicitly disowned by the editor. After a jolly introduction about sailors with toothache, she engages with the debate about women's position in the medical profession and the claim by George Moore that 'woman displays genius only in certain emotional spheres, not in action'. She replies:

> It is hardly yet beginning to dawn upon the male mind that 'authority,' is a doomed weapon. The successful wielding of authority, the imposition of the will of one human being upon another is bad, evil, retarding for the personality imposed upon; it is worse, far more evil and retarding for the personality who imposes. The admission that women display genius in certain *emotional* spheres, not in *action* is an unconscious revelation of an amazing oblivion. Woman might be defined as emotion active, perhaps. Emotion active is the principle of social life, the moving out, by the power of imaginative sympathy, from self towards other selves. The desire for the welfare of other selves. The 'world' of the fighting male has not hitherto been civilised. It is still ruled by force. Force is not power. Might has no enduring potency.[31]

Here the concern with 'welfare of other selves', those other subjectivities which are the products of modernity, but which with which the authority of expert science does not concern itself, to its cost, relates strongly to the project of *Pilgrimage*. In *Pilgrimage* the siting of the subjectivity of the working New Woman in the city as she is made and remade by the new public culture of London acts both to accept and to explore the impact of modernity, in all its forms, in opposition to the masculine expert and what Richardson in another column calls 'the remarkable slowness of the scientific, analytic, relatively inartistic English to perceive the "relationship" of things'.[32] The outlines of Richardson's aesthetic project can be discerned in the balance the 'Layman' admires in 'complete scientific detachment, [but] a detachment, moreover, that does not imply the least indifference to the detailed actualities of the moment'.[33] And, in a reference that anticipates the problems of Richardson's attempts to write the everyday through modernist prose, she welcomes technical language, but argues that the 'truths it has to convey are perfectly translatable into language that can be understood [sic] by the people'.[34]

In this respect, perhaps the best comparison with Richardson as modernist critic of modernity is Walter Benjamin. Her interest in the quotidian, the flotsam and jetsam of everyday life, reflects his fascination for Baudelaire's ragpickers and the collecting mania that lies behind the *Arcades Project*. Richardson's columns are themselves a kind exercise in *bricolage*, with anecdotes about sailors with toothache rubbing up alongside serious social comment. As for Benjamin, what the everyday throws up is not random. Each item chosen can be re-presented as a dialectical image, where the apparently insignificant detail is actually the 'detailed actuality of the moment', which, like Benjamin's example of the everyday, a 'ruffle in a dress', can be folded back into eternity.[35] In the 'Comments by a Layman', nothing is taken as read, it is the job of the 'Layman' to comment and criticise and to place the ephemera of modernity within a wider frame of reference. In this context, expert science is more akin, in Benjamin's distinction, to *Erlebnis*, the unreflecting shock of modernity. Its force cannot be ignored, but a modernist aesthetic has as a task to reflect and reorder the immediate experience into representation as a temporal and spatial constellation.

Afternoon tea was then for Richardson more than a quaint English practice. The rituals of everyday life were (even when she was a vegetarian) the very meat and drink of her aesthetic, an opportunity to show how, as she wrote of Bergson's address to the Society for Psychical Research: 'It leaves one with a sense of step taken, with the sense that one gets from all "live writing", of a piece of actual experience from which there is no going back. It floods, as experience is apt to do, with new meaning much of the current coin of everyday life, the words and phrases whose vitality depends upon one's vision of things as a whole.'[36] In Richardson's dialectical image, in 'the way she pours out tea', form emerges from the everyday, but to reify form and to give it the expert's authority is to separate it artificially from its 'atmosphere'. Behind her perception of the everyday act is a whole technological apparatus, which, if not factored in to an understanding of form, will leave it 'dry' and abstract. In *Revolving Lights* she writes: 'To watch a shape adds interest to listening. But something disappears in listening with the form put first. Hearing only form is a kind of happiness. But in coming back there is a reproach; as if it had been a kind of truancy.'[37]

Scientific modernity offers both too much and too little form for Richardson, but her resort to the alternative views available at the turn of the century does not go so far as to reject scientific form altogether. As for Benjamin, technological modernity is part of the solution as well as part of the problem. It represents a force that cannot be ignored: hence the echo of Hypo's viewpoint in Miriam's head. In another, perhaps less accomplished but no less interesting poem, 'Buns for Tea', Richardson, describes the bun as a 'shadowed world' that incorporates the entire industrial process for which it now stands as dialectical image. The bun incorporates the colonial territories that produce the raw materials, the trade and economic infrastructure that transports them and, most important of all, the 'death-dealing' pain of labour that goes into the bun's production:

> When I buy a bun
> I buy a shadowed world
> Lit by sunlight,
> Dark with shadowed sunlight
>
> Wavering corn I buy.
> Bushes of bright currants
> Tall cane and spices,
> Butter from bright fields.
>
> I see the gathering
> Gold corn and purple berries
> Dark spices, syrup crystals,
> Cream in the pan.
>
> Dark holds of ships;
> Seething souls of toilers,
> Darkness of the town night
> Around the bakery.
>
> Beetles, and the soft
> Death-dealing
> Dust of fine flour,
> Stealthily streaming
>
> Into the life-breath
> Of the baker.
> When I buy a bun
> I buy a world, sun-shadowed[38]

In the first stanza, sun and shadow are the light and dark of the total system that produces the bun as commodity. Work and the poor return for labour make the bun both a product of that system and its potential reward. Thus, for Richardson, a cup of tea is never just a cup of tea, a bun is never just a bun. They are commodities that have both economic and symbolic functions within modernity. Richardson's modernist aesthetic, however, attempts to reinscribe that which capitalist reification would exclude. *Pilgrimage* attempts the creation of an atmosphere akin to the atmospheres Miriam argues women make in everyday life, where the 'welfare of other selves' is included not excluded. In Richardson's work the act of eating becomes a dialectical image for the relationship between work and consumption. A bun and a cup of tea can be read as dialectical images of bodily innervation that extend out to include the industrialisation of food, the medicalisation of diet and the performance of new subjectivities – performances that can become either new modes of consumption or a potential innervation of the collective. Richardson's modernism however opposed a modernity of determined effects, either in diet or in art. Instead it sought to find images that might connect quotidian, corporeal experience with a transformation of the everyday.

11

'Lestrygonians': a place to eat

Miriam's gender identity is as much in process as the tea and buns she consumes. Made and remade in the city, itself a node in a global network of political, social and economic relations, her subjectivity is not fixed, but neither is it free. In some ways an example of what Judith Halberstam calls female masculinity[1], her position moves between the several identities of the New Woman and various masculine identifications: at one moment embodying a feminist political identity, at others reading for statist solutions to social problems. What is clear however is that Miriam's embodied presence in the urban public sphere disrupts earlier moulds of masculinity and femininity.

Leopold Bloom is as extensive and intensive a study as Miriam. The 'Lestrygonians' chapter, which, more than any other part of *Ulysses*, is devoted to food and eating, locates Bloom's embodied masculinity in relation to a process of destruction and renewal. The city in process produces a self in process:

> Cityful passing away, other cityful coming, passing away too: other coming on, passing on. Houses, lines of houses, streets, miles of pavements, piledup bricks, stones. Changing hands. This owner, that. Landlord never dies they say. Other steps into his shoes when he gets notice to quit. They buy the place up with gold and still they have all the gold. Swindle in it somewhere. Piled up in cities, worn away age after age. Pyramids in sand. Built on bread and onions. (135)

Bloom is sometimes cited as an everyman, a full representation of what it is to be human.[2] But, as Kate Soper has pointed out, such a representation ignores the gendered limits of his humanism.[3] Bloom's masculinity is as newly forged as Miriam's uncertain gender identity. Fatherless and not a father to his son, Bloom is cut off from paternal lineage. Destabilising memories of Rudy surface again in 'Lestrygonians'. Bloom's relationship with Molly has never recovered from Rudy's death:

> I was happier then. Or was that I? Or am I now I? Twentyeight I was. She twentythree. When we left Lombard street west something changed. Could never like it again after Rudy. Can't bring back time. Like holding water in your hand. Would you go back to then? Just beginning then. (137)

Bloom's hungers can never be fully satisfied, because he can never fully redeem such losses. In fact, he is never sure whether he wants to go back, for that would mean giving up the pleasures of the moment. He cannot make up his mind whether he would rather redeem past desires or enjoy the possibilities of the present – as represented by memories of his correspondence with Martha Clifford:

> Would you? Are you not happy in your home you poor little naughty boy? Wants to sow buttons for me. I must answer. (137).

At the end of 'Lotus Eaters', the image of the lotus is his penis as 'father of thousands, a languid floating flower' (71). Bloom's masculinity is both negated and multiplied by modernity. The possibilities for conception, biological and otherwise, expand, as do the possibilities of surrogate fatherhood – seen in his symbolic relationship to Stephen Dedalus (see Chapter 6). At issue in 'Lestrygonians' are the spaces in which these new and temporary identifications (improvisations is perhaps a better term) might take place. The chapter begins with the street as offering the minimal conditions for their realisation.

Any new masculine authority Bloom gains has to be recreated in each social encounter he makes, against the current of social expectation. Almost every meeting involves a misrecognition, both of self and other. Half-seeing a religious tract in the hand of a young man, Bloom thinks he sees himself reflected:

> Bloo. . . Me? No.
> Blood of the Lamb (124)

But he has no place in either Christian or Jewish doctrine. In fact, there is a hint here of the anti-semitic 'blood libel', which condenses the myth of the Jews' responsibility for the death of Jesus with the belief that Jews abduct Christian children to use them in their rites. The 'Me? No' signifies a combination of exclusion and self-definition.

Although he is a much more joyful embodiment of modern man than Gissing's embittered characters, Bloom is as discomfited by women's entrance into the public sphere as Sidney Kirkwood in *The Nether World*. Molly's sexual independence means that he is confronted at almost every moment by the limits of a secure sense of self, which now has to be made and remade by acts of evasion, displacement and repression. Although Molly does not leave Eccles Street, the phallic embodiment of her sexual desire walks the streets in the figure of Blazes Boylan, in his straw hat, tan shoes and 'turnup' trousers. Bloom narrowly escapes meeting him at the end of the chapter. Molly's relationship with Boylan connects her to the web of relationships – Penelope's web – that makes up the city's sexual life. Urban promiscuity, as dramatised in the Viennese playwright Arthur Schnitzler's *La Ronde* (1901),[4] makes each part of the web, including Bloom, dependent on the whole and therefore vulnerable. Bloom represses the thought that Boylan might pass on syphilis to Molly:

> If he. . .?
> O!
> Eh?
> No . . . . . . No.
> No, no. I don't believe it. He wouldn't surely?
> No, no.
> Mr Bloom moved forward raising his troubled eyes. Think no more about that. (126)

To this extent, *Ulysses* reproduces a gendered conception of the city, in which women are seen as conduits of disease, desire, energies and information. A few pages later, Bloom considers the usefulness of working women to the police: 'Why those plainclothes men are always courting slaveys. . .Barmaids too, Tobaccoshopgirls' (134). Servants, barmaids (such as Clara Hewett) and shopgirls are all what Benjamin might call guardians of thresholds. They facilitate society's transactions across boundaries. State power has to work through them, but they themselves also constitute a weak power that reinforces Bloom's sense of his own vulnerability. Stable identities can only be secured by closed units, for which the political analogy is the republican cell, which has to internalise the violence of the state in order to protect itself from it: 'James Stephen's idea was the best. He knew them. Circles of ten so that a fellow couldn't round on more than his own ring. Sinn Fein. Back out you get the knife. Hidden hand. Stay in. The firing squad' (134). 'Lestrygonians' thus follows Bloom's search for an oasis where he can find provisional satisfaction, but one that, to fulfil, must recoup all past satisfactions in order to give the most temporary sense of plenitude.

The chapter begins with sweets, food as infantile craving: 'Pineapple rock, lemon platt, butter scotch. A sugarsticky girl shovelling scoopfuls of creams for a christian brother' (124). But, prompted by the presence of the priest, Bloom's thoughts quickly, if playfully, interpellate sweetness into the symbolic orders of state and religion: 'Lozenge and comfit manufacturer to His Majesty the King. God. Save. Sitting on his throne sucking red jujubes white.' He sights the tract with 'Blood of the Lamb' written on it immediately afterwards, an image that brings to the fore not just Bloom's abjected position but the ritual of sacrifice that lies behind all food events. Later, when he sees a couple leaving a vegetarian café, he thinks of the 'Wretched brutes there at the cattlemarket waiting for the poleaxe to split their skulls open' (140).

From the beginning of the chapter, Bloom's thoughts range across a spectrum that spans almost all the uses of food, from the most mundane to the most sophisticated. The context is entirely ordinary, the body's diurnal rhythm: Bloom has digested his breakfast and is getting hungry for lunch. His intellectual enquiries are prompted by bodily need. But the body's rhythm is constantly interrupted by the rhythms of the street, showing a more complex process of cause and effect that is part of a sedimented social history.[5] The sight of one of the Dedalus sisters prompts him to think about malnutrition: 'good Lord, that poor child's dress is in flitters. Underfed she looks. Potatoes and marge, marge and potatoes. It's after they feel it. Proof of the pudding. Undermines the constitution' (125).

Yet Bloom's response to the sight of poverty is typically ludic. He begins a series of idle experiments with seagulls on the Liffey: throwing them first a rolled-up piece of paper (thus finally getting rid of the religious tract – 'Blood of the Lamb'), which they ignore; then pieces of stale Banbury cake, which they devour.[6] The game is an example of Miriam Hansen's conceptualisation of Benjamin's *Spielraum* (see Chapter 7). Bloom creates 'room-for-play' despite the force with which the city channels the bodily functions of its inhabitants. The Liffey here is more than just scene setting. It is a channel for bodily waste, the means by which the city's sewage is removed, as Bloom remembers when he thinks of the son of Reuben J. Dodd (another Jewish Dubliner) who tried to drown himself in it. Tim Armstrong writes that 'Waste production is the point where the man-machine metaphor fails; where the body declares its irreducible presence, and linear time is replaced by the cyclic time of the body'.[7]

Bloom's food-play signifies that, unlike the Dedalus children, he is relatively, temporarily free of necessity, but his game of throwing cake into the river taunts the gulls by throwing their food into what it will become. In 'Hades', Bloom had tried to distract his companions from his own origins by trumping their anti-semitism with a tale of Reuben J.'s meanness with money (78). Now he uses the gulls in the same way, sending them into the river as a way of keeping himself out of the shit. The game is repeated when he sees a line of sandwichmen, the last one – cramming 'a chunk of bread', 'Our staple food' (129), into his mouth – taking the symbolic position occupied by the gull, Reuben J.'s son and Bloom himself. As his thoughts on selling stationary remind the reader, Bloom is himself an advertiser, not so far above the sandwichman in the social order.

Bloom's room-for-play is conditioned by the limits of the public sphere in which he is situated. Dublin's streets allow him a small but significant space in which to forge a self. His encounter with the beefy policeman from College Street station – 'After their feed with a good load of fat soup under their belts' – is a reminder that, on the streets, as elsewhere, the unfed are controlled by the fed. His memory of being chased during an anti-British demonstration reinforces a sense that Bloom is a fugitive, running from thoughts, Boylan, and the imperial state, all of which have the power to discomfort. Nevertheless, given enough space, even the width of the narrow pavement on which he walks, the streets offer sufficient to whet his appetite, if not to satisfy it. For example, Bloom's encounter with Mrs Breen, who evokes the memory of earlier desires, is mixed with the tempting aromas of Harrison's eatery:

> Hot mockturtle vapour and steam of newbaked jampuffs rolypoly poured out from Harrison's. The heavy noonreek tickled the top of Mr Bloom's gullet. Want to make good pastry, butter, best flour, Demerara sugar, or they'd taste it with the hot tea. Or is it from her? (129)

Mrs Breen's position is cruelly analogous to the stale food Bloom threw to the gulls. She describes her children as 'on the baker's list', healthy and hungry, but she herself is looking poor and old:

> Same blue serge dress she had two years ago, the nap bleaching. Seen its best days. Wispish hair over her ears. And that dowdy toque: three old grapes to take the harm out of it. Shabby genteel. She used to be a tasty dresser. Lines round her mouth. Only a year or so older than Molly.
> See the eye that woman gave her, passing. Cruel. The unfair sex. (130)

While Bloom projects these thoughts on to a female passerby, they are his own; and his 'unfair' comparison conjoins the memory of youthful desire and a fresh tart:

> He looked still at her, holding back behind his look his discontent. Pungent mockturtle oxtail mulligatawny. I'm hungry too. Flakes of pastry on the gusset of her dress: daub of sugary flour stuck to her cheek. Rhubarb tart with liberal fillings, rich fruit interior. Josie Powell that was. In Luke Doyle's long ago. Dolphin's Barn, the charades. (130)

In order to satisfy his present desires, Bloom seeks a space in which his various hungers can be sated. Until he finds it, he is one of the unfed, so that he identifies briefly with, and then somewhat callously dismisses, a 'barefoot arab', who stands over the grating of Harrison's, 'breathing in the fumes' of the food he cannot afford: 'Deaden the gnaw of hunger that way'. The street 'arab', for whom the street offers even less scope for satisfaction than Bloom, brings to mind the first in a series of establishments consciously considered as places in which one could have lunch – a space in which satisfaction might be attained: where one might buy a 'Penny dinner. Knife and fork chained to the table' (129). The second, Bloom considers more seriously for himself, 'a sixpenny at Rowe's', finally settling on an 'eightpenny in the Burton' (132). From this point in the chapter, the room for play starts to shift from the public sphere of the streets to that of teashops, vegetarian cafés, restaurants and pubs, all of which offer a wider definition of what that sphere might be capable of.

Once Bloom has a destination in mind, the city streets become oppressive. He feels as if they have eaten him: 'This is the very worst hour of the day. Vitality. Dull, gloomy: hate this hour. Feel as if I had been eaten and spewed' (135). But the memory of past desire strengthens as the destination nears and his hunger grows. Aroused by the sight of silks in a shop window, his heart is 'astir' as he enters the Burton restaurant. His response to what is a typical Victorian eating house is significant. In the nineteenth century, the eating house in Britain and Ireland was, like the pub, an almost exclusively, and to Bloom repugnantly, masculine space (see Chapter 13):

> Men, men, men.
> Perched on high stools by the bar, hats shoved back, at the tables calling for more bread no charge, swilling, wolfing gobfuls of sloppy food, their eyes bulging, wiping wetted moustaches. A pallid suetfaced young man polished his tumbler knife fork and spoon with his napkin. New set of microbes. A man with an infant's saucestained napkin tucked round him shovelled gurgling soup down his gullet. A man spitting back on his plate: halfmasticated gristle: gums: no teeth to chewchewchew it. Chump chop from the grill. Bolting to get it over. Sad booser's eyes. Bitten off more than he can chew. Am I like that? See ourselves as others see us. Hungry man is an angry man. Working tooth and jaw. Don't! O! A bone! That last pagan king of Ireland Cormac in the schoolpoem choked himself at Sletty southward of the Boyne. Wonder what he was eating. Something galoptious. Saint Patrick converted him to Christianity. Couldn't swallow it all however.
> – Roast beef and cabbage.
> – One stew.
> Smells of men. Spaton sawdust, sweetish warmish cigarette smoke, reek of plug, spilt beer, men's beery piss, the stale of ferment.
> His gorge rose. (139)

Bloom's decision to go to Davy Byrne's 'moral' pub defines his different masculine identity, but that identity requires a space in which it can be made. What marks him out from the Burton cannibals is their lack of distinction. They are not conscious of what they eat and therefore are not conscious of themselves. In contrast, Bloom's meal in Davy Byrne's defines his vulnerable, self-reflexive, fugitive masculinity as distinctively cosmopolitan. The famous glass of burgundy, the Gorgonzola sandwich with mustard, served with buttered parsnips, combines the tastes of Europe and invites Bloom's critical engagement: too much mustard, '[t]oo much fat on the parsnips'. The pub offers nothing like complete protection. Nosey Flynn's enquiry about Molly reminds Bloom again of her assignation with Boylan, hitting him at the same time as the hot mustard: 'A warm shock of air heat of mustard hanched on Bloom's heart. He raised his eyes and met the stare of the bilious clock. Two. Pub clock five minutes fast. Time going on. Hands moving. Two. Not yet' (141).

But there is space enough for him to refill, to a certain extent, the hole created by the day's losses. Bloom's Proustian moment comes with a sip of wine, 'a secret touch telling me memory'. Remembrance of the moment when Molly and he exchanged warm seedcake, a moment also remembered by Molly at the culmination of 'Penelope' (643), returns him to state of plenitude, even as he knows himself to be, like the fly buzzing on the window pane 'stuck':[8]

> Oh wonder! Coolsoft with ointments her hand touched me, caressed: her eyes upon me did not turn away. Ravished over her I lay, full lips full open, kissed her mouth. Yum. Softly she gave me in my mouth the seedcake warm and chewed. Mawkish pulp her mouth had mumbled sweetsour of her spittle. Joy: I ate it: joy. (144)

The image of the seedcake exchanged combines the primal mother–child relationship (weaning the infant on chewed pulp), eating together and a utopian scenario of social and sexual intersubjectivity. It offers a brief moment of plenitude in Bloom's day, an epiphany that can be represented only through remembrance. Once he is back on the streets, Bloom is a fugitive once more. He escapes Boylan just in time by turning into the museum. But the image of the seedcake demonstrates the possibility of bringing into harmony, for a moment, bodily rhythm, social and sexual interaction on equal terms, and the technical apparatus that governs the city. The prerequisite for such a moment, which contains the trace of the collective bodily innervation that could transform society, is an enabling public culture.[9] Spaces such as Davy Byrne's make that culture possible, allowing an opportunity to remember, and then to conceive what Habermas calls 'undisturbed intersubjectivity' might look like.[10] The 'moral' pub allows Bloom sufficient room. Part III will look in greater detail at the importance of such spaces to Europe's new urban public cultures.

Part III
Cities

12

Phantasmagoria and the public sphere

a revolutionary is a man who throws himself into space[1]

Rain no longer fell, but the gusty and bitter wind still swept about the black streets. Walking side by side without speech, Clara and her companion left the neighbourhood of the prison and kept in a northward direction until they reached the junction of highways where stands the 'Angel'. Here was the wonted crowd of loiterers and the press of people waiting for tramcar or omnibus – east, west, south, or north; newsboys eager to get rid of their latest batch, were crying as usual, 'Ech-ow! Exteree speciul! Ech-ow! Steendard!' and brass band was blaring out it saddest strain of merry dance–music. The lights gleamed dismally in the rain-puddles and the wet pavement. With the wind came whiffs of tobacco and odours of the drinking-bar.[2]

The final third of this book focuses on the transformation of London's public culture. The chapters that follow pursue three interrelated aspects of the new urban public culture, all of which are present in *The Nether World*: first, work and the changing structure of employment in the period; second, the city as a potential democratic space; and third, phantasmagoria, the semi-hallucinatory experience created by the new cultures of consumption that emerged in the nineteenth century. This latter is the transformation described by Marx whereby the social relations between people assume 'in the eyes of those people, the phantasmagorical form of a relation between things', and which Walter Benjamin, in *The Arcades Project*, described as the nineteenth century's dreamworlds.[3]

In *The Nether World*, the alienated world of work is indicated by Clerkenwell's 'black streets', which keep its working-class inhabitants bound to life on the poverty line. Class is one of the inequalities that limits access to the public sphere, where certain individuals, groups and institutions have more influence than others.[4] Many city spaces invite participation, but, as Ken Hirschkop has argued, the ability to speak and the forms that speech take 'do not struggle on the level surface of the city square, but in the urban maze of an unevenly structured linguistic world'.[5] As Sidney Kirkwood knows, earning power also limits access to the new cultures of consumption and, in the case of Clara, participation involves becoming a commodity oneself.[6]

Gissing is not unaware that London's public spaces could become a democratic sphere, but he is pessimistic about the consequences. Upper Street, with its 'spacious pavement' (broader than the one on which Bloom stands in 'Lestrygonians') is a potential democratic space. But it corresponds to Bakhtin's concept of the 'public square', as described by Hirschkop. It 'represents a response to the problems of a modern, partly democratized linguistic world; it is not that democratized world itself. It constitutes heteroglossia as a desirable end, it does not merely acknowledge its prior existence.'[7] The inequalities of class and gender mean that a democratic linguistic world is never pre-existent.

Gissing criticism has often ignored the phantasmagoric in his texts. As discussed in Chapter 1, Marxist critics in particular (in some ways his strangest promoters), in their urgency to establish Gissing as a realist, have closed down the dreamscapes hidden in his drab urban scenes.[8] Since the belated translation of Walter Benjamin's *Arcades Project* into English, this omission has become more difficult to justify. As will be discussed in Chapter 14, *The Arcades Project* opens up alternative perspectives on Gissing's London as a kaleidoscope of different experiences and states of consciousness. Even in the short passage above, Upper Street is replete with the material structures, the technologies and the architectures that construct a city of dreamworlds. Kirkwood encounters mass communication, in the shape of the evening newspaper; and popular music, in the brass band. City lights[9] and the city streets multiply its reflective surfaces;[10] and public transport, the trams, like Benjamin's Paris Metro, carve new routes through the city, creating new ways to dream.[11] A mobile modernity allows the passage of the urban traveller from one state of consciousness to another as she or he passes from one part of the fragmented metropolis to another.[12]

The impact of a phantasmagoric commodity culture complicates both class relations and the notion of a democratic public sphere. The appearance Marx described of a relationship between things, rather than people, has a mystifying affect on the public culture of the city. Commodity spectacle cloaks, dazzles and distorts the urban dweller's sense of the real and makes it difficult, if not impossible, to imagine a public sphere in which rational debate can take place.[13] In what follows, the concept of 'public culture' is used to describe a public sphere that is both structured by social inequalities and transformed into dreamworlds. It is from such public cultures that modernist masculinities emerge. Modernist texts situate their performances in the productive spaces of the city, on the thresholds where the intimate, the private and the public meet, and where image and actuality clash. What Dorothy Richardson described as the 'elastic' space of the city creates multiple stages for multiple performances.[14] A proper consideration of modernist masculinities requires attention to be paid to these city spaces, which include those more usually associated with performance, such as theatres and music halls, but extend beyond their confines into London's streets with its shops, pubs, clubs, restaurants and cafés.[15] Both spaces of intersubjectivity and phantasmagoric spaces: these formed the material context in which new gendered subjectivities were embodied.

In recent years, opinons about the urban public sphere have undergone some revision. In one of his last lectures, 'When Was Modernism', Raymond Williams argued that modernist movements were

> the products, at the first historical level, of changes in public media. These media, the technological investments which mobilized them, and the cultural forms which both directed the investment and expressed its preoccupations, arose in the new metropolitan cities, the centres of the also new imperialism, which offered themselves as transnational capitals of an art without frontiers. Paris, Vienna, Berlin, London, New York took on a new silhouette as the eponymous City of Strangers, the most appropriate locale for art made by the restlessly mobile émigré or exile, the internationally anti-bourgeois artist.[16]

By making 'public media' the precondition for modernism, Williams effectively challenges the hegemonic aesthetic of Anglo-American modernism, which defined itself by its difference from the new technologies of film, commodity and print production that emerged at the end of the nineteenth century. The modernism versus mass culture debate has been well rehearsed,[17] but the new public culture created by Williams's public media has remained an absent term. One reason, perhaps, is that historians of the public sphere have themselves taken sides. Both Jürgen Habermas and Richard Sennett saw the moment of modernism's emergence, the late nineteenth century, as a period of decline in public life when the bourgeois public sphere that had emerged in the eighteenth century (its 'golden age') was invaded by private interests.[18] In fact, it is tempting to conclude that the dates of their two key works, Habermas's *The Structural Transformation of the Bourgeois Public Sphere* (1962; trans. 1989) and Sennett's *The Fall of Public Man* (1977),[19] made each subject to the powerful, postwar influence of modernism's propaganda about itself: art as a masculine preserve in the face of a rising tide of effeminising commodity consumption.

An alternative approach is suggested in Oskar Negt and Alexander Kluge's reassessment of Habermas's thesis, *The Public Sphere and*

Experience.²⁰ In a view that shares common ground with Williams, Negt and Kluge argue that the late nineteenth century saw not so much a decline as a further transformation of the public sphere, which was now reconstituted in the context of new stages of economic, technical and political organisation. Negt and Kluge's key terms suggest an alternative version of literary production at the turn of the century. As Miriam Hansen explains in her introduction to the English version of *The Public Sphere and Experience*, the German word *Öffentlichkeit* has a broader meaning than the English 'public sphere':

> it implies a spatial concept, the social sites or arenas where meanings are articulated, distributed, and negotiated, as well as the collective body constituted by and in this process, 'the public'. But *Öffentlichkeit* also denotes an ideational substance or criterion – '*glasnost*' or openness. . . – that is produced both within these sites and in larger, deterritorialized contexts; the English word 'publicity' grasps this sense only in its historically alienated form. In the dialectical tension between these two senses, Negt and Kluge develop their concept of *Öffentlichkeit* as the 'general horizon of social experience'.²¹

The dialectic outlined by Hansen might be understood as between space and the social relations that produce space. The term used by Negt and Kluge to understand the social relations that constitute the public sphere is *Lebenszusammenhang*, which Hansen translates as 'context of living', 'connection' or 'relationality'. The concept of *Lebenszusammenhang* gives emphasis to the subject's agency in culture: 'An individual worker – regardless of which section of the working class he belongs to and of how far his concrete labour differs from that of other sections – has "his own experiences". The horizon of these experiences is the unity of the proletarian context of living [*Lebenszusammenhang*].'²² In the transformed public sphere of the late nineteenth century onwards, such experiences are mediated through *Produktionsöffentlichkeiten*, which Hansen translates as 'public spheres of production'. In a striking parallel with Williams, *Lebenszusammenhang* occupies a position somewhere between his 'culture as a way of life' and 'structure of feeling', while *Produktionsöffentlichkeiten* is very close to his 'public media': 'the industrialised public sphere of computers, the mass media, the media cartel, the combined public relations and legal departments of conglomerates and interest groups'.²³ Public spheres of production form the conditions in which experience is produced as contradictory: split between the industrialised public media and a privatised consciousness which is 'rendered "incomprehensible' in terms of social communication'.²⁴ If Negt and Kluge's definitions do not escape some of the vagueness associated with William's theoretical framework, they do provide the starting point for a materialist understanding of an industrialised public sphere as the stage on which modernist masculinities were produced. In this respect, from the late nineteenth century at least, commodity spectacle was part and parcel of what amounted to a new kind of public culture.

In the late nineteenth century, the structure of London's labour market changed and this was paralleled by a change in the service sector catering for its needs. Since the decline of the eighteenth-century coffeehouse, English catering certainly hadn't improved. To get a decent meal you had to have admittance to a gentleman's club, something outside the social experience of most of Gissing's characters. As will be discussed in Chapter 13, in contrast to post-revolutionary Paris, where aristocratic tastes had been democratised by restaurants that prided themselves in the high standard of their cooking, nineteenth-century London gained a reputation for unsanitary and poor-quality food and the masculine culture of its pubs and eating houses.[25] However, partly because of opportunities offered by the railways and the great exhibitions, where companies like Spiers and Pond and Lyons & Co. competed for contracts, the late nineteenth century saw a growth in mass catering designed for London's new workers. Department store cafés and new chains of teashops like the ABCs, (run by the Aerated Bread Company) and the Lyons outlets were specifically designed to appeal to unaccompanied women.[26] The new establishments were both respectable and cheap. Remarkable thought it may seem, these cafés, ordinary and phantasmagoric at the same time, were part of a key transformation in London's public culture, the transformation from which modernist masculinities emerged.

George Gissing, Dorothy Richardson, James Joyce and Franz Kafka all used the public culture of *fin-de-siècle* cities as the raw material for their texts. Despite their different formal modes, their work suggests that the new public culture emerging in the 1880s and 90s was not just the context but a precondition for the production of new gendered subjectivities, of which modernist masculinities were a part. As will be discussed in Chapter 14, against his clear distaste for such subjectivities Gissing's novels provide remarkable evidence of the public culture that enabled them. Chapter 15 will focus on literary representations of London's teashops to discuss the numerous writers who used the city's public spaces as the stages on which their characters perform. Chapter 16 will demonstrate how Richardson's long anti-novel *Pilgrimage* went further to represent specific material spaces – boarding houses, streets, teashops – as the stages on which a new kind of gendered subjectivity could be performed. The concluding Chapter 17 reads Kafka's short story 'The Judgement' in relation to the movement between intimate, private and public spheres that produces the modern itself. The argument is that situating the work of modernist writers relation to the public culture of the city provides a better account of the production of literary masculinities than the binaries that usually govern criticism of modernism's emergence: Victorian versus modern; realism versus modernism; and the avant-garde versus mass culture.

13

Teashop dreams

In London, in 1873, a stroller along one block on the north side of the Strand between Newcastle St and Drury Court would have passed in sequence: The Universe Newspaper Office; Andrew Leonard, tobacconist, Joseph Hitchcock, bootmaker; Gilbert Noble, bookseller; Mary Thick, dressmaker; the Reynold's Newspaper Office; Leon Levy, clothier; Thomas Dark's Oxford Stores; John Priest's dining rooms; Vicker's Henry, publisher. They were all small, independent businesses. The experience of the same stroller, walking the length of the Strand twenty seven years later in 1900, would have been markedly different. The block no longer existed, swept away by the monumental architecture of the Kingsway and Aldwych, a project that had also destroyed the centre of the Victorian pornography industry in Holywell Street.[1] At numbers 14, 132, 149, 263, 294, 355 and 407 the Strand, she would have passed an ABC (Aerated Bread Company)[2] teashop, at numbers 35, 154 a Lyons teashop. By 1890 there were already over fifty ABCs in central London. The first Lyons opened in 1894 and they spread rapidly to cover the same area. The ABCs and Lyons teashops were two of the biggest of the new chains of cheap but respectable cafés and restaurants that sprang up to service London's new consumers, catering for shoppers, theatre goers and workers in central London.[3]

In the space of just over a quarter of a century (during which period London's population grew from 4.2 to 6.5 million), the city street had been transformed by the chains, whose visible presence was matched by their impact on the literary imagination. The teashop became a standard reference point in the literature of the period and seems to have had a particular interest for many early twentieth-century writers. Gissing, not unusually, was ahead of his time, but he was followed by Bram Stoker, H. G. Wells, Arnold Bennett, Somerset Maugham, Bertha Ruck, Dorothy Richardson, Ezra Pound, Katherine Mansfield, Jean Rhys, T. S. Eliot and Virginia Woolf, who all mention the chains by name or make the teashop a key locus for urban encounters.[4] A bohemian haunt, the chain teashop was also a key element in a distinct lower middle-class formation associated with the suburbs, cheap popular fiction and the new entertainments of the West End; and composed of office workers – as Virginia Woolf puts it in her novel *Night and Day*:[5] 'clerk after clerk, solicitor after solicitor', but also women workers, notably typists and secretaries.[6] Their female staff marked out a distinct territory and the teashop was as much a zone of conflict and contestation as it was of refreshment and social encounter.

London's economic growth was boosted in the nineteenth century by the speed with which large quantities of raw materials could be transported from overseas. The distribution of the chain teashops (see Figures 2 and 3, p. 102) can be seen as a visible manifestation of the economic power of Empire: its ability to draw goods to the imperial metropolis and to make them available for popular consumption. While such goods had been imported for centuries, and coffeehouses had been an important aspect of the bourgeois sphere in the eighteenth century, the end of the nineteenth century saw a commercialised public sphere on a new scale. The experience of eating out in chain restaurants makes the example of the eighteenth-century coffeehouse an inadequate model of late nineteenth-century public culture. As Oskar Negt and Alexander Kluge write in *The Public Sphere and Experience*: 'The classical public sphere. . .rests on a quasi-artisanal mode of production. By comparison, the industrialised public sphere. . .represent[s] a superior and more organised level of production.'[7] If not superior from the perspective of the high bourgeoisie, the new teashops were representative of this more organised level of production. The Aerated Bread Company and J. Lyons & Co. were industrial concerns. Their food products were manufactured at a central depot and then distributed to their outlets.[8] J. Lyons & Co. grew throughout the twentieth century to become an international corporation, before eventually being absorbed by other companies.[9]

The power of the new chains was manifest in their ability to dominate and control the suppliers and manufacturers of finished goods. The chain teashops represent the first moves in a process usually recognised in the twentieth century, the shift from an industrial economy, where production dominates, to one where consumption has equal if not greater power. The 1870s saw a transformation in London's retail trade. Department stores such as Harrods, Whiteley's and Selfridges and large chains such as Sainsburys and Lipton all date from this period.[10] Two of the three businessmen who set up J. Lyons & Co. had run a chain of cut-price tobacconists, Salmon and Gluckstein, the success of which helped to provide the capital for the first teashops. As discussed in Chapter 9, the success of Salmon and Gluckstein was guaranteed by buying in bulk and selling cheaply to new markets of consumers such as the growing class of women smokers.

The Lyons vans, horse-drawn at first, but soon motorised, were a familiar and even now a well-remembered sight. Food production followed distribution, when the company started selling individually packaged and priced packets of tea, a commodity that had previously been sold loose. Again, the key was a combination of marketing and careful pricing policy and within three years there were 15,000 agents all supplied by salesmen driving horse vans. As the firm grew, it tried to control every aspect of the business, so that production, distribution and consumption were all in-house. The company went on to become a full-scale imperial corporation with its own tea plantations in Nyasaland (now Malawi), although it never produced enough to supply the business's demands. In its enthusiasm for new manufacturing techniques and processes, Lyons developed a kind of Fordism of food – graphically illustrated by a photograph from 1925 of a banquet when the firm catered for 7,250 Freemasons, all seated at banks of tables and served by serried rows of Lyons waitresses or 'Nippies'.[11] In the 1930s, Lyons boasted of a turnover of three-quarters of a million muffins and crumpets a week. In true Fordist spirit, it aimed to do everything itself, from food production to printing menus, to making its own doors, and in the 1950s, introduced an early computer system. If an example of the industrialisation of everyday life were wanted, J. Lyons & Co. had nearly everything.[12]

Spectacle was a crucial element in the company's success. Its imprint on the city was created by the familiarity of the brand, itself engendered by the sheer number of teashops and the moving presence of their signifiers in the form of the advertising emblazoned on the company's vans as they moved through the city streets. The growth of Lyons might almost be a metaphor for the emergence of consumer capitalism in Britain. Commodity display had been crucial to the success of the tobacconists Salmon and Gluckstein: 'New shops were carefully planned and refurbished, and flamboyant window displays became a feature of the branches.'[13] Joseph Lyons, the eponymous fourth partner in the catering business, was known as something of a showman. He wrote songs and sketches for the music hall and published popular fiction.[14] It is no surprise that the origin of the company was in the great exhibitions of the late Victorian period. Its first success was to win the catering contract at the Newcastle Jubilee exhibition in 1887, the same year Gissing took for his most intensive study of the impact of advertising *In the Year of the Jubilee*. The exotically named 'Indo-Chinese Tea Pavilion' was spectacular in its size and ambition and successful enough to continue after the exhibition itself had closed.[15] If the reminiscences of one of the company's directors are to be believed, J. Lyons' pavilion threatened to outshine the rest of the event. It included a Hungarian orchestra and a shooting gallery. More prosaically, their success was based on selling pots (rather than cups) of good-quality tea at a modest price, but in large quantities.[16]

Millions attended the great exhibitions and if the original aim of Lyons & Co was to bring clean, cheap, practical and efficient mass catering to the spectators of Victorian excess then, like the new department stores, the firm's teashops sought to bring the glitzy culture of the exhibition into the city street. The first teashop opened in 1894 at 213 Piccadilly; the same year the company went public. Such was its success that two years later there were seventeen in London. True to their origins in spectacle, the teashops had impressive shopfronts and were decorated in ostentatious style. The contained polished marble top tables with wrought iron bases, and the walls were hung with large gilt mirrors. In Jean Rhys's *After Leaving Mr Mackenzie* (1930), the heroine, Julia Martin, overhears two women 'with the naïve eyes of children' talking in a 'Lyons':

> 'This place is on a grand scale, you can't deny that.'
> Her companion agreed, and said she thought the ladies' room very fine – all in black and white marble.[17]

Both the exteriors and the interiors of the Lyons teashops were a sensation after the unhygienic conditions of London's pubs, the dirty coffee and eating houses described in George Gissing's fiction, of which the the Burton in *Ulysses* is a Dublin example, or even what the heroine of Dorothy Richardson's *Pilgrimage* calls the 'dowdiness' of the ABCs.[18] The interiors were copied from Parisian cafés and mimicked that city's visual culture,[19] of which Walter Benjamin wrote:

> Women here look at themselves more than elsewhere. . .Before any man catches sight of her, she already sees herself ten times reflected. But the man too, sees his physiognomy flash by. He gains his image here more quickly than elsewhere and also sees himself more quickly merged with this, his image. Even the eyes of passersby are veiled mirrors, and over that wide bed of the Seine, over Paris, the sky is spread out like the crystal mirror hanging over the drab beds in brothels.[20]

As will be discussed in Chapters 14–17, one of the effects of this phantasmagoric reproduction of images was to change the conditions of representation and to allow gendered encounters on different terms. Commodity spectacle changed the nature of the public sphere. But if the surfaces of the teashop offered an ocular feast, inside it was as impressive a monument to industrial efficiency. Its difference from the other businesses around it stopped the stroller in his or her tracks. The teashop, like the huge mirrors Benjamin discusses in *The Arcades Project*, was at once the product of the new industrial technologies of the nineteenth century and part of the city's production of images and reflections. Once the impression of the teashop was fixed in the mind, its repetition in other streets reorganised the visual perception of central London.

Returning to the transformation of the Strand with which this chapter began, it is possible to subject the different experiences of an imaginary stroller, a quarter of a century apart, to what Henri Lefebvre calls rhythmanalysis. Lefebvre describes two levels of approach:

> The first goes from the most general to the most specific (from institutions to daily life) and then uncovers the city as specific and (relatively) privileged mediation. The second starts from this plan and constructs the general by identifying the elements and significations of what is observable in the urban. It proceeds in this manner to reach, from the observable, 'private', the concealed daily life: its rhythms, its occupations, its spatio-temporal organisation, its clandestine 'culture', its underground life.[21]

The experience of walking down the Strand emerges from the interaction between the structure of the street, itself a product of London's economy, and the bodily rhythms of the walker.[22] The two walks in the same area in 1873 and in 1900 constitute two quite different street rhythms. The first, in 1873, responds to a city still divided up into distinct locations and individual units. Localities are defined by certain trades and other forms of economic activity and by their inhabitants. This is what might loosely be called the realist city. Already by 1900, the chain reconfigures the city as a network, bringing together its disparate parts through its trademark sign (above the shopfront) or the traffic (in the form of the companies' vans and lorries (or, as in *Ulysses*, sandwichmen) between its nodes.

For Benjamin, these kinds of changes in the architecture of the city create new states of consciousness that adhere to its surfaces and structures.[23] It is not, perhaps, going too far to say that the presence of multiple outlets of the same chain in the same city space creates the simultaneity of perception that later characterises the visual montage of artists such as Robert Delaunay or the Cubists.[24] The chain as network amounts to a kind of modernist geography that engenders a radically new spatial apprehension of the city.

The origins of Lyons in the exhibitions and the chain teashops' use of reflective surfaces and mirrors all have a clear relationship to the concept of phantasmagoria. But as always the spectacle is distracting. Establishing a relationship between urban phantasmagoria and modernist form locates its emergence in the artistic, theatre and shopping areas of the city, specifically, in London, the West End. This positioning plays into two, now well-established, but equally well-contested, historical narratives about gender and urban modernity. The first argues that, whereas a male flâneur emerged in the eighteenth century, women could participate in the urban public sphere only from the late nineteenth century onwards. Before this period the city streets and places of refreshment, for example eating houses, pubs and clubs, either barred women or were hostile to their presence. There was, according to this argument, no female flâneuse.[25] The second historical narrative argues that women's participation in the urban public sphere began with their increasingly important role as consumers when, for example, they came into the West End to shop or to go the theatre, the music hall or later the cinema.

The first historical narrative has been questioned by Elizabeth Wilson in *The Sphinx in the City*, where she argues not only that women's participation in the public sphere was evident from a much earlier period but that the urban environment produces more not fewer opportunities for women.[26] More recently, Lynda Nead's history of London offers evidence to show that, from at least the eighteenth century, there were certain liminal spaces in the city where encounters between men and women could take place. In an analysis of Whistler's abstract painting of the Vauxhall gardens, she suggests that modernist art and literature drew on such spaces and attempted to represent them.[27]

The second argument is more persistent. Erika Diane Rappaport, for example, argues that:

> gendered identities and physical spaces were constructed through narratives about consumption, whether they took the form of advertisements, newspaper editorials, social criticism, parliamentary legislation, or street protests. These narratives constituted the city and social identities.[28]

Interestingly, this was a narrative that Lyons was very keen to promote as part of the company's vigorous publicity campaign on its own behalf. The Lyons archive includes several references to its service to women, including one that implies that respectable women could enter central London only because Lyons had been kind enough to open facilities that catered for them and allowed them to be safe. In an address to the 'Twenty Club' in 1957 on the company's history, Julian Salmon told his audience that 'In those days it was very indecorous for women, even in pairs, to go our unescorted by a man'.[29] A document updated in 1971 (but clearly adapted from an earlier original) contains the basic narrative developed from the early decades of the twentieth century:

> The opening of the first teashop in Piccadilly during 1894 had considerable social significance; for Lyons' teashops made it possible for Victorian families of suburbia to come to London Town. Hitherto there had been

nowhere 'respectable' for Mama and the children to have a cup of tea or a midday meal. Prices, too, had been extortionate.[30]

In 1978 a sympathetic article in the *Baking Industries Journal* claimed that 'When the first Lyons tea shop opened in Piccadilly during the 1890s [*sic*], it was with the purpose of providing ladies, visiting the West End for their shopping, with suitable refreshment'.[31]

As a company with an eye for public relations, first developed in the context of Victorian commodity spectacle, Lyons were keen to further an interpretation of history endorsed by Rappaport, that 'In Edwardian London, women's emancipation and consumer pleasures had merged to a certain degree'.[32] If this argument seems open to question, it becomes even more so when it appears that it was part of the new service industry's propaganda about itself. In effect, this version, because it focuses on consumption, covers only one side of the modernist city, that which Benjamin describes as its dreamworlds. In *The Arcades Project*, these are subject to the dialectical process of awakening; but this is not to say that city of consumption is an illusion. For Benjamin awakening does not imply that dreaming is false consciousness, nor is being awake the same thing as reality. The dialectical moment of awakening is a threshold moment between sleep and wake. In awakening, the dream has not faded, but is already being wrenched from the dreamworld into waking consciousness. In the Janus-faced portal between the two, the truth of the modern city emerges. Awakening is, Benjamin suggests tentatively, 'perhaps the synthesis of dream consciousness (as thesis) and wakening consciousness (as antithesis)'; and, if this is the case, 'Then the moment of awakening would be identical with the "now of recognisability," in which things put on their true – surrealist – face. Thus, in Proust, the importance of staking an entire life on life's supremely dialectical point of rupture: awakening. Proust begins with an evocation of the space of someone waking up'.[33]

Mapping London's teashops leads to the kind of dialectical awakening Benjamin describes. London's new consumer economy did, as Rappaport suggests, create the material spaces in which new gendered subjectivities could be performed. But consumption is only part of the story. Figure 2 shows the distribution of ABCs in central London in 1890. Figure 3 shows the distribution of Lyons teashops in central London in 1902.

In each case they are concentrated not in the West End but in the City, London's business district, indicating that the expected market came not from shoppers but from workers. As Judith Walkowitz comments, 'the metropolis, besides being a city of consumption and display, was also a city of production, service and exchange'.[34] This suggests an alternative

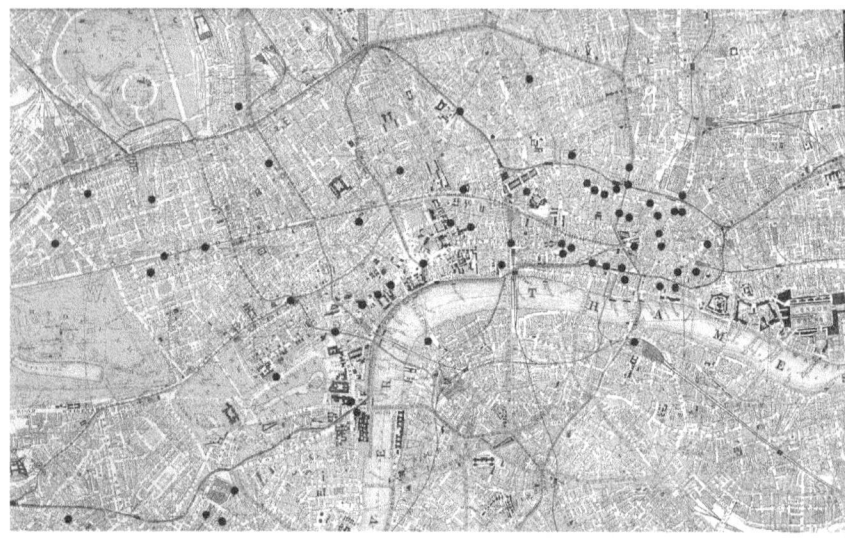

Figure 2 ABC teashops in central London, 1890

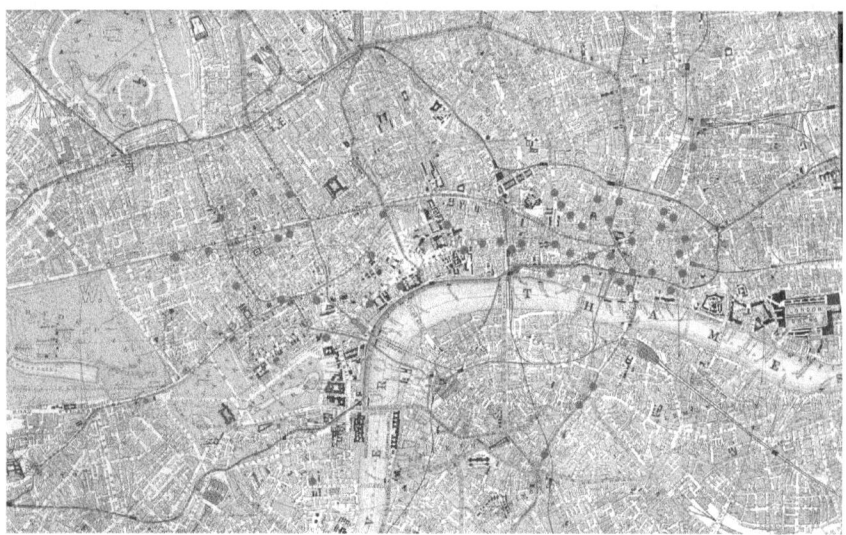

Figure 3 Lyons teashops in central London, 1902

spatial history of London, one borne out by one of the few retrospectives to be found in the Lyons archive written by a woman. On 5 October 1921, to celebrate twenty-five years since the opening of the Trocadero, Lyons took out a whole section of the *Daily Mail* devoted to articles about the company. A piece by Lady Angela Forbes entitled 'The Woman's Point of

View' offers the familiar paean of praise for the company, but focuses on its contribution to women's employment in business rather than to the respectable shopper:

> The City and all commercial centres in those days existed for man alone: for women the simple amenities that make business life possible were non-existent... It may seem at first sight a somewhat far-fetched statement, but I have no hesitation in saying that the opening of Lyons' teashops in the City marked the beginnings of the new era. Here was, for the first time, a place where business women might make their midday meal. With its rooms reserved for ladies, its bright clean atmosphere and its inexpensive fare, it did away in one step with a difficulty that had seemed insurmountable. City men had always had their chop house: now women had at last a restaurant of her own... It was long before the expert typist, doing a man's work, but failing altogether of a man's pay, could hope for more than the merest weekly pittance in return for her services. How they 'managed' it is hard to realise to-day, but one knows that the possibility of obtaining good, inexpensive meals helped them to achieve what approached perilously close to the impossible...Nothing, perhaps, has had a greater influence towards the sensible and natural intermingling of the sexes than the management – the revolutionary management, as it was once regarded – of the Lyons teashop...From every point of view, and most emphatically from a woman's London has changed for the better during the past 25 years; in the metamorphosis the teashops have played a meritorious part.[35]

In this context, Lyons' overemphasis of the opening of their first teashop in Piccadilly and their underemphasis of the number of teashops in the City can be seen to be deliberately misleading. The Piccadilly outlet was important, but atypical. Its position was more to do with publicity and spectacle than with the bulk of the firm's customers. Of the thirty-seven teashops that opened in the the chain's first seven years between 1894 and 1900, only six were in the West End. Their distribution shows a canny understanding of the relationship between the real business of the teashops and marketing and display. In 1896, having overextended financially, the company could afford to open only one teashop and chose to do so in Oxford Street, in the heart of the shopping district. At a time when budgets were tight, a higher rent could be justified because the prominent position established the business in the public eye.

This suggests that the geography of modernist London requires a more dialectical understanding of the relationship between consumption and work. While it is true that the city of images changes the conditions on which subjects participate in the public sphere, many of those subjects would not be there at all if were not for changing structure of employment in London. As interesting as the dreamscapes mapped out by the chain teashops are the boundaries, fractures and thresholds that the site of the teashop reveals in the city's geography. It is a point at which the inequalities of class and gender are refracted through the city of images. It is such boundaries that fascinated Benjamin: 'Nowhere, unless perhaps in dreams, can the phenomenon of the boundary be experienced in a more originary way than in cities.'[36] Rather than dreams themselves, it is the fractured nature of the modernist city as dream that is the true subject of modernist texts.

Thomas Richards has argued that the great Victorian exhibitions offered a fiction of abundance.[37] To see the West End as the key site for the production of modernist subjectivities is probably equally fictional. Or, at least, it should only be seen in Benjamin's dialectic of the dream consciousness as thesis, which needs to be counterposed to the wakened consciousness as antithesis: the teashops as part of a new economy, which has international, global, imperial dimensions. The synthesis, which Benjamin calls awakening comes in the consciousness of both. Such moments occur in flashes, at moments of fracture in the everyday. One of the reasons that the teashop becomes such a resonant location in early twentieth-century literature is because it functions as precisely the kind of threshold Benjamin is interested in. The teashop is one of the points where the new street rhythms of the city intersect with everyday life as experienced by the subject. To have a cup of tea in an ABC or a Lyons is to experience the borderline between the subject's consciousness of the everyday and his or her subjection to the powerful economic forces that position him or her in the city. The experience of the teashop combines or synthesises production and consumption, the economic and the cultural. Not surprisingly, then, the experience of eating out appears again and again in turn-of-the-century fiction as the setting for the intersubjective negotiations that make the new urban public sphere an actuality.

14

Gissing and eating out

An acute social observer, as well as a cultural conservative, Gissing was both dismayed and intrigued by the commercialisation of the public sphere. The commodification of every aspect of life is registered in his 1890s novels such as *In the Year of the Jubilee* (1894). In his short work *The Town Traveller* (1898), this extends even to food and drink. At the public house where the protagonist, Mr Gammon, keeps his dogs, 'the water-bottle on the table' is 'encrusted with a white enamel advertisement of somebody's whisky and had another such recommendation legible on its base', while the 'tray used by the girl in attendance' is 'enamelled with the name of somebody's brandy'.[1] The pervasive presence of advertising marks the penetration of the public sphere by private interests described by Jürgen Habermas. In his words: 'the public sphere assumes advertising functions'.[2] However, rather than heralding the end of the public sphere, it may be that understanding it requires a different approach.

If, as suggested in Chapter 8, the playful aspects of Gissing's prose have been almost universally and systematically downplayed in favour of the image of the lonely and embittered man, then the city that has been built up to house the man has been mapped on to that depressing biography. Gissing's irony, the satirical elements that abound in the novels of the 1890s, but which are by no means absent in the novels of the 1880s, are matched by his keen observations of the transformed public culture of a new commercial age. As David Glover has pointed out, the panoramic visions of the city in *In the Year of the Jubilee* configure a new experience of urban modernity.[3] But, if the late nineteenth century is often seen as a period in which the public sphere goes into decline, Gissing is too often read just for his negative aesthetic.[4]

Such a reading underestimates the dialectic of modernity that takes place in Gissing's texts, including his diary where, in his trips to Italy and Greece, the overwhelming impression is of the ancient world as pervading the present. Gissing frequently picks out customs, forms of speech and even burial practices that echoed the Roman or Greek past.[5] The diary shows that Gissing's own movements in the late 1880s, despite the image of the lonely and embittered man, were not confined to London, let alone its poorer areas. Far from being static, by the end of the 1880s Gissing was making annual trips to the continent on the proceeds of his novels. In the porous zone that is Naples Gissing meets Walter Benjamin, not of course, in time, but in a common space in which modernity is understood to absorb earlier epochs, rendering them trivial by reducing the past to the ephemerality and forgetfulness of fashion, so that history itself becomes an exhibition or an arcade.[6] Gissing describes Naples as a space in which past and present interpenetrate. A description of that matches that of Benjamin, for whom ancient myth and superstition mingle with the modern in the city, a process that is enabled by its 'porous' material structure.[7]

Even *The Nether World*, usually seen as one of Gissing's bleakest visions of London, operates a dialectic between antiquity and modernity, moving between the different levels of reality produced by the city's phantasmagoric spaces. Chapter 12, 'Io Saturnalia', is a case in point. The chapter's title celebrates the festival of Saturn, which involved public spectacles and banquets, when presents were exchanged and class relations inverted. The chapter's style borrows from classical satire to describe a Bank Holiday trip by working-class inhabitants of the East End to visit Crystal Palace, which, like the Parisian arcades studied by Benjamin, was made from the new industrial technologies of iron and glass. Crystal Palace blurred the boundaries between past and present, inside and outside, nature and culture. Built sufficiently tall to include the trees of Hyde Park, as a phantasmagoric space it absorbed not just London but, in its lavish display, the whole world from which the commodities exhibited were drawn.[8] By the 1880s, now moved to South London, it had become a popular holiday destination, a role that replicated a function of the great exhibitions as 'a day out' for the Victorian public. However, they may also have had a political function, acting as a public space in which socialist activists from different countries could meet. French delegations to the London exhibitions of 1851 and 1862 were met by parties of English workers and the rendezvous marked a milestone in co-operation between French and English workers' organisations.[9] Georgi Plekhanov, the Russian Marxist argued that:

> The world exhibition has given the proletariat an excellent idea of the unprecedented level of development which the means of production have reached in all civilized lands – a development far exceeding the boldest utopian fantasies of the century preceding this one . . .
>
> The exhibition has further demonstrated that modern development of the forces of production must of necessity lead to industrial crises that,

given the anarchy currently reigning in production, will only grow more acute with the passage of time, and hence more destructive to the course of the world economy.[10]

If, on the one hand, this latter statement seems of a piece with the mechanistic form of scientific Marxism for which Plekhanov is best known, on the other, anarchy is exactly the state of affairs Gissing depicts as the holiday degenerates from festival to food fight, and then to fist fight. Conflict is sparked after an encounter on the threshold of the 'Shilling Tea-room' – like the Newcastle exhibition, Crystal Palace demanded catering on a mass scale. The Tea-room is a less ostentatious, but none the less impressive, version of Lyons' Indo-Chinese Tea Pavilion:

> Having paid at the entrance, they were admitted to feed freely on all that lay before them. With difficulty could a seat be found in the huge room; the uproar of voices was deafening. On the tables lay bread, butter, cake in hunches, tea-pots, milk-jugs, sugar-basins – all things to whomso could secure them in the conflict. Along the gangways coursed perspiring waiters, heaping up giant structures of used plates and cups, distributing clean utensils, and miraculously sharp in securing the gratuity expected from each guest as he rose satiate. Muscular men in aprons wheeled hither the supplies of steaming fluid in immense cans on heavy trucks. Here practical joking found the most graceful of opportunities, whether it were the deft direction of a piece of cake at the nose of a person sitting opposite, or the emptying of a saucer down your neighbour's back, or the ingenious jogging of an arm which was in the act of raising a full tea-cup.[11]

In this passage, many of the themes discussed in Chapter 8 are reprised. But the exhibition refreshment room appears as a superb example of the kind of space in which London's new public culture was generated. At a shilling, it was within reach of a working man's wage. It is a carnivalesque space of 'imbecile joviality' and, in Bahktinian terms, proto-democratic. Its position within the exhibitive space makes it what might be called part of the popular phantasmagoric, but the passage resists empathy with the commodity.[12] Instead, the tearoom as public space is fractured and contentious. The stimulation of commodity desire, the text suggests, does not necessarily impede a critical perspective.

The good-humoured interaction of the tea-room later becomes a real conflict, when battle is joined by the rivals, Bob Hewlett and Jack Bartley:

> Near St James's Church Jack Bartley made a stand and defied his enemy to come on. Bob responded with furious eagerness; amid a press of delighted spectators swelled by people just turned out of the public-houses, the two lads fought like wild animals. Nor were they the only combatants. Exasperated by the certainty that her hat and dolman were ruined,

> Pennyloaf flew with erected nails at Clem Peckover. It was just what the latter desired. In an instant she had rent half Pennyloaf's garments off her back.[13]

Here a defined space is exceeded by the energy of the combatants as are the constraints of the law: 'There was no question of making arrests. . . it was the night of the Bank holiday and the capacity of police cells is limited.'[14] At a different level to Plekhanov, and envisaging a different outcome, Gissing suggests that anarchy is the converse of commodity culture, that the riot of goods and pleasures offered by Crystal Palace has its corollary in social disorder. For Gissing, the violence is internal to the working class, not directed towards its masters. It is part of the cycle of despair of the Nether World that is working-class life. But, as ever in his texts, there is a contradiction between plot and the novel's textuality.[15] If the failure of philanthropy condemns the novels' characters to further circuits of their particular circle of hell, the language of the novel suggests that the city's phantasmagoric spaces are equally contradictory. They offer the possibility of free, unregulated debate, even if here it ends in violence. The city's exhibitive spaces suggest the possibility of abundant riches, even while that vision must, ultimately, appear as unattainable to its working-class audience. But behind that combination, of free speech and the possibility of freedom from material want, lies a third possibility: that the question might be asked: 'Why can't *we* have *that*?'

If, at one level, the level of 'realism', Gissing's fiction argues that, if they did get *that*, they wouldn't know what to do with it, at another it is drawn to the phantasmagoric spaces that pose such questions. The 'Shilling Tea-room' is one such 'sphere of delight'. Although the exhibition was in the vanguard, such spaces were beginning to be found also in the city's streets. Pubs, cafés, eating houses and restaurants are key sites in Gissing's work. He was fascinated by the dialectic between specific material spaces and the social relations that produce that space. If, as discussed in Chapter 8, the meal in his novels is always indicative of social structure, where the meal takes place is equally significant. In a scene from *Demos: A Story of English Socialism* (1886) Daniel Dabbs, 'the proletarian pure and simple',[16] fetches a tumbler of pickled walnuts from the local pub for Alice Mutimer to eat at the family meal:

> Alice emptied half a dozen into her plate and put one of them whole into her mouth. She would not have been a girl of her class if she had not relished this pungent dainty. Fish of any kind, green vegetables, eggs and bacon, with all these a drench of vinegar was indispensable to her. And she proceeded to eat a supper scarcely less substantial than that which had appeased her brother's appetite. Start not, dear reader; the Princess is only a subordinate heroine, and happens, moreover, to be a living creature.[17]

The passage is a piece of classic Gissing. It combines the kinds of prejudice – 'a girl of her class' – that give his texts the reputation for political reaction, with the eye for cultural distinction that marks his genuine knowledge of the East End diet. The overt sensuality of Alice's mouthful participates at once in a gaze that renders working-class women available as sexualised beings and is, at the same time, a provocative critique of an ideology of domesticity that would deny women an embodied sexuality at all. The mocking, 'dear reader', is a masculinist response to the Victorian literary discourse that sustained that ideology; while the implicit comparison of Alice, a subordinate heroine, as a 'living creature' with the 'superior' heroine, Adela, is an apt one, as Adela rarely achieves a characterisation that could be called embodied.

The trajectory of the pickled walnut is revealing. It moves from *public* house to private house, and then from public view to private mouthful, from outside to inside. This progress, culminating in the walnut's incorporation by Alice, maps the co-ordinates of a distinctive public sphere: moving between the 'intersubjectivity of a self-constituting public sphere', in this case the pub, and the 'subjectivity rooted in the intimate sphere', the family.[18] In the movement of the walnut, the boundaries of public and private are not so much defined but actually produced.[19] Where Gissing's public sphere differs from Habermas's model is in the period (late nineteenth rather than eighteenth century), the central position of a working-class (rather than the bourgeois) family and in a woman's, Alice's (rather than public man's), assertive and embodied public role. In these respects, Gissing's documentation of working-class life in his early novels already suggests an alternative or counterpublic sphere. In the novels of the 1890s, his focus shifts from pubs to eating houses, cafés and restaurants, which come to signify that alternative public sphere as (using Negt and Kluge's term) the 'context of living' for his characters.

Contemporary social studies of eating out have tended to demote its role in a public culture, seeing it as an example of bourgeois display.[20] Lydia Martens and Alan Warde's 1997 study of eating out in northern British cities argues that:

> The restaurant is not exactly a public place, rather it is a quasi-public place. The restaurant is a space containing a number of private reservations (tables), from which mutual inspection of the tenants of other reservations is permitted, and where one's own behaviour is restrained by the gaze (and power) of others. So, eating out is not necessarily commendable for its encouragement of public conviviality and coexistence. Rather it is private behaviour in a public place. To that extent, it has limited potential for encouraging a public sphere or civil society.[21]

For Martens and Warde, 'Restaurants offer possibilities and opportunities for a somewhat sanitised version of the urban experience, a dip into the maelstrom of modernity, without being exposed to too much danger'.[22] But this is to separate the public and the private, reproducing a binary between the polite, and by implication tame, experience of the restaurant and a more risky and exciting culture of the streets. The experience of the restaurant is removed from its 'context of living'. Such accounts of an incomplete public sphere can be situated in the long narrative of decline initiated by Habermas and Sennett. The sense of loss that lies behind it can be traced back to the central role that going out to eat and drink, particularly to drink coffee, has in their accounts of the formation of the 'golden age' of the eighteenth century. The London coffeehouse stands as the paradigmatic space in which the public sphere flowered and, as with any narrative of decline, that space can only be evoked nostalgically. Sennett charts its loss in *The Fall of Public Man*. Where noise and discussion characterised the eighteenth-century coffeehouse, nineteenth-century bourgeois English and French culture valued silence. He cites eating alone in one's club, the exclusion of pubs from middle-class areas and Haussman's aim to eliminate *tavernes* and *caves* in Paris as examples of the divide between public and private spheres: 'Silence is order, because silence is the absence of social interaction.'[23] In the commercial sphere, Sennett gives the department store as an example where discussions over price were replaced by a silent agreement to buy or not to buy at a pre-fixed charge. Like Habermas, he adheres to a narrative that moves from a critical public to a public of cultural consumers.

As a social critic Gissing seemed to share that thesis. His narratives of alienated intellectuals express a yearning for an earlier phase of cultural life, a kind of golden age, not specifically embodied in the early eighteenth century but reaching back even further into Greek and Roman antiquity. His disgust at the saturation of life and letters by brand names amounts to the same degraded public sphere that is the object of Sennett's or Habermas's critique. On the other hand, it can be argued that Gissing was a better, if still partial, social observer than either Sennett or Habermas. He documents a public sphere that existed below the level of Sennett's high, ordered and silent bourgeoisie and which cannot be consigned to a hermetically sealed autonomous and masculine working-class culture – the jollity of the pub. The social strata that are the particular object of Gissing's novels span across the skilled working class up to clerical workers and salesmen, including his declassed, disenfranchised artistic intellectuals *and*, significantly gendering the notion of the public, shopgirls, clerical workers, female students and theatre attendants.

In *The Town Traveller*, two characters drawn from London's new economy, Polly Sparks, a programme seller in a theatre, and Christopher Parrish, a 'minor clerk', splash out at a relatively expensive restaurant, which has adopted the Parisian style favoured by Lyons & Co. They are 'seated amid plush and marble, mirrors and gilding, in a savoury and aromatic atmosphere'.[24] The restaurant is one of the many that sprang up in the period to cater for the theatre audience, offering meals before and after shows. However, the delights of the new generation contrast with the disgust of Polly's father, a disgruntled head waiter and victim of the new fashion, who is appalled by the glitzy revolution in restaurant design in which his daughter basks. The meal also comes at a cost to Parrish, who foots the bill. He makes 'a rapid calculation [that] told him that he must dine at the Aërated Bread Shop [an ABC teashop] for several days to come'.[25] In *The Town Traveller*, as always with Gissing's representation of the meal, not only is the reference to an ABC up to date but the context of its invocation locates it in the economy and public culture of the new service class. Thus, despite the nostalgia that pervades Gissing novels for an earlier, purer public sphere, the sheer accuracy of the social detail is a contemporary voice calling into question the thesis of the decline and disintegration of public culture in the 1890s. Neither does Habermas's account of its transformation fully capture the world depicted in *The Town Traveller*, a world we catch glimpses of in all Gissing's work, and which is always its 'context of living'. It is as noisy and argumentative as any eighteenth-century coffeehouse: 'two first-rate quarrels in one day put Polly Sparkes into a high good humour'.[26] In the novel, meals are the chosen battlefields, offering the ideal terrain on which the boundaries between public and private can be crossed and recrossed. The text is structured as an episodic narrative punctuated by significant encounters in pubs, cafés and restaurants. The key protagonist is called Gammon and a minor character Mr Cheeseman. Thus, eating out is not just a meal but a socially symbolic act, in which the entire economic and social structure of the city participates.

In *Born in Exile* (1892), a restaurant is the mark of shame that drives the hero, Godwin Peak, from public (academic) life. If eating is an act of distinction in itself, his uncle's planned establishment, 'Peak's Refreshment an' Dinin' Rooms' (28), pronounced 'with the offensive purity of [a] Cockney accent' (24), represents the invasion of the England's streets by the new commercialism. Godwin's reaction to the mere appearance of his Uncle is bodily, a form of corporeal disgust: 'For an instant he was clay colour, then a hot flush broke upon his cheeks' (24). His next response is to break away from his student friends and to try and confine the source of disruption to the private sphere, his lodgings; but Andrew Peak, acting like the force of commerce he is (a precursor of Luckworth Crew in *In the Year of the Jubilee*) impels them both into the public space of a teashop opposite the college. Godwin manages to direct his uncle to a quieter, more private, room, but he cannot prevent his open questions to the waitress concerning the viability of the business. The dialogue between uncle and nephew enacts, at a personal level, a battle for the high street. The teashop, like the chandler shop where Yule encounters his wife in *New Grub Street*, represents an old and outdated artisanal economy: the waitress is asthmatic, as if to emphasis the exhausted state of the business; the eating area almost empty.

As with *The Town Traveller*, the novel is an accurate document of the period's public culture. It opens in 1874, the year that saw the very beginnings of the transformation of Britain's city streets, when individually owned shops and businesses began to be replaced with chains of retail outlets, teashops and restaurants. Andrew Peak remarks that what the area needs is a 'Spiers and Pond', a branch of one of the new successful London restaurant chains run by the catering company. As always the choice demonstrates Gissing's eye for historical and social accuracy. Spiers and Pond opened their famous Criterion restaurant in Piccadilly in 1874, but Andrew Peak's admiration also indicates his social class. In W. S. Gilbert's Ballad, 'Fanny', the firm is associated with downmarket tastes:

Fanny and Jenny in Paris did dwell,
Miss Jane was a dowdy,
Miss Fanny a swell –
Each went to dine at a quarter to four –
At her own little favourite *Restauratore* –
Fanny of Bertram and Roberts was fond
While Jenny she worshipped her Spiers and Pond

Godwin cannot swallow the prospect of his family name becoming a brand: his uncle's ambition to 'flare his name upon a placard' (60). A piece of toast he 'was endeavouring to masticate', as his uncle unveils the idea, 'turns to sawdust upon his palate'. Godwin's distaste stems from his resistance to being visibly associated with a burgeoning, phantasmagoric commercial culture, to becoming, like the sandwichmen in 'Lestrygonians', one of its signs. This is not just a question of being associated with Uncle's lower-class origins, but a sense of being incorporated into a system of exchange in which his intellectual successes will become one form of value amongst many. In his later novels Gissing came to see consumer culture as the medium through which all social relations are lived and this is nowhere more the case than in his short novel *Eve's Ransom* (1895).

The biblical story of the Fall presents Eve with a prohibition that defies 'natural' law. The divine command not to eat takes food out of the sphere of nature and into that of culture. In *Eve's Ransom* the basic necessity of eating is taken through a series of dialogic levels that correspond to the co-ordinates outlined in Chapter 8. If biological necessity stands as the first level (Social Darwinist theories of nutrition), hunger in the story also stands as an implicit metaphor for sexual desire (bodily pleasure). The relationship between Hilliard and Eve is conducted through a series of 'food events', including three meals, of which two involve eating out. These events define the boundaries of their relationship (the meal as socially symbolic act); but the semi-private, semi-public character of eating out situates the performance of a gendered subjectivity at the threshold between private and public spheres. Finally, eating out itself is conducted in the midst of the new phantasmagoric public culture of the two cities, London and Paris, in which the couple's encounters take place. Thus, Gissing's text explores the transformations of biological necessity through to limits of food's capacity to act as a form of display in consumer culture. The culture of consumption, as much as eating, becomes the narrative's theme.

Hilliard's first meeting is not with Eve herself, but with her image, a photograph belonging to his landlady in Birmingham, which he consumes in her absence. The moment has to be read in terms of the complex representation of the male gaze in Gissing's fiction. For example, in two of the novels of the 1890s, the heroines are presented to the reader posed on their beds in the tradition of the female nude. In *The Odd Women* (1893), the image of Rhoda Nunn, writhing on the bed as she resists her desire for Everard, adds a sadistic element to that of voyeurism: 'she shed bitter tears; and not only wept, but agonized in mute frenzy, the passions of her flesh torturing her until she thought of death as a refuge'.[27] It is difficult to see this image as anything other than a form of masculine revenge on the woman who dares to lead an independent public career. In *In the Year of the Jubilee*, the representation of Nancy Lord, naked on a hot summer night, is explicitly sensual, but, as Arlene Young has pointed out, Nancy's sexual self-confidence is directly related in the passage to her new-found public confidence at the Jubilee celebrations.[28] Here, Nancy is not just presented for the consumption of the desiring male reader. She is herself a consumer. The famous crowd scene in the novel offers the male reader an experience of cross-dressing, where he experiences the crowd through the eyes of a woman in a series of public encounters where her self-assurance does not falter. Nancy offers an early example of the experimental third space explored by Dorothy Richardson in Miriam (discussed in Chapter 16), the heroine of *Pilgrimage*.

The relationship between Hilliard and Eve does not offer so self-assured a heroine, but Eve combines Rhoda's resistance to masculine advances with some of Nancy's confidence in her own sexual power. Eve's mystery is not her sexuality but the question of how much agency she possesses in the new public culture, caught as she is between her position as (limited) consumer and as object of a consuming male gaze: in Rachel Bowlby's words, 'seducer and seduced, possessor and possessed' at the same time.[29] The power difference between Hilliard and Eve is signified, as with Yule's social status in *New Grub Street*, by their different purchasing power, endowed by the greater and lesser sums of money each unexpectedly receives. Eve and Hilliard's different positions within the new consumer economy are then played out at meals eaten out. Restaurants act as a space of intersubjectivity, where the new inequalities of London's public culture can be played out.

For Hilliard, the money he has received, £436, buys him out of the 'black streets' of an alienated life, life as a machine: 'Before long there'll be machines for washing and dressing people – machines for feeding them.'[30] After yielding to 'London's grossest lures', his more virtuous life in Paris is figured by meals that offer good value. He eats 'at restaurants where dinner of several courses costs two francs and a half'. His mind turns to Eve's address, given to him by his landlady on leaving Birmingham, over a 'bowl of coffee and *petit pain*' (20).

Significantly, Hilliard's first exchange with Eve is at an exhibition, the 1884 International Health Exhibition at Kensington, a celebration of the advances in public sanitation that characterised the modern city. As discussed in Chapter 13, the Victorian exhibitions were opportunities not only for the celebration of technological advancement or commodity display but also for huge catering contracts competed for by firms like Spiers and Pond and later companies like J. Lyons & Co. These companies saw the emegent workforce of women as a new market looking for respectable dining at a reasonable price. In that context, Eve's autonomy is figured by sitting down at one of the open-air tables, where, like Bloom in Davy Byrne's, she orders and consumes a glass of wine and a sandwich. For Hilliard, the pre-lapsarian Eve, 'the meek, the melancholy, the long-suffering, the pious', all but disappears in this new Eve who has an assignation, for which exhibition is the venue. Eve willingly consumes the fruit that London has to offer: 'She had the look, the tones, of one bent on enjoying oneself, of one who habitually pursued pleasure, and that in its most urban forms' (25). If the tale is read as an updated account of the Fall, then this man, who has the 'external attributes of a gentleman', plays the part of the serpent, luring Eve away from the path of righteousness. However, this would be the scene as understood by Hilliard. The reader learns that the man lacks the devil's attractions or, apparently, his ill intent: 'He was plain of feature, but wore a pleasant, honest look and his demeanour to the girl showed not only good breeding but unmistakeable interest of the warmest kind' (27). This apparent benevolence throws Hilliard's position as moral judge into doubt. In fact, the passage suggests that Hilliard and Eve begin from a position of relative equality in the public sphere, where their equivalence is figured by independent acts of consumption. Hilliard, who has followed her from her lodgings, orders a bottle of beer, which he drinks at a neighbouring table before plucking up the courage to approach her. At this point, Hilliard's proletarian and parochial bottle of beer, when compared with Eve's sophisticated and cosmopolitan glass of wine, makes him, if anything, the lesser party, far less confident in the spectacular space of the exhibition. Eve, on the other hand, follows in the footsteps of Clara Hewett, Clem Peckover, Totty Nancarrow (see Chapter 8) or Alice Mutimer in her new-found confidence in the city.

Their second meeting is at the theatre, another place to see and be seen in the city. At their third, an encounter in the street engineered by Hilliard after more liquid courage, he invites her to dine. The restaurant they go to combines the scale of exhibition catering – 'a great hall, where some scores of people were already dining' with the possibility of privacy, 'a nook' (42), allowing 'private behaviour in a public place'. Whereas each consumed separately and differently at the exhibition, eating together the difference in their economic positions is enacted through their relationship to food. This time Eve's autonomy, in contrast to that of Hilliard, is expressed not through consumption but through abstinence: 'Hilliard began his dinner with appetite and gusto; the girl, after a few sips, neglected her soup and glanced about the neighbouring tables (43); 'Hilliard drank a glass of wine and saw that Eve just touched hers with her lips' (44).

Eve's reluctance to eat is at once a performance in tune with Social Darwinist theories and, at the same time, a symbolic resistance to the power Hilliard has acquired over her as a consequence of his greater spending power. She is, to follow Geddes and Thomson's terminology (see Chapter 8), the passive, 'anabolic' body; Hilliard the active, hungry, 'catabolic' male-in-pursuit. She is in a state of dependence on Hilliard for her nutrition that equates both with Charlotte Perkins Gilman's 'sexuo-economic' relation and Olive Schreiner's 'sex-parasitism'. But while the dining scene reflects Darwinist discourse it also subverts it. Eve's distracted glances to other tables indicate both her dissatisfaction with her present situation and the other possibilities the city has to offer. Hilliard's pompous celebration of dining as a form of higher civilisation is gently punctured by Eve's humility. His grandiose plans of excess are countered by her practicality:

> When the fruit had been set before them – and as he was unpeeling a banana:
> 'What a vast difference,' said Hilliard, 'between the life of people who dine, and of those who don't! It isn't the mere pleasure of eating and the quality of the food – though that must have a great influence on mind and character. But to sit for an hour or two each evening in quiet, orderly enjoyment, with graceful things about one, talking of whatever is pleasant – how it civilises! Until three months ago I never dined in my life, and I know well what a change it has made in me'. (45)

In contrast to Hilliard's phallic display, 'unpeeling a banana', Eve deflatingly remarks on her continuing lack of access to what in London particularly was still a very masculine sphere of public life and civility.

> 'I never dined till this evening,' said Eve.
> 'Never? This is the first time you have been in a restaurant?'
> 'For dinner – yes.' (45)

Eve's answer suggests that while she has taken advantage of the daytime opportunities now available to women, she has eschewed London's more dangerous nightlife. Where Richard Sennett sees silence in public as a retreat to the private sphere,[31] Eve's reticent response to Hilliard's advances suggests that abstinence and silence may also be a reaction to public inequalities that debar free and frank speech. Hilliard receives her brief statement with joy. If she has not dined out 'there could not have been much intimacy between her and the man she met at the exhibition'.

Furthermore, there is another, more political, reading of Eve's fasting. In *Thyrza*, Totty Nancarrow boycotts her local shop as a protest against the owner's treatment of a tenant. A few years later, the hunger strike would become a part of the armoury of the women suffragists.[32] Eve's resistance can be read as a reaction to the new economy that offered women the opportunity to consume, but no political rights other than a decision to abstain.

Their second meal takes place under different circumstances. Eve is now kept by Hilliard in Paris, the city that was, to paraphrase Benjamin, the capital of nineteenth-century consumerism. Hilliard tells of his recent trip to the Alps, 'whilst he nibbled an olive' (72). Eve's consumption or lack of it is not described, but she is far from reticent. Instead, she is hungry for news of the journey and in particular for amusing stories of Hilliard's rich friend (and her future husband) Narramore. This hunger replaces the distraction at the earlier meal and it becomes clear Eve has learnt, or gained sufficient confidence, to manage Hilliard's dominant position at the table:

> The dinner went merrily on, and when the coffee was set before them:
> 'Why not have it outside?' said Eve. 'You would like to smoke, I know.' (73)

When Hilliard takes this opportunity to tell Eve of his prospects as an architect, she takes advantage of the new position she has engineered to avoid a direct response, 'gazing across the street' (73). Once again, she finds the view of the city more interesting than Hilliard. Thus, feminine autonomy is achieved through evasion and denial. A couple of pages later we are told that when she arrived in London, 'I was obliged to dress decently, and that came out of my food' (75). Where Gissing's male characters often undergo hunger to buy books, in other words to participate in an intellectual public sphere, Eve's participation, also involving bodily cost, is at the expense of becoming a commodity herself. As with the women suffragists, her engagement often has to be framed as a refusal. When at the end of this encounter 'Her eyes drew him with the temptation he had ever yet resisted', her acquiescence is represented as a double negative: 'Eve did not refuse his lips' (80).

Eve's limited opportunities for freedom recede when they both return to Dudley with its far less developed public culture. She lacks the employment opportunities open to her in London, and Hilliard feels far more secure about their relationship. While his hunger continues, hers recedes and is replaced with a sense of obligation that enrages Hilliard:

> 'Your gratitude be hanged! Pay me back with your lips – so – and so! Can't you understand that when my lips touch yours, I have a delight that would be well purchased with years of semi-starvation? What is it to me how I won you? You are mine for good and all – that's enough'. (90)

In Dudley, Eve is always seated inside, situated so that she has no view of beyond the private. Her appetite diminishes again: 'she pretended to eat, but in reality scarce touched her food' (94). She also refuses a gift of port given to Hilliard by Narramore. Again her desire for Hilliard mirrors her desire for food and once again it is the mouth and particularly the lips that figure her refusal: 'If she granted him her lips they had no fervour respondent to his own: she made a sport of it, forgot it as soon as possible' (96). Her self-control becomes a method for controlling Hilliard as:

> Upon Hilliard's vehement nature this acted provocatively; at times he was all but frenzied with the violence of his sensual impulses. Yet Eve's control of him grew more self-assured the less she granted of herself; a look, a motion of her lips, and he drew apart, quivering but subdued. (96)

Eve, in effect, spits out her lover before leaving him.

Eve's subsequent approach to Hilliard's wealthy friend, Narramore, is, in a Darwinian sense, a rational move. She goes at first for work (that is, to secure an independent income), when Hilliard refuses to act as an intermediary, but Narramore's attraction is clear at once. For Eve, the brass bedstead business, an almost absurd parody of bourgeois marriage (bolstered by Narramore's own irony – 'if brass bedsteads keep firm' (92)), offers a better basis for financial security than Hilliard's still uncertain prospects and volatile character. Narramore, as his name punningly suggests, offers the narrow *amour* of middle-class matrimony. Eve is quite open about her choices: 'If I had been free I would have married him – just because I am sick of the life I lead, and long for the kind of life he offered me. . .It's your mistake to think me a crafty plotting, selfish woman. I'm only a very miserable one' (117). Released by Hilliard and married to Narramore she becomes almost unrecognisable: 'He. . .only just persuaded himself of her identity.' It is not clear whether this is because she is better fed or even, to fulfil the biological destiny designated by Geddes and Thomson, pregnant. Instead, the final chapter stresses the excellence of her performance: 'Mrs Narramore was perfect in society's drill' (123).

Eve's Ransom is not really a novel either in length or in terms of its narrative structure. It is rather a literary novella that takes a parable as its source. Eve's final appearance in an English garden is deeply ironic- despite her fall she has returned to, not left, Eden. The final image of the novel is of fruit, still unplucked: 'Thick-clustered berries arrayed the hawthorns, the briar was rich in scarlet fruit' (124). But the biblical parallels are only one intertext in a work that demonstrates the richness of Gissing's best fiction. The metaphor of eating structures the whole text and its meanings modulate between Darwinian discourse, the meal as social ritual and the new possibilities of the city streets, transformed by shops, restaurants and exhibitions that offer new opportunities for public interaction between the sexes.

In this context, Hilliard's masculinity, like that of Sidney Kirkwood, is shown to be vulnerable in the city streets. Eating out in the novella acts as a microcosm of the gendered balance of power on the city's new terrains. The difference in spending power between Hilliard and Eve is paradigmatic of the different economic positions of men and women in London's new economy. Each is subject to the new culture of consumption, where social relations are conducted through the mirage of images the city projects; but Eve again is positioned as object of the gaze. Yet, at the same time, cafés and restaurants offer spaces of intersubjectivity, which constitute a partially democratised public sphere. The suggestion is that, before Hilliard begins to exert his economic power, Eve is functioning better than he does in London's exhibitive spaces. In the restaurants of London and Paris, Eve, albeit at a cost to herself, is able to control the situation and to position herself as consumer of the city's alluring images, even while Hilliard attempts to consume her. The novella's resolution dodges the implications of Eve's wider public success, but later modernist texts return to these questions and to the urban spaces in which they are posed.

15

Modernism's ABC

Richard Aldington reported that 'Like other American expatriates, Ezra [Pound] and H[ilda].D[oolittle]. developed an almost insane relish for afternoon tea'.¹ Although Aldington reports their taste as more upmarket than ABCs or Lyons – 'they insisted on going to the most fashionable and expensive tea-shops (which I thought a sad waste of money) not only in London, but in Paris' – his description of their meetings in 'some infernal bun-shop full of English spinsters' doesn't suggest too different a milieu, however 'prissy'. It is not surprising then that 'the Imagist *mouvemong* was born in a tea-shop – in the Royal Borough of Kensington'.² While Pound remembered the location differently, his poem 'The Teashop', (1916) shows a significant interest in the relationship between place and form. The Vorticists too were conscious of the distinction offered by different locations, insisting on meeting in the more downmarket ABC rather than a Lyons, while the editorial team of *The New Age* took tea in 'a grimy ABC in Chancery Lane'.³

A brief extract from Bertha Ruck's novel *The Official Fiancée* (1914), where the eponymous heroine gives her reasons for marriage, indicates the struggles for social distinction that took place in ABCs and elsewhere on the city streets:

> No more lining up with the crowd to wait for that beastly old workman's tram at the 'Elephant!' No more strap-hanging! No more packed motor buses with flower-women, and goodness knows what, shoving their baskets into you and trampling on your feet as they get in!. . .No more having to keep on at it if you *are* ready to drop and your eyes popping out of your head – no more A.B.C. girls not taking the slightest notice of your order and *then* giving you sauce because you've waited half an hour for your lunch.⁴

As this indicates, the habitus of the ABC was defined as often by opposition to its distinctive spaces as by a sense of belonging. In 'A Cooking Egg', T. S. Eliot expresses a typical ambivalence to its world, which, the narrator suggests, will not make it to paradise, but will be missed none the less:

> But where is the penny world I bought
>   To eat with Pipit behind the screen?
> The red-eyed scavengers are creeping
>   From Kentish Town and Golder's Green;
>
> Where are the eagles and the trumpets?
>   Buried beneath some snow-deep Alps.
> Over butter scones and crumpets
>   Weeping, weeping multitudes
> Droop in a hundred A.B.C.'s.[5]

Despite the poem's attempt to distance them, the wider impact of the ABC and Lyons teashops extended beyond a lower-middle-class habitus. Their ubiquity made them an image of mass urban culture. In Virgina Woolf's *Jacob's Room* (1922), Florinda, who cannot understand Shelley, spends her public life trailing 'along the shopping streets': she 'opened her bag and powdered her cheeks in omnibuses; read love letters, propping them against the milk pot in the A.B.C. shop'.[6]

The threat this new feminine constellation posed to a masculine subjectivity is clear in Somerset Maugham's novel of 1915, *Of Human Bondage*. The hero, Philip Carey, a failed modernist artist, is both attracted to and repelled by Mildred, a waitress in an ABC in Parliament Street. Mildred has the androgynous body of the New Woman: 'She was tall and thin, with narrow hips and the chest of a boy' (267). She is both aestheticised and seen as representative of mass culture. She has 'green', unhealthy-looking skin characteristic of decadent representations of New Women and 'the broad low brow which the Victorian painters, Lord Leighton, Alma Tadema, and a hundred others, induced the world they lived in to accept as a type of Greek beauty' (267). At first she ignores Philip by reading a 'cheap novelette' (271). For Philip, this locates her firmly in the sphere of 'low', commercial culture; but it is an early demonstration of the comparative weakness of Philip's masculine authority when faced with the power of the ABC (271). As with the waitresses described by Bertha Ruck, Mildred is a powerful figure within the confines of the teashop: 'She had the art of treating women who desired refreshment with just that degree of impertinence which irritated them without affording them the opportunity of complaining to the management' (268).[7]

Indistinguishable in dress from the other waitresses, who all wear 'plain black dresses, with a white apron, cuffs, and a small cap' (271), the same uniform that would become famous as that of the Lyons 'Nippies',

Mildred is at home in Benjamin's city of reflections. She is characterised by a kind of acquisitive narcissism, in love with her own image and fascinated by the images other women project in the street or music hall:

> She was much interested in the women who surrounded them in the stalls. She pointed out to Philip those who were painted and those who wore false hair.
> 'It is horrible, these West End people,' she said. 'I don't know how they can do it.' She put her hand to her hair. 'Mine's all my own, every bit of it.' (276)

Yet, if Mildred is identified with the commodity, it is the chain teashop that provides the space in which she achieves the power to resist Philip's desiring gaze. In contrast with the established norm in the nineteenth century (when waiting was done by men like Polly Sparks's father in *The Town Traveller*), the ABCs were a feminine space, staffed and managed by women. When Wyndham Lewis in *Tarr* (1918) describes Alan Hobson's 'strong, piercing laugh' as capable of throwing 'A.B.C. waitresses into confusion', far from citing the vulnerablity of the waitresses, he is describing the unusually powerful masculinity he believes is necessary to inhabit the new public culture of Europe's cities.[8]

In Katherine Mansfield's short story, 'Pictures', the exclusion of Ada Moss, an ageing, unemployed singer, from an ABC signifies her exclusion from London's new sexual economy:

> But when she came to the A B C she found the door propped open; a man went in and out carrying trays of rolls, and there was nobody inside except a waitress doing her hair and the cashier unlocking the cash-boxes. She stood in the middle of the floor but neither of them saw her.
> 'My boy came home last night,' sang the waitress.
> 'Oh, I say – how topping for you!' gurgled the cashier.
> 'Yes, wasn't it,' sang the waitress. 'He bought me a sweet little brooch. Look, it's got "Dieppe" written on it.'
> The cashier ran across to look and put her arm round the waitress' neck.
> 'Oh, I say – how topping for you.'
> 'Yes, isn't it,' said the waitress. 'O-oh, he is brahn. "Hullo," I said, "hullo, old mahogany." '
> 'Oh, I say,' gurgled the cashier, running back to her cage and nearly bumping into Miss Moss on the way. 'You are a *treat*!' Then the man with rolls came in again, swerving past her.
> 'Can I have a cup of tea, Miss?' she asked.
> But the waitress went on doing her hair. 'Oh,' she sang, 'we're not *open* yet.' She turned round and waved her comb at the cashier.
> '*Are* we, dear?'
> 'Oh, no,' said the cashier. Miss Moss went out.[9]

The dejected Miss Moss is rejected on a number of levels before she is eventually ejected from the ABC. The teashop as industrial enterprise is figured by the delivery of rolls 'swerving past her', which would have come from the company's central depot in Camden and the cashier who rings out the same response over and over again like the machine she operates. In *Jacob's Room*, Woolf suggests that conditions in a rival firm, the Express Dairy Company, induce a mechanical response from the customers:

> Damp cubes of pastry fell into mouths opened like triangular bags.
> Nelly Jenkinson, the typist, crumbled her cake indifferently enough. Every time the door opened she looked up. What did she expect to see?
> The coal merchant read the *Telegraph* without stopping, missed the saucer, and, feeling abstractedly, put the cup down on the table-cloth.[10]

In 'Pictures', Miss Moss, unable to pay her rent and unable to find work has no place in that economy, even as a consumer willing to spend her last 'one and thrippence', the approximate cost of the cheap ABC meal (as also bought by Miriam Henderson in *Pilgrimage*, see Chapter 16).[11] The waitress who 'sings' her merry receipt of gifts further underlines Miss Moss's redundancy. Miss Moss is a contralto by training, looking for acting work only because she cannot find employment as a singer. The present from Dieppe and the 'brahn' boyfriend summon up a cosmopolitan world of slang ('topping'), sexual freedom and international exchange, in which the midst of which Miss Moss, 'in the middle of the floor', is invisible: 'neither of them saw her'.[12]

According to Judith Walkowitz, popular romances published in women's periodicals such as the *Girl's Friend* 'glamorized the workgirl's life, insisting that "there is much to wonder at even in the life of a mere tea waitress"'.[13] As representative of and participant in this world of wonder, the ABC waitress signified a whole cultural tendency. In *Of Human Bondage* Philip identifies Mildred not so much as an individual, but as a part of the chain of teashops in which she works. Mildred's ability to disorientate the male gaze, to disturb Philip's sense of his own autonomy, relates to more than the teashop being working-class, feminine territory. It is as much a product of the power of the chain discussed in Chapter 13, as a network of signs that pervade the city.[14]

After their first break-up, when it becomes clear that Mildred does not see their relationship as exclusive, Philips is plagued with the idea that the backs of unidentified women in the street might also be Mildred:

> he would see a girl who looked so like Mildred that his heart seemed to stop beating. Then he could not help himself, he hurried to catch her up, eager and anxious, only to find that it was a total stranger. (287)

He attempts to escape her presence only to find himself at another branch of the chain:

> The well-known uniform made him so miserable he could not speak. The thought came to him that perhaps she had been transferred to another establishment of the firm for which she worked, and he might suddenly find himself face to face with her. The idea filled him with panic. (287)

This combination of attraction and disgust is not so much the product of Freud's 'universal tendency towards debasement in the sphere of love'[15] but the sense in which Mildred's power, small as it is in social terms, is multiplied by the way the chain permits a proliferation of the spaces in which an assertive femininity might be produced. As suggested in Chapter 13, once the impression of the teashop was fixed in the mind, its repetition in other streets reorganised the visual perception of central London. In *Of Human Bondage*, the network of cafés produces a dreamscape in which repetition draws the dreamer back to the scene of trauma.

In Dorothy Richardson's *Pilgrimage*, the sign of a of a tea company, Teetgen's teas, has a similar affect. It reminds Miriam of her mother's suicide, which occurs at the end of the third 'chapter-novel' in the series, *Honeycomb*. As Miriam wanders London's streets in a semi-dream state, the kind of reverie or fugue the new modernist geography of the city seems to induce, Miriam is drawn back unconsciously to the company's sign and the repressed memory of her mother's death: Why do I always forget there's this piece . . . always be hurrying along seeing nothing and then suddenly, Teetgens Teas and this row of shops? [. . .] I don't know where this bit is or how I get to it.'[16]

Usually however, Miriam finds the networks of ABC and Lyons teashops enabling as she navigates across the city. They open up the possibility of new dreamworlds rather than becoming part of a nightmare. *Pilgrimage* and other novels of the period bear out Lyons' claim that the new teashops were safe havens for women. In H. G. Wells's *Ann Veronica* (1909), a novel that uses information about women's experience of the city partly gathered during Wells's relationship with Richardson, Ann uses a British Tea Table Company (a thinly disguised ABC) teashop to attempt to escape, unsuccessfully in this case, from a man who has been following her in the street.[17] Part of the sense of liberation Miriam experiences in the city is the ability to operate in a non-realist mode that the chain facilitates. The state of dreaming appropriate to the modernist city contrasts with the street rhythms of the earlier Victorian period, where the small, independent businesses described in Chapter 13 required a conscious attention to each door, business or house as one passed. Most of Miriam's movements through the city are accompanied by reflection, memories and distractions, the mode typical of European modernist prose and its important city texts: *Ulysses, A La Recherche du Temps Perdu, The Trial, Nightwood* and *Good Morning Midnight*. The example of the chain teashops suggests that that state of mind is facilitated by the new economy of which the chains were part, creating new maps of the city, both real and imaginary.

For example, In the 'Lotus Eaters' chapter of *Ulysses*, a display of tea in the 'Belfast and Oriental Tea Company' shop window sends Bloom into an orientalist fantasy worthy of Lyons' Indo-Chinese tea pavilion:

> choice blend, made of the finest Ceylon brands. The far east. Lovely spot it must be: the garden of the world, big lazy leaves to float about on, cactuses, flowery meads, snaky lianas they call them. Wonder is it like that. Those Cinghalese lobbing about in the sun in *dolce far niente*, not doing a hand's turn all day. Sleep six months out of twelve. Too hot to quarrel. Influence of the climate. Lethargy. Flowers of idleness. The air feeds most. Azotes. Hothouse in Botanic gardens. Sensitive plants. Waterlilies. Petals too tired to. Sleeping sickness in the air. Walk on roseleaves.[18]

As for Miriam, tea as everyday commodity performs a magical transformation to become part of the dreamscape that is the proper, phantasmagoric realm of commodity capitalism. Thus, the sight of 'Bolton's Westmoreland house' (the Westmoreland Street branch of William Bolton & Co., grocers and tea, wine and spirit merchants) in 'Lestrygonians' returns Bloom to the train of thought he had begun in 'Lotus Eaters': 'Tea. Tea. Tea. I forgot to tap Tom Kernan' (132). Kernan is, as we learn in 'Ithaca', 'agent for Pulbrook, Robertson and Co, Mincing Lane, London, E. C., 5 Dame street, Dublin' (597). Bloom regrets not asking him for some tea; although, when the thought first occurs he thinks it would be inappropriate to make the request at Paddy Dignam's funeral. Ithaca, the chapter in *Ulysses* that, more than any other offers a representation of the rationalised systems-world that supports the city,[19] makes the connection between the global economic networks of the everyday modern and the thoughts that have been filtering through Bloom's consciousness all day.

Dublin's relationship to those networks is routed through London, the centre of Empire. The city stands like the branch of Kernan's firm, which imports from Ceylon via London, at one, dependent remove from the imperial metropolis, mimicking its structures and outlets on a smaller scale. The teashop that appears in *Ulysses* is not an ABC, but the DBC in Dame Street, standing for 'Dublin Bakery Company' (the historical Dublin Bread Company), its name a clear allusion to the successful London chain. Buck Mulligan mocks its pretensions at nationalism, claiming – after ordering not only a *mélange* (a mixture of nuts and thick cream),[20] but scones and cakes – that it stands for 'damned bad cakes' (204); while the Englishman, Haines, whose anthropological interest in all things 'authentically' Irish is satirised throughout the novel, asks, 'with forbearance': 'this is real Irish cream, I take it . . . I don't want to be imposed on' (205).

The DBC emerges at a semi-conscious level in the consciousnesses of both Bloom and Molly. In 'Lestrygonians', the DBC allows Bloom to position himself geographically and politically while wandering the city streets while his mind is elsewhere, but it also filters into his reverie. The evocation of the teashop permits a meditation that mingles political reflections about Irish nationalism with bodily sensations, notably the hunger of which he is not yet conscious – but which will shortly be satisfied at Davy Byrne's. Political debate emerges as the 'gas' that is the byproduct of human consumption:

> Gas about our lovely land. Gammon and spinach. The Dublin Bakery Company's tearoom. Debating societies. That republicanism is the best form of government. That the language question should have precedence of the economic question. (134)

Politics is part of the, not so fragrant, atmosphere of a place to eat. Food buys influence:

> Stuff them up with meat and drink. Michaelmas goose. Here's another lump of thyme seasoning under the apron for you. Have another quart of goosegrease before it gets too cold. Halffed enthusiasts. Penny roll and a walk with the band. No grace for the carver. The thought that the other chap pays best sauce in the world. Make themselves thoroughly at home. Show us over those apricots, meaning peaches. The not far distant day. Homerule sun rising up in the northwest. (134)

Yet, despite the mockery of Mulligan, Haines's pretensions and the material interests that drive and influence political debate, the DBC offer a space in which the politics of nationalism can be articulated. The tearoom is brought to mind twice in 'Lestrygonians'. The second time, by a sighting of John Howard Parnell, brother of the late Charles Stewart, who can be found playing chess in the DBC in Dame Street. In 'Wandering Rocks', Mulligan and Haines see him in the corner, his image once again associated with his dead brother: 'his eyes looked quickly, ghostbright' (204). The DBC is a point at which past and present, as well as deliberations about Ireland's future, meet. The teashop acts as what Benjamin calls a threshold in the city:

> It is only from the thresholds of these gates of imagination that lovers and friends like to draw their energies; it is from thresholds in general. . .A *Schwelle* <threshold> is a zone. Transformation, passage, wave action are

in the word *schwellen*, swell, and etymology ought not to overlook these senses.²¹

Benjamin's threshold might be described as the site where two of Lefebvre's urban rhythms intersect (see Chapter 13). The teashop is a place where the everyday, including the bodily, intersects with the larger forces of which the new service economy is a part. Typically for Bloom, he recognises the other function of the teashop for women navigating the city. The sequence of references to DBCs begins with the need for public urinals for women: 'Ought to be places for women. Running into cakeshops' (133). The tea that goes in must come out again: 'such a long one I did', remembers Molly, for whom the Dame Street DBC is a place of flirtation and opportunity – the beginning of her affair with Boylan – and bodily constriction, where Bloom's sexual demands, in the shape of 'black closed breeches', interfere with her ability to function independently in the public sphere

> theyre all so different Boylan talking about the shape of my foot he noticed at once even before he was introduced when I was in the D B C with Poldy laughing and trying to listen I was waggling my foot we both ordered 2 teas and plain bread and butter I saw him looking with his two old maids of sisters when I stood up and asked the girl where it was what do I care with it dropping out of me and that black closed breeches he made me buy takes you half an hour to let them down wetting all myself always with some brandnew fad every other week such a long one I did I forgot my suede gloves on the seat behind that I never got after some robber of a woman and he wanted me to put it in the *Irish* times lost in the ladies lavatory D B C Dame street finder return to Mrs Marion Bloom and I saw his eyes on my feet going through the turning door he was looking when I looked back and I went there for tea 2 days after in the hope but he wasn't. (613)

Molly's reverie is also 'a long one', a stream that transforms the city into dreamscape. But the teashop represents a space of intersubjectivity in which participation in the public sphere is enabled, albeit on limited and somewhat uncertain terms. Ezra Pound's poem 'The Teashop' attempts to capture its elusive magic:

> The girl in the tea shop
>   Is not so beautiful as she was,
> The August has worn against her.
> She does not get up the stairs so eagerly;
> Yes, she will also turn middle-aged,
> And the glow of youth that she spread about us
>   As she brought us our muffins
> Will be spread about us no longer.
>   She also will turn middle-aged.²²

The 'girl' is the new waitress of the new economy, who would have been dressed, like Mildred, in the standard uniform of the teashop worker. She induces the same feelings of attraction and repulsion in the male viewer as Mildred did for Philip; and the passing of her allure is almost imperceptible, a mere month, an impression or image rather than the 'real' time of nineteenth-century realism. The lyric represents an awakening in the Benjaminian sense, but one that stops short of recognising the moment where dream and wakeful consciousness intersect and enlighten one another.[23] The dream in which the waitress appeared as beautiful is broken by the sense of her new 'worn' image; her previously unremarked movements are suddenly heavy on the stairs. The moment of summer gives way to a sense of a longer duration, youth ceding to middle age. Yet, these classic elements of the (here parodied) *carpe diem* poem (gather ye muffins while ye may) have to be read in the context of the teashop as spectacular space in the new commodity culture. The muffins are a signifier of quaint Englishness and an industrial product (Lyons, remember, produced 750,000 muffins and crumpets a week). The dream is produced by the teashop as site of spectacle, including sexual spectacle. The dream is broken by the consciousness of the teashop as a site of work and production: as a place of employment that in which the employees are 'worn' down. Part of Mildred's threat in *Of Human Bondage* is that she is not just representative of the new culture of consumption, she is also a worker and it is her place of work that gives her some of her allure. Significantly, Ann Veronica seeks invisibility and final escape from the attentions of her pursuer in a crowd of rush-hour workers rather than shoppers. But Pound's poem draws back from exploring this aspect of the teashop. The inversion of 'will' and 'also' between lines 5 and 9 has a quasi-biblical effect,[24] turning the waitress from particular case to phantasmal presence, from individual, exploited worker to abstract value. The poem evades Benjamin's 'now of recognisability', when 'things put on their true – surrealist – face' and seeks refuge in the fantasy that maintains the waitress as object. It is ironic that Pound, sexist and condescending as usual, is in many ways running behind the modernism of the teashop rather than, as he believes, forging ahead of it. For, although he doesn't appear to know it, Pound's modernist masculinity has already been franchised.

A more dialectical representation of the battle over images that constitutes the new public sphere is given by Katherine Mansfield in her exquisite short story 'A Dill Pickle' (1920).[25] Cafés and cups of coffee and tea appear regularly in Mansfield's fiction as scenes of ritual that lend themselves to her sparing art. That the reader already knows the codes allows her to give every nuance proper weight and significance.

The scenario is rehearsed in an earlier story, 'In a Café' (1907), but 'A Dill Pickle' abandons the more conventional narrative of the earlier piece, taking the encounter's setting in the new urban public culture as read. It begins: 'And then, after six years, she saw him again. He was seated at one of those little bamboo tables decorated with a Japanese vase of paper daffodils.'[26]

The orientalism of the *japonaiserie* is reminiscent of Lyons' 'Indo-Chinese' tea pavilion at the Newcastle exhibition, the orientalist displays at shops such as Liberty's or the more recent Japan-British Exhibition, in White City in 1910, which Andrew Thacker argues had a deep impact on the Imagists.[27] The woman, Vera, speaks very little, but from the opening sentence it is the unnamed man who is held in her gaze, reversing Pound's viewpoint, so that he is part of the spectacle of the café.[28] In the context of the café as a phantasmagoric public sphere, their dialogue develops as a contest over image and memory rather than a direct engagement. In what is a coded battle for position, she achieves his recognition, accepts his offer of coffee, but not food, and agrees to sit. He then makes the running, remembering her, 'Ah, no. You hate the cold', and giving narrative form to his memory of their relationship. His remembrance of a day at Kew Gardens, another exhibitive space, is an act of possession. She becomes his dream:

> I don't what it is – I've often wondered – that makes your voice such a – haunting memory [. . .] But whenever it is very fine and warm, and I see some bright colours – it's awfully strange – I hear your voice saying: 'Geranium, marigold and verbena.' And I feel those three words are all I recall of some forgotten, heavenly language . . . You remember that afternoon? (272)

In contrast, her memory of the exhibitive space is as intersubjective. Another orientalist tearoom, 'in a Chinese pagoda', made him an object of ridicule because he did not recognise it as a partly democratised sphere, in which what he signifies is open to public criticism:

> A great many people . . . and he behaving like a maniac about the wasps – waving them away, flapping at them with his straw hat, serious and infuriated out of all proportion to the occasion. How delighted the sniggering tea drinkers had been. And how she had suffered.

The story proceeds dialogically, as she is by turns pulled into his dream and then repulsed by one of her own memories – never communicated to him – of his egoism or his pettiness. Accepting a Russian cigarette, she is drawn into his traveller's tales of Russia, and the story's turning point is reached when she imagines putting a dill pickle offered by the Russian coachmen in her mouth:

> She saw the carriage drawn up to one side of the road, and the little group on the grass, their faces and hands white in the moonlight. She saw the pale dress of the woman outspread and her folded parasol, lying on the grass like a huge pearl crochet hook. Apart from them, with his supper in a cloth on his knees, sat the coachman. 'Have a dill pickle,' said he, and although she was not certain what a dill pickle was, she saw a the greenish jar with a red chilli like a parrot's beak glimmering through. She sucked in her cheeks; the dill pickle was terribly sour . . .
> 'Yes, I know perfectly what you mean,' she said. (274)

The image encompasses its prelude, inhaling on the Russian cigarette, actually ingesting the dill pickle, and a sexual fantasy of polymorphous perversity: The 'red chilli like a parrot's beak' is ambiguously, but suggestively, sexed. The fantasy seems to include not only her former lover but the Russian coachman and perhaps also the 'woman outspread' 'with her folded parasol, lying on the grass like a huge pearl crochet hook'. The fantasy dissolves boundaries, creating an imagined moment of pure intersubjectivity (not unlike the moment with the seedcake remembered by Bloom and Molly), in which mutual comprehension seems possible again: 'In the past when they had looked at each other like that they had felt such a boundless understanding between them.' But London's new public sphere, such mutual understanding (the perfect speech act) is quickly put into doubt. She feels he holds back. He is mocking her. She remembers an example of his pettiness. He authorises her rejection of him, narrating a masochistic fantasy in which she walks on him and he turns 'into a magic carpet', carrying her 'to all those lands you longed to see' (275). Only then does he draw back, bathetically, into a psychological rationalisation of her isolation, to find:

> She had gone. He sat there, thunderstruck, astounded beyond words . . . And he asked the waitress for his bill.
> 'But the cream has not been touched,' he said. 'Please do not charge me for it.'

It is not, of course, the case that Vera has self-knowledge and he does not. Nor that she does not try and control the situation. She initiates the meeting, having first been disappointed that he does not recognise her right away. Her self-fashioning is as evident as his. But she is aware of that which he refuses to recognise, the intersubjective context of their speech acts. In effect, the short story does for their dialogue what the story of the tea room in the Chinese pagoda does for his memory. It reveals a masculinity not ready for a democratic public culture. The male speaker is, like Pound's franchised masculinity, still trapped in the dream. She leaves him for the freedom of the streets. She responds to his old 'trick of interrupting her' (271) with her own conversation interruptus, giving a wicked double meaning to his lament to the waitress: 'the cream has not been touched'.

Mansfield was perhaps the most acute observer of gendered social interactions amongst the English modernists, but it was Dorothy Richardson who gave the best account of a woman's lived experience of London's new public culture. In *Pilgrimage*, the relationship between consumption and work is embodied in the figure of Miriam Henderson, who is both a New Woman worker in the city and a consumer of the city's delights, albeit limited by her income in what she can buy.

16

Miriam, teashops and the industrialised public sphere

In 1921, Dorothy Richardson was delighted to discover a Lyons newspaper, an event she recounted in a letter with a characteristic mixture of appreciation, satire and some envy:

> Talking of periodicals makes me think of a curious little shock I had yesterday rushing out of a Lyons whither I had retired for a coffee in the midst of a long round of shopping. I was paying my bill & looking at the same time at the cover of something lying on the counter . . . the Lyons Mail[.] I read & saw Henry Irving in a series of dramatic situations. I read other things & drifted out into the street taking them in – & a list of names & something about 2/- monthly, or quarterly. Then I saw which Lyons was intended . . . I long now for Monday & a chance of getting a copy of the bun monthly. A delightful idea to write only, & with one's whole soul for a bun monthly. Think of the size of your audience.[1]

In standard histories, the newspaper was, with the coffeehouse, the key facilitator of the classic bourgeois sphere. Here, the description of the company or 'industrial' newspaper is characteristic of Richardson's fiction in that it places the experience of the chain café in its 'context of living'.[2] The café is situated 'in the midst' of shopping and the contents of the paper reveal its relations with consumerism, theatre, popular journalism, scandal and gossip. It is in these relations that the 'industrialised' teashop might be understood as one of Negt and Kluge's public spheres of production, in which new counter-publics were produced. As they argue, *'industrialized public spheres of production . . . tend to incorporate private realms in particular the production process and the context of living'*.[3] Dorothy Richardson was one of the first film critics to notice that the cinema produced such an alternative public sphere, commenting in the process on the gendered make-up of that audience. It consisted largely, she remarked in her column, 'Continuous Performance', of working-class women.[4] But she first developed an idea of such a counter-public in her representations of teashops in *Pilgrimage*.

Miriam Hansen theorises the concept of a counter-public as follows:

> Even in their parasitic and illusory grasp of human needs and qualities, these new public spheres make visible a substantially different function of the public sphere in general, i.e., to provide a medium for the organization of human experience in relation to rather than, as in the classical model, separation from – the material sphere of everyday life, the social conditions of production.[5]

As an experiment in modernist writing, *Pilgrimage* attempted to represent the interpenetration, rather than the separation, of material and symbolic production. Its urban heroine's labour as a New Woman is the precondition for her ability to participate in a public sphere. *Pilgrimage* is extraordinarily detailed about the social relations that produce space, not just the space of the chain café but the complicated codes of access and disbarment that define the difference between a lodger and a boarder. At first, as a lodger not a boarder, Miriam does not take her meals in the 'boarding house' and is excluded from some of its common spaces. Instead, she eats out, usually at an ABC teashop, an arrangement she prefers because it allows her to elude the surveillance of her landlady, Mrs Bailey. Later, when she gains some of the privileges of a boarder in return for giving French lessons, she wins the right to cross the boarding house's internal thresholds; but this right is won at the expense of her own privacy:

> The whole house was hers; she was a *boarder*; but the right to linger freely in any part of it was bought by Sissie's French lessons, and being Sissie's teacher meant that the Baileys could approach familiarly at any moment. All her privileges were bought with a heavy price, here and at Wimpole Street. It's us; our family; always masquerading.[6]

Miriam's masquerade extends to cafés. She describes her position as neither lodger nor boarder as 'amphibious'.[7] In the early 'chapter-novels' of *Pilgrimage*, the ABCs allow her to be similarly 'amphibious', when they act as staging posts or thresholds between her private room in the boarding house and the public life of the city. In this context, the café not only allows 'private behaviour in a public place', but, between her room and the street, it is a space where public and private meet. As such, the chain teashop is a productive space, the narrow stage upon which Miriam can perform a new kind of gendered subjectivity, which is neither conventionally masculine nor feminine. Far from being a tame copy of modernity, the chain café provides an intermediate zone in which Miriam can participate in London's public culture because of, not despite, its relationship to her material 'context of living'.

Two key dream sequences in *Pilgrimage* dramatise Miriam's relationship with London's new public culture. The first occurs in *The Tunnel*

(1919), the fourth 'chapter-novel' in Dorothy Richardson's *Pilgrimage*. The second has already been discussed in relation to Richardson's aesthetic (in Chapter 10). It occurs in *Revolving Lights* and also involves a long walk through central London. At the end of Chapter 3 of *The Tunnel*, Miriam begins a walk from her place of work in Wimpole Street (just off Oxford Street) that is destined to remain lost in the depths of her unconscious.

> The door opened and closed with its familiar heavy wooden firmness, neatly, with a little rattle of its chain. Her day scrolled up behind her. She halted, trusted and responsible, for a long second, in the light flooding the steps from behind the door. The pavement under her feet and the sparsely lamplit night all around her. She restrained her eager steps to a walk. The dark houses and the blackness between the lamps were elastic about her.[8]

At the beginning of Chapter 4 she resurfaces in the Strand with no memory of how she got there and, to her relief, finds sanctuary in an ABC teashop. The gap in her consciousness, where the memory of the walk should be, is intriguing. Walter Benjamin suggests that both dreams and cities are characterised by boundaries, thresholds and crossing places.[9] The hiatus in Richardson's text writes such a boundary into the narrative. As elsewhere in *Pilgrimage*, Miriam has crossed London in a dream: 'she wondered what she had been thinking since she left Wimpole Street, and whether she had come across Trafalgar Square without seeing it or round some other way' (II, 75). But the gap between the chapters also marks a crossing between two identities: the worker and the consumer. All forty-three pages of Chapter 3 are devoted to an account of Miriam's day at work as a dental receptionist. In Chapter 4 she reawakens – 'she came to herself' (II, 75) – transformed from New Woman employee to woman about town. The narrative break figures her identity as fractured. She is here again 'amphibious', able to be worker and consumer, masculine and feminine, public and private, to walk through the realist city or swim through the dreamscape of the modernist city. But the joins between these different subjectivities are incomplete. The appearance of the ABC, part of the 'industrialised' public sphere, figures a space in which the contradictions in a fractured social self can be negotiated.

At one level, the hiatus between the chapters marks a moment of narrative difficulty in Richardson's project: the problem of siting the performance of a New Woman subjectivity in relation to the new gendered division of labour in late Victorian London. As Nancy Fraser has pointed out in her critique of Habermas's distinction between material and symbolic reproduction, the division between worker and consumer has always been gendered.[10] Conventionally, male workers are understood to exist in the real world of capitalist production; female consumers buy the goods produced by men either for the family or to adorn themselves as part of the same world of commodities.[11] The journey Miriam takes between chapters marks a transgression of these conventional boundaries; and, in addition, each chapter represents a form of troubled embodiment that goes beyond the constraints of Victorian femininity. But if Miriam's missing moments signal a difficulty in the narrative, they also create a problem for a cultural criticism that would seek to site the performance of new subjectivities in a history of material practices. As suggested in Chapter 13, histories of identity formation in this period have paid insufficient attention to the alienating effects of work under capitalism, preferring to dwell on consumption as the key site for the constitution of identity.[12] On the one hand, Miriam's lost, transitional passage from worker to consumer demonstrates the difficulty of achieving a coherent account of what Elizabeth Grosz calls 'an embodied subjectivity or a psychical corporeality'.[13] On the other, the contradictions that emerge between the world of work and that of consumption demonstrate the social complexity of what Judith Butler calls the 'gendered matrix of relations' that produce the subject.[14]

In Richardson's fiction, dentistry and the culture of the Wimpole Street practice become exemplary metaphors for the interpenetration of material and symbolic reproduction. The workplace is recognised as a key site for the production of a New Woman subjectivity, but it also has a dialectical relationship to women's consumption. For Miriam, as for thousands of other women who entered London's labour force in the period, work is both an economic necessity and an opportunity to enter London's public culture.[15] She earns £1 a week. This was the wage that was to become the subject of a famous Fabian pamphlet, *Round about a Pound a Week*, which described the survival of whole working-class families on between 18 and 30 shillings. But even as a single woman, the margin beyond subsistence is tiny.[16] Like Gissing's characters, she often has to choose between books and eating. None the less, her limited ability to make choices is significant. In his history of eating in England and France, Stephen Mennell argues that political security and economic surplus are prerequisites for 'the cultural syndrome of bourgeois rationality as a whole'.[17] Alone in the city, Miriam's pound a week provides the minimal material conditions for an identity beyond the Victorian, middle-class family. Thus, if the opportunities for performing a New Woman subjectivity appear most clearly in the forms of consumption (clothes, smoking, cycling, eating out) permitted by that small surplus, work is a key determinant of what Judith Butler calls the 'regulatory norms' of a new kind of femininity.[18]

Miriam's employment provides her with a basic wage and the possibility of a marginal existence in the city, but the practice in Wimpole Street is also a symbolic site in which social identities are produced. Miriam's experience of work is, at the same time, the history of her contradictory relationship to consumption. Many of the rituals associated with food are designed to distance the eater from the physical processes involved.[19] The culture of dentistry as a medical practice concerned with the consequences of eating has to perform a double distancing from food and bodily decay. In chapter 3 of *The Tunnel*, dental instruments – as both the cold, clinical consequence of indulgence and the tools that construct the technological body – symbolise Miriam's alienation from her work. One of her last tasks before she leaves the practice is to cover the tools of the trade:

> Leaving the dried instruments in a heap with a wash-leather flung over them she gathered up the books, switched the room into darkness, felt its promise of welcome, and trotted downstairs through the quiet house. (II, 74)

Work alienates Miriam from her own appetites. Keeper of order of the practice's instruments and finances, she is also in charge of intellectual consumption in the practice. Her cultural capital outweighs her actual capital and in recognition of this fact she is put in charge of ordering the practice's library books (stretching the definitions of bourgeois good taste, she orders Zola);[20] but more often her position within the firm relies on self-deprecation and denial. Meals at work dramatise the regulation of social boundaries. The ritual of the practice's lunch is described in detail and is punctuated by Miriam's refusal of food: 'Have some pâté, Miss Hens' – No? despise pâté?' (II, 56). Scared of 'contemptible self-indulgence' (II, 56). Miriam, like Eve in *Eve's Ransom*, constructs a disciplined feminine self through abstinence.[21] The meal as social event underlines her own subordination. Her attempts to make relationships on the basis of equality are constrained by the rigid boundaries constructed by position and gender. If she drops her guard for a moment, she slips back:

> '. . . Have a biscuit and butter Miss Hens'n.'
> Miriam refused and excused herself.
> On her way upstairs she strolled into Mr Leyton's room. He greeted her with a smile – polishing instruments busily.
> 'Mr Hancock busy?' he asked briskly.
> 'M'm.'
> 'You busy? I say, if I have Buck in will you finish up these things?'
> 'All right, if you like,' said Miriam, regretting her sociable impulse. (II, 58)

In this encounter, Miriam's subordinate position is signified by her relationship not only to Mr Leyton, but to the medical systems-world he represents. The reader becomes aware of the ironically named Mr Buck's condition. He is suffering from syphilis, a condition of which Miriam is only dimly conscious. Mr Buck is a victim of the over-consumption and self-indulgence from which dental masculinity 'protects' the young Miriam. Her subjectivity as a feminine worker is produced against and between the horror of Buck's unregulated body and the hygienic Mr Leyton's professional power and knowledge:

> 'I boil every blessed thing after he's been . . . if that's any indication to you.'
>
> 'Boil them!' said Miriam vaguely distressed and pondering over Mr Leyton standing active and aseptic between her and some horror . . . something infectious . . . it must be that awful mysterious thing . . . how awful for Mr Leyton to have to stop his teeth.
>
> 'Boil 'em,' he chuckled knowingly.
>
> 'Why on earth?' she asked.
>
> 'Well – there you are,' said Mr Leyton – 'that's all I can tell you. I boil 'em.'
>
> 'Crikey,' said Miriam, half in response and half in comment on his falsetto laugh, as she made for the door. (II, 59)

Women's exclusion from medical knowledge about venereal disease was a campaigning focus for feminists in the period.[22] Here, Mr Leyton's 'that's all I can tell you' is an act of biopolitical power. But a few pages later, subversive revenge is wreaked upon him in the practice common room, where, like the man in a 'A Dill Pickle', he fails to recognise his performance as open to public criticism. Miriam observes his grotesque form failing abysmally in the feminine art of taking tea that is later theorised in *Revolving Lights*:

> His shirt and the long straight narrow ends of his tie made a bulging curve above his low-cut waistcoat. The collar of his coat stood away from his bent neck and its tails were bunched up round his hips. His trousers were so hitched up that his bent knees strained against the harsh crude Rope Brothers cloth. The ends of his trousers peaked up in front, displaying loose rolls of black sock and the whole of his anatomical walking shoes. Miriam heard his masticating jaws and dreaded his operation with his teacup. A wavering hand came out and found the cup and clasped it by the rim, holding it at the edge of the lifted newspaper. She busied herself with cutting stout little wedges of cake. Mr Leyton sipped, gasping after each loud quilting gulp; a gasp, and the sound of a moustache being sucked. (II, 69)

Comic retribution for masculine pretension is one of the key strands of *Pilgrimage*. However, it does not obscure the fact that Miriam's femininity is produced in relation to a division of labour that makes her the subordinate party. She has to wash the instruments used on Mr Buck and add up his bills. None the less, her identity is not just that of office skivvy. Work puts her, geographically at least, at the centre of things. Her job in Wimpole Street and her lodgings in Bloomsbury are an escape from the 'backwater' that lies beyond the Euston Road: 'by day and by night, her unsleeping guardian, the rim of the world beyond which lay the northern suburbs, banished.' (II, 15). Paid employment is an entry ticket to *fin-de-siècle* London. The 'elastic' darkness of the city just outside the office opens up the possibility of participation in an expanded public culture which might allow multiple stages on which new subjectivities can be rehearsed.

Miriam's lost journey between Chapters 3 and 4, between work and her evening meal, takes her through the major shopping, restaurant and theatre districts of the West End in a kind of dream state. A reconstruction of her route suggests that she might have walked along Oxford Street, through Soho, which, with its many French and Italian cafés and restaurants, epitomised the transformation in London's public culture in the period.[23] However, Miriam does not frequent Soho restaurants until much later. At this early stage in her odyssey, her destination is the humbler ABC, in which the transitions performed during her walk can be recovered. Miriam's path through the city figures the dialectical relationship between the labouring and the consuming body. The complexity of late nineteenth-century consumer capitalism means that the connections between the two are indeed obscure, but they are, nevertheless, different sides of the same coin. The presence of New Women workers, like Miriam, created the conditions for new forms of consumption; but, at the same time, those new forms permit new kinds of embodied subjectivity to emerge. The chain teashop acts as a threshold, in Benjamin's sense, between the two, a point at which the worlds of work and consumption meet, and a newly gendered subjectivity can be reconstituted. In other words, the ABC acts as an imaginative space drawn from the new industrialised public sphere in which the contradictions of the urban dreamscape can be negotiated.

Tracing the genealogy of the ABC in *Pilgrimage* reveals a legacy of childhood pleasures and adult interdependence. The chain is mentioned in the first volume, *Pointed Roofs* (1915), as one of the childhood treats Miriam will miss when she leaves England to take up her first teaching post in Germany: 'No more all day *bézique* . . . No more days in the West End . . . No more matinées . . . No more A.B.C. teas . . .' (I, 18). However, when Miriam gets to Germany her relationship with cafés changes. She shares her pupils' childish view of a visit to Kreipe's, a local café, as a much-anticipated treat, but finds that the café offers a space in which she can observe a new assertive form of adult femininity:

> There were only women there – wonderful German women in twos and threes – ladies out shopping, Miriam supposed. She managed intermittently to watch three or four of them and wondered what kind of conversation made them so emphatic – whether it was because they held themselves so well and 'spoke out' that everything they said seemed important. She had never seen women with so much decision in their bearing. She found herself drawing herself up. (I, 89)

Miriam, 'drawing herself up', is able to imagine the possibility of a new embodied subjectivity, constituted in relation to both the memory of childhood pleasures and her intersubjective relationship with the 'wonderful German women'.

> Three cups of thick-looking chocolate, each supporting a little hillock of solid cream arrived at her table. Clara ordered cakes.
> At the first sip, taken with lips that slid helplessly on the surprisingly thick rim of her cup, Miriam renounced all the beverages she had ever known as unworthy. (I, 89)

She soon discovers, however, that she is not free to enjoy the pleasures of a feminine public culture unconstrained. As with her consumption of the cigarette in *Honeycomb*, her position as paid employee limits her ability to enjoy. Under the surveillance of her employer, Fräulein Pfaff, Miriam's moment of bliss, enjoying 'the familiar looking *éclair*' is interpreted as an instance of over-indulgence. Later at dinner Fräulein Pfaff 'went round the table with questions as to what had been consumed at Kreipe's' (I, 89), requiring each cake to be described. An ascetic biscuit receives a smile, but Miriam's *éclair* makes her almost alone in her 'excesses'. In what can be taken as a lesson in how to behave as an employee, the excessive moment of consumption is used to fix Miriam into an economy in which she is the weaker party, imposing the model of self-discipline she later employs at the Wimpole Street practice.

It is, then, significant that the next appearance of an ABC, in the subsequent volume, *Backwater* (1916), is when Miriam takes her mother out to tea rather than the other way round. Miriam's forced cheerfulness is ostensibly an attempt to recreate the atmosphere of the family treat, but its real purpose is to show off her new-found independence and knowledge of the city:

> 'You'll see our A B C soon. You know. The one we go to after the Saturday pops. You've been to it. You came to it the day we came to Madame Schumann's farewell. It's just round here in Piccadilly. Here it is. Glorious. I must make the others come up once more before I die. I always have a

> scone. I don't like the aryated bread. We go along the Burlington Arcade too. I don't believe you've ever been along there. It's simply perfect. Glove shops and fans and a smell of the most exquisite scent everywhere.'
> 'Dear me. It must be very captivating.'
> 'Now we shall pass the parks. Oh, isn't the sun A1 copper bottom!'
> Mrs Henderson laughed wistfully. (I, 199)

The inviting mention of an arcade sites Miriam as a female flâneuse, at home in the city's spaces of consumption; but as important is the location of the ABC in relation to what Kevin Lynch in the *Image of the City* calls a path, one of the routes through which the city space is mapped by its inhabitants.[24] Miriam, significantly, is the one who maps, who knows the city's slang, its attractions and dangers. The excess of goods – gloves, fans and scents – with their associations of a dangerously public femininity makes her mother nervous; but if in the workplace Miriam's subordinate position as employee is clear, on the streets as a consumer she is able to define herself against her mother's more timid relationship to the city. The consumption of the scone, not the 'ayrated' bread, misspelled perhaps to emphasise the point, marks her distinctive and authoritative taste and it is this new-found 'elastic' space into which Miriam walks at the end of a day's work.

Reached without conscious thought, the Strand, in keeping with its name, is represented as a liminal space. A nexus of commerce, theatre and the restaurant trade, it marks (at least in the middle-class Miriam's opinion) the end of the respectable West End. This diversity of contradictory urban spaces provides the conditions for what Butler calls a 'proliferative catachresis', permitting the production of new gendered subjectivities.[25]

> Most of the shops were still open. The traffic was still in full tide. The jeweller's window repelled her. It was very yellow with gold, all the objects close together and each one bearing a tiny label with the price. There was a sort of commonness about The Strand, not like the cheerful commonness of Oxford Street, more like the City with its many sudden restaurants. She walked on. But there were theatres also, linking it up with the West End and streets leading off it where people like Bob Greville had chambers. It was the tailing off of the West End and the beginning of a deep dark richness that began about Holywell. Mysterious important churches crowded in amongst little brown lanes . . . the little dark brown lane . . . She wondered what she had been thinking since she left Wimpole Street, and whether she had come across Trafalgar Square without seeing it or round some other way. (II, 75)

On the edge of the West End, Miriam is between what Franco Moretti, in his study of literary geography, calls (after Adorno) two 'half Londons, that do not add up to a whole'.[26] In Richardson's complex rewriting of London she draws on the representation of the East End established by realist writers such as George Gissing and Arthur Morrison. Their imagery of penetration and contamination, Gissing's 'corners and lurking-holes',[27] is reproduced here in the anal imagery of 'little brown lanes . . . the dark little brown lane'. Yet, characteristically, Richardson's text enjoys imagining the bodily pleasures of the city's otherness, the 'deep dark richness that began about Holywell', the centre of the Victorian pornography industry. The urban imaginary opens up the possibility of new subjectivities of which Miriam is not yet conscious. Certainly, her awakening brings a repulsion for bourgeois marriage as represented by the jeweller's window, 'yellow with gold'.

Still, her experience of the streets is far from utopian. The constraints on her movement are brought home by her immediate encounter with male violence:

> They were fighting; sending out misery and suffocation into the surrounding air . . . she stopped close to the upright balanced threatening bodies, almost touching them. The men looked at her. 'Don't' she said imploringly and hurried on trembling. (II, 75)

And this threat underlines the importance of the ABC, which appears at the moment of crisis, 'suddenly at her side'. While 'nearly full of men' and 'not one of her own ABCs' (the ABC closest to her lodgings becomes 'her A.B.C.' (II, 329), a first port of call before she ventures out into less hospitable parts of the city), the teashop signals a safe, homely space: 'its panes misty in the cold air'. In this more distant hostelry, the interior creates a strange hybrid of work and consumption, public and private, masculine and feminine spaces. In effect, the ABC allows the gap between Chapters 3 and 4 to be filled.

The 'City men' who occupy it make for an atmosphere of masculine work with their 'uncongenial scraps of talk that now and again penetrated her thoughts'; but the restaurant also has a 'feminine' space: its own domestic hearth:

> The shop turned at a right angle showing a large open fire with a fireguard, and a cat sitting on the hearth-rug in front it. She chose a chair at a small table in front of the fire. The velvet settees at the sides of the room were more comfortable. But it was for such a little while tonight. (II, 76)

Amongst the city men, Miriam chooses the feminised space, constructed within a masculine world, but on the boundary between the two her own performance on the fractured stage of the ABC is not, and indeed cannot be, the domestic role of Victorian ideology. As discussed in Chapter 9,

Miriam feels her way gradually towards a new kind of gendered subjectivity. Her ambivalent relationship to femininity is explored in *Honeycomb*, the volume that precedes *The Tunnel*, where the Wilde trial exerts a powerful effect on her, pulling her towards the city and its possibilities. In her entrance into the teashop she adopts a masculine pose that borders on the camp: 'She walked confidently down the centre, her plaid-lined golf-cape thrown back.'

Again, work is a necessary precondition for her performance as well as a crucial element in its staging. Transgressing gender boundaries, Miriam also transgresses the gendered roles of worker and consumer. The dialectic between work and consumption finds its dialectical image, once again, in what she eats and drinks. Miriam's meal, a boiled egg, roll and butter and a small coffee, is the cheapest available that allows her to participate in London's public culture. This is not the treat of the childhood tea, the indulgence of the German *éclair*, nor the daring idiosyncrasy of the scone in the home of aerated bread. It is the meal of the white-collar worker on round about a pound a week.

Later in *Pilgrimage* a boiled egg, roll and butter become a kind of currency against which other commodities are measured (II, 150). At one point she compares them with home cooking, 'the lovely little loaf and the wholesome solid fish would cost less' (II, 259), but Miriam's preference for mass catering over miraculous loaves and fishes cannot just be put down to her lack of culinary skills. Her wage and situation give her access to a limited public life and the ABC provides the narrow stage upon which she can perform her new subjectivity. The image of the boiled egg, roll and butter and small coffee figures the material constraints which defined the embodiment of that subjectivity. Miriam's spartan meal cannot be divorced from the circulation of commodities in which her labour plays a small, but crucial part. As she gains confidence in the city at night, she starts to frequent late-night Soho cafés and to meet her lovers in more expensive restaurants, widening the public sphere in which she participates. But her ability to meet men on more equal terms is enabled by her earlier colonisation of the ABCs, each of which, to a greater or lesser extent, she makes her own.

The material and symbolic role of the café in *Pilgrimage* is further demonstrated in the long promenade taken by Miriam in the first section of *Revolving Lights* (1923). This is the same walk that frames her remembrance of the dialogue with Hypo Wilson (discussed in Chapter 10). Held within the embodied experience of the walk are a series of related reflections and other remembered conversations about not only women and aesthetics but also her relationship with her Jewish lover, Michael Shatov, her own bisexual identity and literature. These reflections constitute the shifting constellation of relations that produce Miriam's urban subjectivity. That they are represented within the walk as their 'context of living' makes the point that Miriam's identity is produced by the dialectic between space and the social relations that produce that space. It is the public culture of the city that allows her to be amphibious in a different but related sense and experience an ambivalent sexuality:

> Within me . . . the *third* child, the longed-for son, the two natures, equally matched, mingle and fight? It is their struggle which keeps me adrift, so variously interested and strongly attracted, now here, now there? Which will win?
> . . . Feeling so identified with both, she could not imagine either of them set aside. Then her life would be the battlefield of her two natures.[28]

It is tempting here to see 'the *third* child' as including the idea of the third intermediate sex theorised by writers like Edward Carpenter in the period.[29] In her superb cultural history of the emergence of a distinct lesbian identity in the period after the First World War, Laura Doan argues that before 1928 'Knowledge of lesbianism was. . . never "common" . . .most important, lesbianism in any formulation was not yet generally connected with style or image'.[30] Thus, in *Revolving Lights*, which is set in 1903 and was published in 1923, Miriam's position and the space it might occupy are still unclear, although the challenge her sense of herself presents to masculine hegemony is not.[31]

Unsure of her identity, on the walk Miriam actively seeks a 'third space' in which this ambivalent third position might be expressed, one where she might comfortably continue the reflections produced by the contradictions of public and private, masculine and feminine, consciousness and embodiment: 'Why hadn't she a club, down here; a neutral territory where she could finish her thoughts undisturbed?'.[32] In the context of that loss the memory of a Lyons intervenes as the place in which she read Conrad and encountered the possibility of a differently gendered form of writing:

> it was not like reading a book at all . . . Expecting good difficult 'writing', some mannish way of looking at things, and then . . . complete forgetfulness of the worst time of day on the most grilling day of the year in a crowded Lyons's at lunch-time and, afterwards, joyful strength to face the disgrace of being an hour or more late for afternoon work.[33]

Chain cafés, as an enabling space in a fractured public culture, allow Miriam to develop an urban, intellectual identity. They also provide her with the confidence to cross over into more liminal zones, such as the Piccadilly café frequented by prostitutes she enters before returning home. This act of defiance, which chooses the café as an alternative third space in place of the gentleman's club, is prompted by an encounter with an old, male friend of her sisters'. The meeting rewrites a canonical text in the literature of the flâneur, Baudelaire's 'A une Passante':

> He had seen her, and his unawakened face told her that she would neither pause nor speak [. . .] He was obviously embarrassed by the sense of having placed her amidst the images of his preoccupation. She rushed on, passing him with a swift salute, saw him raise his hat with mechanical promptitude as she stepped from the kerb and forward, pausing an instant for a passing hansom [. . .] It was done. It had always been done from the very beginning. They had met equally at last. This was the reality of their early association [. . .] Tommy of all people wakened thus out of his absorption in the separated man's life that so decorated him with mystery in the feminine suburbs.[34]

Where in Baudelaire the look of the 'passante' is a kind of sexual rebirth – 'Un éclair . . . puis la nuit! – Fugitive beauté/Dont le regard m'a fait soudainement renaître' ('A flash . . . then night! – O lovely fugitive, / I am suddenly reborn from your swift glance') – in Richardson, the rebirth is in the rejection of a sexuality constructed as subordinate. The cup of coffee she orders in the café is an extension of this triumphant refusal: 'Here, still on the Circus, was the little coffee-place. Tommy was going home. *She* was rescuing the last scrap of a London evening here at the very centre and then going home, on foot, still well within the charmed circle.'[35]

If the late-night café on Piccadilly enables the production of a new kind of gender subjectivity, set free from the 'feminine suburbs', chain cafés act as the thresholds over which Miriam can step to more exciting encounters. Significantly, in the last 'chapter-novel' of *Pilgrimage*, Richardson sets the moment when Miriam is publicly recognised as a professional writer in a Lyons: 'Important, I felt, a writer to whom this Harley Street doctor was humbly appealing.'[36] At this point, Miriam finally becomes the unalienated worker. The Lyons teashop, hitherto a place of consumption of food, drink and books, is now the space in which she is recognised as a producer: not the office skivvy, not even the knowledgeable library assistant, but an artist in her own right, who can write her own version of a public identity.

17

Kafka, masculinity and the public sphere

In the climactic final lines of Franz Kafka's short story 'The Judgement', Georg Bendemann, a young businessman, performs a spectacular feat of gymnastics, the prelude to his death by drowning in the river below:

> He swung himself over, like the distinguished gymnast he had once been in his youth, to his parents' pride. With weakening grip he was still holding on when he spied between the railings a motor bus coming which could easily cover the noise of his fall, called in a low voice: 'Dear parents, I have always loved you, all the same,' and let himself drop.
> At this moment an almost endless stream of traffic was going over the bridge.[1]

The image of Georg's leap is an example of the performance as the expression, even the apotheosis, of modernist art. From the image of the dancer in the poetry and art of the 1890s to the choreographed play of self-referentiality in modernist texts, modernism defines itself by its performativity. The performative step has been repeated over the last decade, originally in the work of Judith Butler, but now danced by all critics who have taken up queer theory's tune. As with modernism, the early examples were drawn from the stage. Where Symons, Wilde or Beardsley represented the ambivalent position of the male spectator viewing the self-reflective and narcissistic figure of the female dancer who 'dances for her own delight', for Butler the cue for performativity is the drag queen or even Aretha Franklin, rehearsing an imitation of gendered identity without an original.[2] As with many aspects of poststructuralist criticism, it is tempting to see here an extension of modernism, repeating in theory what has already been done in art.

But reading for masculinity in Kafka's nightmarish interior spaces requires them also to be related to a public sphere. Like London, Prague's public sphere was defined by its café culture. The city was split along ethnic lines and its cafés reflected those cultural faultlines. The Casino complex was the centre of German culture. The Café

Continental, situated on the first floor of a baroque palace, was the meeting place for German-Jewish businessmen, doctors, lawyers, journalists and literary figures. Kafka's circle, which was, even before the First World War, breaking through the barrier between German and Czech culture, met in the Café Arco, where international avant-garde journals were available. The Café Chantant Montmartre was another venue for the German and Czech avant-garde and put on events in Czech. Less respectable cafés included the Balkan and the Café Savoy; the latter, situated in the red light district of the old Ghetto, put on performances of Yiddish drama.[3] These cafés were the context for Kafka's art and, sometimes, the venues for its performance in the form of public readings.

Despite Kafka's reputation as a writer of enclosed spaces, his letters show a fascination with public life, especially, as Mark Anderson has documented, the world of commerce and fashion,[4] the same industrialised public sphere that was the context for the modernist texts discussed in this book. As described in Chapter 5, in the 'Letter to His Father' Hermann Kafka's fancy goods business stands as an example of this world and Kafka's masculinities are produced at the borderline between public and private.

Despite the glittering image of his fall, Georg's masculinity is also produced by a sequence of transactions between public and private spheres, transactions that are figured in the final image of the story: 'At this moment an almost endless stream of traffic was going over the bridge.' The German word for traffic, *Verkehr*, is, as Mark Anderson has pointed out (see Chapter 5) central to Kafka's fiction. Of the end of 'The Judgement', Anderson writes, 'The traffic that streams across the bridge is not just an image of urban life, but the liberated energy of the writer, the *Verkehr* of literary creation'.[5] But this is a somewhat romantic interpretation, where urban identity, and implicitly here the subjectivity of the male artist, is reflected by a sense of dynamic movement: the circulation of vehicles and commodities in the city. In this sense, the city is itself the performance. Instead, it might be suggested, Kafka's 'The Judgement' is structured around clearly defined thresholds between the public and the private spheres and that Georg Bendemann's masculinity, like the Miriam Henderson's ambivalent gender identity, is produced through the traffic across them.

The story opens with Georg in his 'private room [*Privatzimmer*]' gazing from interior into exterior space: 'out of the window at the river, the bridge and the hills on the farther bank with their faint [*schwachen*] green'.[6] His viewpoint or subject position thus relates to the tri-partite universe described in the 'Letter to His Father':

Hence the world was for me divided into three parts: one in which I, the slave, lived under laws which had been invented only for me and which I could, I did not know why, never completely comply with; then a second world, which was infinitely remote from mine, in which you lived, concerned with government, with the issuing of orders and with the annoyance about their not being obeyed; and finally a third world where everybody else lived happily and free from orders and from having to obey.[7]

In 'The Judgement' these three parts correspond to: the domestic in which a tyrannical father holds sway; the city, which offers an alternative mode of governance to that of the father, but which is still haunted by an archaic patriarchal power; and Kafka's 'faint' or 'weak' (*schwach*) utopia, which is a third space (like that sought by Miriam) beyond both.

Kafka uses the term *schwach* for his own masculine self in 'Letter to His Father'.[8] Georg has just finished writing a letter to a friend in St Petersburg and the letter represents what might be described as a 'weak' transaction between two businessmen in two European cities. Georg's friend is cut off from social interaction or 'traffic': 'he had no regular connection with the colony of his fellow countrymen out there, but also almost no social intercourse [*Verkehr*] with native families'.[9]

In Georg's fantasy, for his friend to return home would be to expose himself to public humiliation: 'to come back home and be always gaped at by everyone as the one who came back'.[10] In contrast, Georg's successful masculinity is produced through his successful transactions within the public sphere. The friend's failure is sustained by Georg's reticence with him. He attempts to cordon him off from a public life: 'one could not send him any real news'.[11] As Georg's own public life has expanded he has endeavoured: 'to leave undisturbed the idea of the home town which his friend must have built up to his own content during the long interval'.[12] As if to underline the successful balance between public and private Georg has achieved, or feels he has achieved, he is greeted through the window by a passing acquaintance, a greeting he only just acknowledges with 'an absent smile'.[13]

The second threshold in the story is between Georg's room and his father's. In contrast to Georg's room, the father's room is dark, overlooking interior not exterior space, a narrow courtyard, the window shut. Since his mother's death Georg's relations or 'traffic' with his father have been entirely public and commercial: 'he dealt with [*verkehrte mit*] his father daily at business'.[14] They eat together in public, taking their midday meal 'at the same time in an eating house'.[15] Georg has not entered his father's private room for months. In the evenings, they sit in their own rooms reading their own newspapers. Newspapers function in the text to figure the public sphere. Read in their 'common living room', each paper ties the private life of father and son to a public world. They may be two different papers. Christoph Stölzl details two German newspapers, which it might be possible to associate with each generation: the father perhaps reading the older, more established *Bohemia*, Georg reading the newer *Prager Tagblatt*, which prided itself on its financial pages, something which, according to Stölzl, made it indispensable for Jewish businessmen in Bohemia.[16] Yet, the father's connection with public life is, both literally and metaphorically, an oblique one. He reads the newspaper 'held to one side before his eyes in an attempt to overcome a defect of vision'.[17] His view of the commercial public sphere is also obscured: 'There's many a thing done in the business I'm not aware of.'[18] Later, as the father becomes a more threatening figure, his newspaper seems to grow in size, as if to emphasise his growing public power.[19]

The father's startling question, 'Do you really have this friend in St Petersburg?', challenges Georg's apparently stable balance between public and private. It works because it upsets the whole constellation of social relations Georg has established to construct a public masculinity. When Walter Benjamin writes that the father 'throws off a cosmic burden' (see Chapter 4), he eschews a narrow psychoanalytic approach and recognises that Kafka was writing not of the self-evidence of the law of the father but of the rerouting of masculinity through the complex social relations of modernity. These relations are unimaginable outside the context of the modern city. In response to his father's aggression, it is Georg who attempts to repress the public construction of his identity, suddenly offering to close down the business and to take his father into his new home with his bride-to-be. His father's ravings, by contrast, reveal one after another the transactions between private and public spheres that create what Adorno calls Kafka's 'parabolic system without a key', a phrase that is reminiscent of Adorno's description of theoretical thought as a constellation in *Negative Dialectics*:

> As a constellation, theoretical thought circles the concept it would like to unseal, hoping that it may fly open like the lock of a well-guarded safe deposit box: in response not to a single key or a single number, but to a combination of numbers.[20]

In the same way, the father utters a sequence of claims and threats, the combination of which, rather than any single one, drives Georg to his death. The father attacks his son's sense of himself as a successful businessman: 'I've established a fine connection with your friend and I have your customers here in my pocket.' He puts in doubt Georg's forthcoming marriage, the event that has precipitated this crisis: 'Just take your bride on your arm and try getting in my way! I'll sweep her from your very side, you don't know how!' The son's construction of himself through his friend's abjection is undermined by his father's declaration of his relations with his other: 'He knows it already, you stupid boy, he knows it all! I've been writing to him, for you forgot to take my writing things away from me.' More threatening than anything else is the father's apparent lack of concern for public life: ' "Do you think I concern myself with anything else? Do you think I read my newspapers? Look!" and he threw Georg a newspaper sheet which he had somehow taken to bed with him. An old newspaper, with a name entirely unknown to Georg.'

It is this combination of connections – the traffic between cities, marriage as a transaction, writing as a transaction and the old newspaper, representative of some public sphere the son has not even connected with – that provoke Georg's tragi-comic reaction to his father's sentence, death by drowning. Together, they take apart his 'context of living'. As if to emphasise this, his flight takes him over several thresholds, from his father's room, from inside to outside, 'across the roadway', and only then into his leap over the railings: 'Already he was grasping at the railings as a starving man clutches food. He swung himself over.'

Georg's plunge to his death is a paradoxical celebration of failure.[21] But what Adorno calls Kafka's 'expression through repudiation'[22] (see Chapter 5) can be read as a dissection of masculinity, the success or failure of which is dependent on a constellation of social relations, which holds in place the traffic between public and private spheres that make up modern, urban, gendered subjectivities. Moving from Gissing's naturalism to the embodied modernism of Richardson and Joyce to Kafka's more abstract and opaque parables suggests that the production of masculinities in as canonical a modernist as Franz Kafka has to be read in relation to the social relations that allow their staging in the material and imaginative spaces of the early twentieth-century city. His work should not be confined to narrow co-ordinates of the Freudian family or the individual psyche, but its metaphors rerouted through the transformed public sphere described by Negt and Kluge and which figures so prominently in early twentieth-century European literature. Of the other writers discussed in this book: Gissing may not have grasped the aesthetic opportunities they offered, but he at least recognised the formation of new counterpublics even while he opposed them; Joyce draws his material directly from the streets; while Richardson's experiment, still underestimated, amounts to a theorisation of the potential inherent in a transformed public sphere for producing new gendered subjectivities like that embodied in Miriam Henderson.

Thus, if Kafka's work seems, at least on first impression, to be concerned primarily with the private and the interior, the centrality of thresholds to his fiction argues otherwise, and a comparison with other modernist writers suggests that a public sphere as the other side of private life is always implied. Mapping modernist masculinities requires not just a move from private to public sphere, but that there be 'an endless stream of traffic' between the two.

Notes

Preface

1. Lane argues against social constructionism that sexual desire 'is not *constructed* as such, but is instead the point of identificatory *failure*'. Psychoanalysis 'alone grasps the "internal difficulties" – the lapses, fault lines, and blind spots – that desire inevitably fosters'. Christopher Lane, *The Burdens of Intimacy: Psychoanalysis and Victorian Masculinity* (University of Chicago Press, 1999), p. xiii.
2. Walter Benjamin, *The Arcades Project*, trans. H. Eiland and K. McLaughlin (Cambridge, MA: Belknap Press, 1999), [N1, 6] p. 458.
3. 'The painfully acquired techniques of significant *dis*connection are relocated, with the help of the special insensitivity of the trained and assured technicists, as the merely technical modes of advertising and commercial cinema. The isolated, estranged images of alienation and loss, the narrative discontinuities, have become the easy iconography of the commercials, and the lonely, bitter, sardonic and sceptical hero takes his ready-made place as star of the thriller.' Raymond Williams, *The Politics of Modernism: Against the New Conformists*, ed. T. Pinkney (London: Verso, 1989), p. 35.
4. Siegfried Gideon, *Bauen in Frankreich* (1928), cited in Benjamin, *The Arcades Project*, [G2, 3], p. 175.
5. Franco Moretti, 'The Spell of Indecision', *New Left Review*, 164 (July/August 1987), 28.
6. Andreas Huyssen, 'Introduction', *After the Great Divide: Modernism, Mass Culture, Postmodernism* (Bloomington: Indiana University Press, 1986), p. vii.
7. See Kevin Dettmar and Stephen Watts (eds), *Marketing Modernisms: Self-Promotion, Canonization, Rereading* (Ann Arbor: University of Michigan Press, 1996); Lawrence Rainey, *Institutions of Modernism: Literary Elites and Public Culture* (New Haven: Yale University Press, 1998); Paul Delany, *Literature, Money and the Market* (Basingstoke: Palgrave, 2002); and Gail McDonald, 'Product Placement: Literary Modernism and Crisco', *Modernist Cultures* (forthcoming 2006).
8. John Carey, *The Intellectuals and the Masses: Pride and Prejudice among the Literary Intelligentsia 1880–1939* (London: Faber, 1992), p. 21.

9 Michael Tratner, *Modernism and Mass Politics: Joyce, Woolf, Eliot, Yeats* (Stanford University Press, 1995).
10 Eric Hobsbawm, *The Age of Empire* (London: Weidenfeld and Nicolson, 1987), pp. 219–242.
11 Perry Anderson, 'Modernity and Revolution', *New Left Review*, 144 (March–April 1984), p. 104.
12 John Xiros Cooper, *Modernism and the Culture of Market Society* (Cambridge University Press, 2004), p. 192.
13 See Perry Anderson, 'Renewals', *New Left Review*, 1 (January–February 2000), 5–24; and Timothy Bewes and Jeremy Gilbert, 'Politics After Defeat', Introduction to T. Bewes and J. Gilbert (eds), *Cultural Capitalism* (London: Lawrence and Wishart, 2000).
14 Karl Marx, 'Theses on Feuerback', in *Karl Marx: Early Writings*, (Harmondsworth: Penguin, 1975), p. 421.

Introduction

1 George Gissing, *The Nether World* [1889] (Brighton: Harvester, 1974), p. 31.
2 Ibid., p. 56.
3 Ibid., p. 23.
4 Ibid.
5 On the New Woman see Lucy Bland, *Banishing the Beast: English Feminism and Sexual Morality, 1885–1914* (London: Penguin, 1995); Linda Dowling 'The Decadent and the New Woman in the 1890s', *Nineteenth Century Fiction*, 33, 4 (March 1979), 177–186; Bridget Elliot, 'New and Not so "New Women" on the London Stage: Audrey Beardsley's Yellow Book Images of Mrs Patrick Campbell and Réjane', *Victorian Studies*, 31 (Autumn 1987) 33–57; Ann Heilmann, *Feminist Forerunners: New Womanism and Feminism in the Early Twentieth Century* (London: Rivers Oram, 2003); Sally Ledger, *The New Woman: Fiction and Feminism at the Fin de Siècle* (Manchester University Press, 1997); Jill Liddington and Jill Norris *One Hand Tied Behind Us: The Rise of the Women's Suffrage Movement* (London: Virago, 1978); Patricia Marks, *Bicycle, Bangs and Bloomers* (Lexington: Kentucky University Press, 1990); Lisa Tickner, *The Spectacle of Women: Imagery of the Suffrage Campaign 1907–14* (London: Chatto & Windus, 1987); and Martha Vicinus *Independent Women: Work and Community for Single Women, 1850–1920* (London: Virago, 1985).
6 For an excellent discussion of the cultural significance of the Victorian barmaid see Peter Bailey, 'Parasexuality and Glamour: The Victorian Barmaid as Cultural Prototype', *Gender and History*, 2, 2 (Summer 1990), 148–172.
7 For more discussion of London's public culture see Part III, 'Cities', below.
8 Gissing, *The Nether World*, p. 30.
9 Ibid., p. 31
10 Ibid., p. 33.

11 On gender and the public sphere see David Glover and Cora Kaplan, *Genders* (London: Routledge, 2000), pp. 125–156.
12 This term is taken from Miriam Hansen, 'The Mass Production of the Senses: Classical Cinema as Vernacular Modernism', *Modernism/Modernity* 6, 2 (1999), 59–77. Hansen argues for 'a wider notion of the aesthetic, one that situates artistic practices within a larger history and economy of sensory perception . . . cultural practices that both articulated and mediated the experience of modernity, such as the mass-produced and mass-consumed phenomena of fashion, design, advertising, architecture and urban environment' (p. 60).
13 Virginia Woolf, *Night and Day* (London: Grafton, 1978), p. 399.
14 Dorothy Richardson, *Interim, Pilgrimage* II, (London: Virago, 1979), pp. 382–385.
15 Richardson, *Revolving Lights, Pilgrimage* III, (London: Virago, 1979), p. 276.
16 Ken Hirschkop writes that intersubjectivity is 'elaborated cooperatively among subjects, and the roles assigned to the *I* or the *other* in this process are not fixed . . . An intersubjectivity with these options is one which makes history in a discriminating fashion. It does not endorse every claim to symbolic authority, no matter what its substance, nor does it accept every narrative shaping of words or actions which subjects have to offer. It picks and chooses and often says no.' Ken Hirschkop, *Mikhail Bakhtin: An Aesthetic for Democracy* (Oxford University Press, 1999), p. 263.
17 See Raymond Williams, *The Politics of Modernism: Against the New Conformists*, ed. T. Pinkney (London: Verso, 1989), p. 34. See Chapter 12 below.
18 See J. Dollimore and A. Sinfield (eds), *Political Shakespeare: New Essays in Cultural Materialism* (Manchester University Press, 1985), pp. vii–viii, 2–3.
19 Rita Felski, 'Modernist Studies and Cultural Studies: Reflections on Method', *Modernism/modernity*, 10, 3 (September 2003), 511. It might be more accurate to add here that the political import of a text cannot be inferred *just* from its internal form or logic, as Felski goes on to suggest that cultural studies pays more attention to formal questions than is usually recognised. Felski's key examples of 'cultural studies' are: B. Singer, *Melodrama and Modernity: Early Sensational Cinema and its Contexts* (New York: Columbia University Press, 2001); Laura L. Doan, *Fashioning Sapphism* (New York: Columbia University Press, 2001); and L. Conor, *The Spectacular Modern Woman* (Bloomington: Indiana University Press, 2004). Exemplary studies that employ a cultural materialist approach would include Jonathan Dollimore, *Sexual Dissidence: Augustine to Wilde, Freud to Foucault* (Oxford University Press, 1991) and Judith Walkowitz, *City of Dreadful Delight: Narratives of Sexual Danger in Late-Victorian London* (London: Virago, 1992).
20 The teashops were also the site of economic struggles. Lyons' waitresses went on strike over a reduction in their rate of commission in 1895 and again over

union recognition in 1920: see Peter Bird, *The First Food Empire: A History of J. Lyons & Co.* (Chichester: Phillimore, 2000), pp. 45, 110–111. Reports of the Aereated Bread Company in *The Times* record examples of prosecutions for customers who left without paying and theft of food by workers at the ABC factory in the Camden Road. See: 'An Unpaid "A.B.C." Meal', *The Times*, 21 February 1919, p. 7; Issue 42030; col. E; and 'Thefts By "A.B.C." Workers', *The Times*, 24 February 1919, p. 6; Issue 42032; col. C.

21 Arnold Bennett, *The Author's Craft*, ed. S. Hynes (Lincoln: University of Nebraska Press, 1968), p. 7. My thanks to Meirion Owen for pointing out this passage to me.

22 Raymond Williams, *Marxism and Literature* (Oxford University Press, 1977), pp. 121–127.

23 On the cultural history of masculinity see: George Mosse, *The Image of Man: The Creation of Modern Masculinity* (Oxford University Press, 1996); and Glover and Kaplan, *Genders*.

24 Peter Dews, *Logics of Disintegration: Post-structuralist Thought and the Claims of Critical Theory* (London: Verso, 1986), p. 228.

25 Ibid., p. 228.

26 Jessica Benjamin, *The Bonds of Love: Psychoanalysis, Feminism and the Problem of Domination* (New York: Pantheon, 1988), p. 181.

27 This is what John Xiros Cooper calls 'the urbanization of consciousness', *Modernism and the Culture of Market Society*, p. 171.

28 On the 'law of the father' see Jacques Lacan, *Ecrits: A Selection*, trans. A. Sheridan (New York: Norton, 1977), p. 199, and also Kaja Silverman, *Male Subjectivity at the Margins*, (New York: Routledge, 1992), pp. 35–42.

29 Toril Moi, *What Is a Woman?* (Oxford University Press, 1999), p. 63.

30 Ibid., p. 65.

31 Ibid., p. 197.

32 On Victorian masculinities see Herbert Sussman, *Victorian Masculinities: Manhood and Masculine Poetics in Early Victorian Literature and Art* (Cambridge University Press, 1995); Donald E. Hall (ed.), *Muscular Christianity* (Cambridge University Press, 1994); and James Eli Adams, *Dandies and Desert Saints: Styles of Victorian Masculinity* (Ithaca and London: Cornell University Press, 1995).

33 Eve Kosofsky Sedgwick, *Between Men: English Literature and Homosocial Desire* (New York: Columbia University Press, 1985). Sedgwick gives an account of these institutions largely based on literary evidence. See for example her account of the Victorian class system, pp. 172–179. For a more historically grounded account see Regenia Gagnier, *Subjectivities: A History of Self-representation in Britain, 1832–1920* (Oxford University Press, 1991), particularly chapter 5, 'The Making of Middle-Class Identities: School and Family', pp. 171–219.

34 Alan Sinfield has convincingly challenged any link between effeminacy and same-sex relations between men in Britain until the Wilde trial in 1895. See Sinfield, *The Wilde Century: Effeminacy, Oscar Wilde, and the*

Queer Moment (New York: Columbia University Press, 1994); see also David Alderson, *Mansex Fine: Religion, Manliness and Imperialism in Nineteenth-century British Culture* (Manchester University Press, 1998). However, Matt Cook argues that, although 'a problematic and imprecise signifier of homosexuality', effeminacy 'was used repeatedly in descriptions of men who had sex with other men' (*London and the Culture of Homosexuality, 1885–1914* (Cambridge University Press, 2003) p. 8). It is probably important to distinguish between effeminacy and the feminine. Effeminacy may have been an imprecise signifier, but 'feminine' always signified subordinate to masculine.

35 Perhaps the best approach to the sex/gender question is to treat it always as a problem, rather than an answer, much as Fredric Jameson suggests the base/superstructure opposition should be treated in Marxist theory.

36 This overload was also noted by Georg Simmel and Siegfried Kracauer. See Singer, *Melodrama and Modernity*, chapter 4, 'Making Sense of the Modernity Thesis', pp. 101–131.

37 Walter Benjamin, 'On Some Motifs in Baudelaire' [1940], in *Selected Writings* Vol. 4: 1938–40, eds H. Eiland and M. Jennings (Cambridge, MA: Belknap Press, 2003), pp. 313–355 (p. 319). See also Andrew Benjamin, 'Tradition and Experience: Walter Benjamin's "On Some Motifs in Baudelaire"', in Andrew Benjamin (ed.), *The Problems of Modernity: Adorno and Benjamin* (London: Routledge, 1989), pp. 129–139.

38 Conversely, Benjamin's *The Arcades Project* mimics the shock effect of *Erlebnis* in its form, demanding that the reader responds in a reflective, considered and creative manner. See Peter Buse, Ken Hirschkop, Scott McCracken and Bertrand Taithe, *Benjamin's Arcades: An Unguided Tour* (Manchester University Press, 2006).

39 Benjamin, *The Arcades Project*, trans. H. Eiland and K. McLaughlin (Cambridge, MA: Belknap Press, 1999), [C3, 3] p. 88. Elsewhere in *The Arcades Project* Benjamin distinguishes the threshold from the boundary as point of transformation, [O2a, 1], p. 494.

1 George Gissing, urban modernity and modernism

1 See Joseph Allen Boone, *Libidinal Currents: Sexuality and the Shaping of Modernism* (University of Chicago Press, 1998).

2 Williams asks why nineteenth-century realists like 'Gogol, Flaubert or Dickens', who 'devised and organized a whole vocabulary and its structure of figures of speech with which to grasp the unprecedented social forms of the industrial city', or the Impressionists of the 1860s, who 'defined a new vision and a technique to match in their rendering of modern Parisian life', are not included as modernists with writers like Proust, Kafka and Joyce or the post-Impressionists and Cubists. Williams's definition of the boundaries of modernism makes the point about the difficulty of marking the break, because many critics (including myself) would include Flaubert and the

Impressionists amongst the early modernists. There is a strong argument to be made that modernism begins earlier in France than in England with Baudelaire and Flaubert, but Williams's key point is of a continuing response to urban modernity 'without Dickens no Joyce': *The Politics of Modernism: Against the New conformists*, ed. T. Pinkney (London: Verso, 1989), p. 32.

3 See Sally Ledger, *The New Woman: Fiction and Feminism at the Fin de Siècle* (Manchester University Press, 1997); Ann Ardis, *New Women, New Novels: Feminism and Early Modernism* (New Brunswick: Rutgers University Press, 1990), *Modernism and Cultural Conflict, 1880–1922* (Cambridge University Press, 2002); and Ann Heilmann, *New Woman Fiction: Women Writing First-wave Feminism* (London: Macmillan, 2000). Also Sandra Gilbert and Susan Gubar, *No Man's Land: The Place of the Woman Writer in the Twentieth Century*, 3 vols (New Haven: Yale University Press, 1987–94); Rita Felski, *The Gender of Modernity* (Cambridge, MA: Harvard University Press, 1995); Lyn Pykett, *Engendering Fictions: the English Novel in the Early Twentieth Century* (London: Edward Arnold, 1995); and Bonnie Kime Scott, *Refiguring Modernism* (Bloomington: Indiana University Press, 1995).

4 For two recent accounts of Gissing that see him as a proto-modernist, see Martin Ryle and Kate Soper, *To Relish the Sublime: Cultural Self-realization In Postmodern Times* (London: Verso, 2002), pp. 164–165, and Martin Ryle, '"To Show a Man of Letters": Gissing, Cultural Authority and Literary Modernism', in M. Ryle and J. Bourne Taylor (eds), *George Gissing, 1903–2003 Voices of the Unclassed* (Aldershot: Ashgate, 2005), pp. 119–132.

5 Raymond Williams, *Culture and Society* (Harmondsworth: Penguin, 1963), p. 177.

6 Ibid., p. 179.

7 Ibid., p. 279.

8 Ibid., p. 181.

9 Ibid.

10 Ibid., p. 284.

11 The novel opens: 'It was a bright cold day in April, and the clocks were striking thirteen. Winston Smith, his chin nuzzled into his breast in an effort to escape the vile wind, slipped quickly through the doors of Victory Mansions, though not quickly enough to prevent a swirl of gritty dust from entering along with him' (George Orwell, *1984* (Harmondsworth: Penguin, 1983), p. 7).

12 Ledger, *The New Woman*, especially pp. 162–169.

13 John Goode, *George Gissing, Ideology and Fiction* (London: Vision, 1978), p. 9.

14 Ibid., p. 39. For Lukács, the moment of disruption coincides with the 1848 revolution in France (*Studies in European Realism* (New York: Grosset and Dunlap, 1964), p. 72). As Goode implies, the process was more gradual in England.

15 Goode, *Gissing*, p. 35.

16 Ibid., pp. 45–46.
17 T. W. Adorno, *Negative Dialectics*, trans. E. B. Ashton (London: Routledge & Kegan Paul, 1973), p. 12.
18 Goode, p. 201.
19 Antonio Gramsci, *Prison Notebooks* (London: Lawrence and Wishart, 1971), pp. 5–23.
20 Goode, *Gissing*, p. 201.
21 Ibid.
22 Charles Booth, *Inquiry into the Life and Labour of the People in London* (New York: Augustus M. Kelly, 1969).
23 Goode, *Gissing*, p. 74.
24 Ibid., p. 77.
25 Ibid., p. 80.
26 Ibid., p. 107.
27 Susan Buck-Morss, *Dialectics of Seeing: Walter Benjamin and The Arcades Project* (Cambridge, MA: MIT Press, 1989), pp. 78–80.
28 Fredric Jameson, *The Political Unconscious: Narrative as a Socially Symbolic Act* (London: Methuen, 1981), chapter 1, 'On Interpretation: Literature as Socially Symbolic Act', pp. 17–102.
29 Ibid., p. 186.
30 Ibid., pp. 190–191.
31 Ibid., p. 204.
32 Ibid., pp. 203–204.
33 Ibid., p. 204.
34 Judith Halberstam, *Female Masculinity* (Durham: Duke University Press, 1998).
35 See Gillian Hanscombe, *The Art of Life: Dorothy Richardson and the Development of Feminist Consciousness* (London: Peter Owen, 1982).

2 Dorothy Richardson and New Woman fiction

1 Penny Boumelha *Thomas Hardy and Women: Sexual Ideology and Narrative Form* (Brighton: Harvester, 1982); A. R. Cunningham 'The "New Women Fiction" of the 1890s', *Victorian Studies*, 17, 1 (September 1973), 177–186; Gail Cunningham, *The New Woman and the Victorian Novel* (New York: Barnes and Noble, 1978); Sandra M. Gilbert and Susan Gubar, *No Man's Land Vol. 1: The War of the Words* (New Haven and London: Yale University Press, 1988); Wendell V. Harris, 'Egerton: Forgotten Realist', *Victorian Newsletter*, 33 (Spring 1968), 31–55; Wendell V. Harris, 'John Lane's Keynotes Series and the Fiction of the 1890s', *PMLA*, 83 (October 1968) pp. 1407–1413; Sally Ledger, *The New Woman: Fiction and Feminism at the Fin de Siècle* (Manchester University Press, 1997); Ann Heilmann, *New Woman Fiction: Women Writing First-wave Feminism* (London: Macmillan, 2000), *New Woman Strategies: Sarah Grand, Olive Schreiner, Mona Caird* (Manchester University Press, 2004); Terry Lovell,

Consuming Fiction (London: Verso, 1987); and Lynn Pykett, *The Improper Feminine: The Sensation Novel and the New Woman Writing* (London: Routledge, 1992).

2. See e.g. Scott McCracken, 'A Hard and Absolute Condition of Existence: Reading Masculinity in *Lord Jim*', *The Conradian*, 17, 2 (Spring 1993), 17–38, 'Postmodernism a Chance to Reread?', in Sally Ledger and Scott McCracken (eds), *Cultural Politics at the Fin de Siècle*, (Cambridge University Press, 1995), pp. 267–289; Andrew Michael Roberts, *Conrad and Masculinity* (Basingstoke: Macmillan, 2000).

3. See Scott McCracken, 'A Novel from/on the Margins: George Egerton's *Wheel of God*', in T. Foley, L. Pilkington, S. Ryder and E. Tilley (eds), *Gender and Colonialism* (Galway University Press, 1995), pp. 145–163; and Rosie Miles, 'George Egerton, Bitextuality and Cultural Representation in the 1890s', *Women's Writing*, 3, 3 (1996), 246–248.

4. George Egerton, *Keynotes* (London: Virago, 1983), p. 123.

5. George Egerton, *The Wheel of God* (London: Grant Richards, 1898), p. 68.

6. On the novel's complex ending see Carolyn Burdett, *Olive Schreiner and the Progress of Feminism: Evolution, Gender, Empire* (London: Palgrave, 2001), pp. 31–45; and Lane, *The Burdens of Intimacy*, pp. 116–118.

7. See Ruth First and Ann Scott, *Olive Schreiner* (New York: Schocken, 1980), pp. 119–124.

8. Ibid., p. 185.

9. See Scott McCracken, 'Stages of Sand and Blood: The Performance of Gendered Subjectivity in Olive Schreiner Colonial Allegories', in A. Jenkins and J. John (eds), *Rereading Victorian Fiction* (Basingstoke: Macmillan, 2000), pp. 145–158.

10. Sarah Grand, *The Heavenly Twins* (London: Heinemann, 1893), p. 231.

11. Ledger, *The New Woman*, p. 181.

12. Ibid., p. 194.

13. Miles, 'George Egerton, Bitextuality and Cultural Representation in the 1890s', pp. 244–246.

14. See Sally Ledger, 'The New Woman and the Crisis of Victorianism', in S. Ledger and S. McCracken (eds), *Cultural Politics at the Fin de Siècle* (Cambridge University Press, 1995), pp. 22–44.

15. See also, on this question, Rita Felski, *Beyond Feminist Aesthetics: Feminist Literature and Social Change* (Cambridge, MA: Harvard University Press, 1989).

16. 'While jobs in offices and shops were invariably represented as stifling and narrow for men, for women they were more often seen as a means of escape from the even more restrictive confines of domestic bondage': Peter Bailey, *Popular Culture and Performance in the Victorian City* (Cambridge University Press, 1998), p. 193.

17. See Patricia Marks, *Bicycles, Bangs and Bloomers: The New Woman in the Popular Press* (Lexington: University Press of Kentucky, 1990).

3 Going up in smoke: Mr Richardson

1 Dorothy Richardson, *Pointed Roofs, Pilgrimage* I, (London: Virago, 1979), p. 9.
2 Ibid., pp. 16, 33.
3 Ibid., p. 22.
4 Ibid., p. 26.
5 Ibid., p. 27.
6 Ibid., pp. 27–28.
7 Richardson, *Honeycomb, Pilgrimage* I, (London: Virago, 1979), p. 474.
8 Judith Butler, *Bodies that Matter* (New York: Routledge, 1993), pp. 82–83. See also 'the phallus is a transferable phantasm' (p. 86). This allows her to posit a lesbian sexuality that is not 'only or even primarily structured by the phallus', rather 'the phallus constitutes an ambivalent site of identification and desire that is significantly different from the scene of normative heterosexuality to which it is related' (ibid., p. 85). In Butler's thesis the phallus persists as the trace of the continuing hegemony of masculine power and compulsory heterosexuality, so that the articulation of lesbian sexuality always exists in its shadow, as 'that which is abjected by heterosexist logic' (p. 86). The counter-hegemonic politics she proposes would protest that 'the phallus is but one signifier amongst others in the course of lesbian exchange, neither the originating signifier nor the unspeakable outside' (p. 87).
9 Richardson, *Revolving Lights* [1923], *Pilgrimage* III, (London: Virago, 1979), p. 250.
10 Richardson saw each of the individual 'novels' as a 'chapter' in *Pilgrimage*, which should be treated as one work. See Gillian E. Hanscombe, *Dorothy Richardson and the Development of Feminist Consciousness* (London: Peter Own, 1982), pp. 11–13.
11 For an account of the relationship between smoking and femininity in the period, which describes Richardson's novel as the 'classic story of women's smoking', see Matthew Hilton, 'Consuming the Unrespectable: Smoking and Femininity', in *Smoking and British Popular Culture, 1800–2000: Perfect Pleasures* (Manchester University Press, 2000), pp. 138–161. As will be discussed in Chapter 10, Miriam's identity is more complex than a generalised 'femininity'.
12 Richardson, *Backwater* [1916], *Pilgrimage* I, p. 208.
13 See Chapter 9.
14 Ibid., p. 209.
15 Ibid., pp. 209–210. 'For Sartre, the idea that a cigarette tastes better when you roll it yourself has nothing to do with any intrinsic quality of the object; rather, it has to do with the appropriative – creative act that produces it. Its taste lies more in my hands than in my tongue.' Richard Klein, *Cigarettes Are Sublime* (Durham: Duke University Press, 1993), p. 33.
16 Benjamin, 'Surrealism: The Last Snapshot of the European Intelligentsia', in *Selected Writings Vol. 2: 1927–1934* (Cambridge, MA: Belknap Press,

1999), p. 210. The surrealist slogan called for winning 'the energies of intoxication for the revolution' (p. 216).
17 Richardson, *Backwater*, I, p. 210.
18 Fred Botting, in his incendiary essay on the act of smoking, cites Jacques Derrida, 'the fact that nothing natural remains does not mean, on the contrary, that nothing symbolic remains. The annihilation of the remainder, as ashes can sometimes testify, recalls a part and performs the role of memory': 'The Act of Smoking in an Age of Techno-Moral Consumption', *new formations*, 39 (Winter 1999–2000), p. 83.
19 Klein, *Cigarettes Are Sublime*, p. 38.
20 Ibid., p. 4.
21 Richardson, *Pointed Roofs*, I, p. 185.

4 Fathers and cities

1 See Ann Ardis's excellent reading of masculinities in Lawrence and Lewis in *Modernism and Cultural Conflict, 1880–1922* (Cambridge University Press, 2002), pp. 78–113.
2 Pierre Bourdieu, *Masculine Domination*, trans. Richard Nice (Cambridge: Polity, 2001), pp. 82–83.
3 Benjamin, *Arcades Project*, trans. (H. Eiland and K. McLaughlin, Cambridge, MA: Belknap Press, 1999), [B3, 6], p. 69.
4 See Graeme Gilloch, ' "The Return of the Flaneur": The Afterlife of an Allegory', *new formations*, 38 (Summer 1999), 101–109. This discussion is indebted to Peter Buse and Andrew Stott's introduction to their edited collection, *Ghosts: Deconstruction, Psychoanalysis, History* (London: Palgrave, 1999), pp. 1–20.
5 Franz Kafka, *Collected Stories* (New York: Alfred A. Knopf, 1993), p. 35.
6 Franz Kafka, *Sämtliche Erzählungen*, (Frankfurt: Fischer, 1970), p. 29.
7 Susan Buck-Morss, *Dialectics of Seeing: Walter Benjamin and The Arcades Project* (Cambridge, MA: MIT Press, 1989), pp. 78–80.
8 Walter Benjamin, 'On Some Motifs in Baudelaire', in *Selected Writings Vol. 4: 1938–40* (Cambridge, MA: Belknap Press, 2003), pp. 333–334, translation modified; *Gesammelte Schriften*, vol. 1.2, ed. R. Tiedemann and H. Schweppenhäuser (Frankfurt: Suhrkamp, 1974), pp. 638–639.
9 Benjamin, *The Arcades Project*, [J71a, 5], pp. 355–356.
10 Ibid., p. 356.
11 Benjamin, 'Franz Kafka', in *Selected Writings Vol. 2: 1927–1934* (Cambridge, MA: Belknap Press, 1999), p. 796.
12 See Walter Benjamin, *The Origin of German Tragic Drama* (usually now translated as *The Origin of the German Mourning Play*), trans. John Osborne (London: New Left Books, 1977), p. 34. On constellations see Esther Leslie, 'Stars, Phosphor and Chemical Colours Extraterrestiality in *The Arcades*', *new formations*, 54 (Winter 2004/5), 13–27; and Thesis XVIIIA in 'On the Concept of History', *Selected Writings Vol. 4*, p. 397.

13 Walter Benjamin, 'Berlin Chronicle', *Selected Writings, Vol. 2: 1927–1934* (Cambridge, MA: Belknap Press, 1999), p. 596, translation modified; *Gesammelte Schriften*, vol.VI (Frankfurt am Main: Suhrkamp Verlag, 1985), p. 466.
14 Benjamin, 'Berlin Chronicle', p. 614; *Gesammelte Schriften*, vol. VI, p. 490.
15 Ibid., p. 614.
16 Ibid., p. 614, translation modified; *Gesammelte Schriften*, vol. VI (Frankfurt am Main: Suhrkamp Verlag, 1985), p. 490.
17 On Mass Observation see L. Marcus (ed.), special issue of *new formations*, 44, (Autumn 2001); for Benjamin on surrealism see 'Surrealism: The Last Snapshot of the European Intelligentsia', in *Selected Writings Vol. 2: 1927–1934* (Cambridge, MA: Belknap Press, 1999), pp. 207–221.
18 Benjamin, 'Berlin Chronicle', pp. 614–615. Miriam Hansen writes: 'Benjamin undeniably participates in a patriarchal discourse on vision insofar as the auratic gaze depends upon a veil of forgetting, that is, a reflective yet unacknowledged form of fetishism which reinscribes the female body as source of both fascination and threat. In his most obsessive and experimental undoing of that very defense, however, he seems to be seeking a position in relation to vision, to the image and the eye, which has traditionally been assigned to women, as a group historically excluded from scopic mastery.' 'Benjamin, Cinema and Experience: "The Blue Flower in the Land of Technology"', *New German Critique*, 40 (Winter 1987), 215–216.
19 Benjamin, 'Berlin Chronicle', p. 600; *Gesammelte Schriften*, vol. VI, p. 472.
20 Interestingly, Ben Knights argues that it is the text as network that undermines patriarchal authority: *Writing Masculinities* (Basingstoke: Palgrave, 1999), p. 72.

5 On the threshold: Franz Kafka

1 Franz Kafka, 'Letter to His Father', in H. Kiesel (ed.), *Kafka's The Metamorphosis and Other Writings* (New York, London: Continuum, 2002), pp. 209–210.
2 Ibid., p. 210.
3 Elizabeth Boa, *Kafka: Gender, Class, and Race in the Letters and Fictions* (Oxford: Clarendon Press, 1996), p. 111.
4 Christa Bürger and Peter Bürger, *Prosa der Moderne*, (Frankfurt: Suhrkamp, 1988), p. 306.
5 Benjamin, 'Franz Kafka: On the Tenth Anniversary of His Death', in *Selected Writings Vol. 2: 1927–1934* (Cambridge, MA: Belknap Press, 1999), p. 807.
6 Boa, *Kafka*, p. 45.
7 Kafka, 'The Cares of a Family Man', *Collected Stories* (New York: Alfred A. Knopf, 1993), p. 184.
8 Ibid., p. 183.
9 Ibid., pp. 184–185.

10 Mark Anderson, *Kafka's Clothes: Ornament and Aestheticism in the Habsburg Fin de Siècle* (Oxford: Clarendon, 1992), p. 23.
11 Ibid., p. 2.
12 Cultural histories of England in the same period also suggest the importance of fashion for the construction of modernist identities. See Christopher Breward, *The Hidden Consumer: Masculinities, Fashion and City Life 1860–1914* (Manchester University Press, 1999) and Laura Doan, *Fashioning Sapphism: The Origins of a Modern English Lesbian Culture* (New York: Columbia University Press, 2001), especially pp. 95–125.
13 Kafka, 'Letter to His Father', p. 192.
14 Anderson, *Kafka's Clothes*, p. 23.
15 Benjamin's interest in interiors is interesting in this respect. See Convolute 'I', 'The Interior; The Trace', *The Arcades Project* (Cambridge, MA: Belknap Press, 1999), pp. 212–227.
16 Franz Kafka, *The Trial* [1925] (Harmondsworth: Penguin, 1984), p. 123.
17 Ibid., p. 123.
18 Ibid., pp. 123–124.
19 *Verschollene* means 'missing, disappeared, presumed dead' – Kafka's title for the book usually published as *Amerika* was *Der Verschollene*, 'the one who is missing'.
20 As Adorno describes it: 'All of his stories take place in the same spaceless space . . . all of America, however, is incorporated into that space in the image of steerage.' T. W. Adorno, 'Notes on Kafka', in *Prisms* (Cambridge, MA: MIT Press, 1983), p. 256.
21 Ibid., p. 246.
22 Ibid., p. 247.
23 Ibid., p. 246.
24 Walter Benjamin, 'Franz Kafka', *1927–1934*, p. 796.
25 Walter Benjamin, 'Notes from Svendborg, Summer 1934', in *Selected Writings Vol. 2: 1927–1934* (Cambridge, MA: Belknap Press, 1999), p. 787. See also Benjamin's letter to Gershom Scholem of 12 June 1938, in *Walter Benjamin Selected Writings Vol. 3: 1935–1938* (Cambridge, MA: Belknap Press, 2002), p. 325.

6 Journeys through the city: James Joyce

1 James Joyce, *A Portrait of the Artist as a Young Man* [1916] (New York: Signet, 1991), p. 103.
2 T. W. Adorno, 'Reconciliation under Duress', in E. Bloch et al., *Aesthetics and Politics: Debates between Bloch, Lukács, Brecht, Benjamin, Adorno* (London: Verso, 1980), pp. 158–159.
3 Joyce, *A Portrait of the Artist as a Young Man*, p. 76.
4 Ibid.
5 Mark Anderson, *Kafka's Clothes: Ornament and Aestheticism in the Habsburg Fin de Siècle* (Oxford: Clarendon Press, 1992), p. 23.

6 Joyce, *A Portrait of the Artist as a Young Man*, p. 76.
7 Ibid.
8 On Joyce's relationship with Wilde see Margot Norris, 'A Walk on the Wild(e) Side: The Doubled Reading of "An Encounter"' and Jean-Michel Rabaté, '"On Joycean and Wildean Sodomy"' in J. Valente (ed.), *Quare Joyce* (Ann Arbor: University of Michigan Press, 2000), pp. 19–33, 35–44.
9 Benjamin, 'Berlin Chronicle', p. 614.
10 Joyce, *A Portrait of the Artist as a Young Man*, p. 89.
11 See James Joyce, *Ulysses* [1922] (London: The Bodley Head, 1993), pp. 73, 79–80, 91, 124, 137, 357–358, 497.
12 Joyce, *A Portrait of the Artist as a Young Man*, p. 107.
13 George Gissing, *Demos: A Story of English Socialism*, (Brighton: Harvester, 1982), p. 26.
14 Joyce, *A Portrait of the Artist as a Young Man*, p. 108.
15 Ibid. See Steve Watts, 'The Construction of the Artist as a Young Man: Masculinity in Joyce's *A Portrait*', unpublished paper, 1985.
16 On the significance of the urban walk in modernist fiction see Deborah Parsons, *Streetwalking the Metropolis: Women, the City and Modernity* (Oxford University Press, 2000); and Tamar Katz, *Impressionist Subjects* (Urbana: University of Illinois Press, 2000), pp. 152–157.
17 Joyce, *A Portrait of the the Artist as a Young Man*, p. 222.
18 Ibid.
19 'She was a figure of the womanhood of her country': ibid., p. 223.
20 Ibid., p. 221.
21 See Parsons, *Streetwalking the Metropolis*, p. 76.
22 Joyce, *Ulysses*, p. 170.
23 In 'Lotus Eaters': 'From me. Just a chance. Must have been that morning in Raymond terrace she was at the window watching the two dogs at it by the wall of the cease to do evil. And the sergeant grinning up. She had that cream gown on with the rip she never stiched. Give us a touch Poldy. God, I'm dying for it. How life begins.' Joyce, *Ulysses*, pp. 73–74; and in 'Lestrygonians': 'Swish and soft flop her stays made on the bed. Always warm from her. Always liked to let herself out. Sitting there till near two taking out her hairpins. Milly tucked up in beddyhouse. Happy. Happy. That was the night' (p. 128).
24 A striking example of this retrospective writing of the father–son relationship is the young Patrick Dignam's sense of its confirmation in the newspaper report of his father's death: 'Do they notice I'm in mourning? Uncle Barney said he'd get it into the paper tonight. Then they'll all see it in the paper and read my name printed and pa's name' (Joyce, *Ulysses*, p. 206).
25 Ibid., p. 170.
26 Ibid, p. 156.
27 For a fascinating psychoanalytic account of Miriam's relationship to her mother see Jean Radford, *Dorothy Richardson* (Hemel Hempstead: Harvester Wheatsheaf, 1991), pp. 86–105.

28 The two pioneering works of criticism on *Pilgrimage* were: Gloria Fromm, *Dorothy Richardson: A Biography* (Urbana: Illinois University Press, 1977); Gillian Hanscombe, *The Art of Life: Dorothy Richardson and the Development of Feminist Consciousness* (London: Peter Owen, 1982). For more recent work see Jean Radford, *Dorothy Richardson* (Hemel Hempstead: Harvester Wheatsheaf, 1991); Carol Watts, *Dorothy Richardson* (London: Northcote House, 1995); Kristen Bluemel, *Experimenting on the Borders of Modernism: Dorothy Richardson's Pilgrimage* (Athens: University of George Press, 1997); Tamar Katz, *Impressionist Subjects: Gender, Interiority, and Modernist Fiction in England* (Urbana: University of Illinois Press, 2000), pp. 138–168; and Jane Garrity, *Step-daughters of England: British Women Modernists and the National Imaginary* (Manchester University Press, 2003), pp. 85–139. Perhaps the most outstanding piece of Richardson criticism is Joanne Winning, *The Pilgrimage of Dorothy Richardson* (London, Madison: University of Wisconsin Press, 2000).

7 Bodily innervation: food, eating and the everyday

1 George Gissing, *The Nether World* [1889] (Brighton: Harvester, 1974), pp. 30–31.
2 On window displays, see Ben Highmore, *Cityscapes: Cultural Readings in the Material and Symbolic City* (Basingstoke: Palgrave Macmillan, 2005), pp. 45–53.
3 Franz Kafka, *The Trial* (Harmondsworth: Penguin, 1984), p. 7.
4 Ibid., p. 11.
5 Ibid., p. 12.
6 'Bones mustn't be cracked with the teeth, but you could. Vinegar must not be sipped noisily, but you could. The main thing was that the bread should be cut straight. But it didn't matter that you did it with the knife dripping with gravy. Care had to be taken that no scraps fell on the floor. In the end it was under your chair that there were most scraps. At table one wasn't allowed to do anything but eat, but you cleaned and cut your fingernails, sharpened pencils, cleaned your ears with a toothpick.' Kafka, 'Letter to His Father', pp. 182–183.
7 Walter Benjamin, 'Franz Kafka, On the Tenth Anniversary of His Death', *Selected Writings, Vol. 2: 1927–1934* (Cambridge, MA: Belknap Press, 1999), p. 796.
8 James Joyce, *Ulysses* (London : Bodley Head, 1993), p. 45.
9 Ibid., p. 56.
10 Ibid., p. 130.
11 Marcel at one point attributes the anguish he experiences at the end of his relationship with Gilberte to his intake of caffeine: *In Search of Lost Time II: Within a Budding Grove*, trans. C. K. Scott Moncrieff, T. Kilmartin, D. J. Enright (London: Vintage, 2002), pp. 181, 215.

12 Tim Armstrong comments: 'Modernism is ... characterized by the desire to intervene in the body, to render it part of modernity by techniques which may be biological, mechanical or behavioural.' *Modernism, Technology and the Body: A Cultural Study* (Cambridge University Press, 1998), p. 6.
13 The origin of the term is medical, where 'innervation' means the supply of nerve-force to some organ by means of the nerves. In the work of Freud, it can refer to internal, psychic excitation that has a bodily manifestation, or, as in the case of war trauma, external shock, which can also result in the paralysis or reduction of other psychical functions: Miriam Bratu Hansen, 'Benjamin and Cinema: Not a One-Way Street', *Critical Inquiry*, 25, 2 (Winter 1999), 316–317.
14 Ibid., 317.
15 Walter Benjamin, 'A Berlin Chronicle', *Selected Writings Vol. 2: 1927–1934* (Cambridge, MA: Belknap Press, 1999), pp. 217–218.
16 Hansen, 'Benjamin and Cinema', 325.
17 Ibid., p. 321.
18 Ibid., p. 332.
19 Joyce, *Ulysses*, pp. 144–145.
20 Miriam Hansen, '"Room-for-Play": Benjamin's Gamble with Cinema', *October*, 109, 1 (Summer 2004), 3–45. Benjamin uses the term in relation to Kafka's modernism: 'Kafka's gestures of horror are well served by the glorious *Spielraum* of which the catastrophe will know nothing.' Letter to Gerschom Scholem, in *Walter Benjamin Selected Writings Vol. 3: 1935–1938* (Cambridge, MA: Belknap Press, 2002), p. 326.
21 Cited in Frank Budgen, *James Joyce and the Making of Ulysses* (London: Grayson and Grayson, 1934), p. 21. 'Lestrygonians' is discussed in detail in Chapter 12 below.
22 For an extension of this argument about Benjamin and the everyday see Scott McCracken, 'The Completion of Old Work: Walter Benjamin and the Everyday', *Cultural Critique*, 52 (Fall 2002), 145–166.
23 Walter Benjamin, *The Arcades Project* (Cambridge, MA: Belknap Press, 1999), [O2a, 1], p. 494.
24 Two exceptions to this tendency are Diane E. McGee, *Writing the Meal: Dinner in the Fiction of Early Twentieth-century Women Writers* (University of Toronto Press, 2001), which focuses on the symbolics of the meal; and Tim Armstrong's study *Modernism, Technology and the Body: A Cultural Study* cited above.
25 Terry Eagleton, 'Edible Ecriture', in S. Griffiths and J. Wallace (eds), *Consuming Passions: Food in the Age of Anxiety* (Manchester: Mandolin, 1998), p. 207.
26 See Claude Lévi-Strauss, *The Raw and the Cooked*, trans. J. and D. Weightman (New York: Harper & Row, 1969); and Mary Douglas, *Food in the Social Order: Studies of Food and Festivities in Three American Communities* (New York: Russell Sage Foundation, 1984).

27 Deborah Lupton, *Food, the Body and the Self* (London: Sage, 1996), p. 9.
28 McGee, *Writing the Meal*.

8 George Gissing and the cultural politics of food

1 The full theorisation of the distinction between systems and life-worlds can be found in Jürgen Habermas, *The Theory of Communicative Action*, trans. T. McCarthy (Cambridge, MA: MIT Press, 1984). For a summary and explanation of the arguments see Jürgen Habermas, 'The Dialectics of Rationalization', in *Autonomy and Solidarity: Interviews* (London: Verso, 1986). On system versus life-worlds, see pp. 105–117.
2 See Elspeth Probyn, *Carnal Appetites: FoodSexIdentities* (London: Routledge, 2000), for an exploration of the meaning of food in contemporary culture.
3 See Peter Bird, *The First Food Empire: A History of J. Lyons and Co.* (Chichester: Phillimore, 2000), pp. 2–11. Ben Highmore, *Cityscapes: Cultural Readings in the Material and Symbolic City* (Basingstoke: Palgrave Macmillan, 2005), pp. 45–69.
4 'As a visual field, modernity marked an era in which industrialized and commodified image production provided a new way to articulate sexual difference. Although this articulation reinforced the status of the woman-object, it also opened up new cultural spaces for women to occupy. Women were enjoined to make themselves in the image of feminine spectacles they encountered, which produced new meanings of their visibility, such as social, political and sexual agency. The very spectacularization of women which reiterated their object status also encouraged and sometimes explicitly instructed women in the techniques of appearing, which enabled them to enact different types of subject position of the modern appearing woman. Through these historical negotiations new ways of seeing and being seen were created for women in the modern scene.' Liz Conor, *The Spectacular Modern Woman: Feminine Visibility in the 1920s* (Bloomington: Indiana University Press, 2004), p. 35.
5 Peter Bailey argues that the Victorian barmaid was 'an assertive and competent modernist', 'Parasexuality and Glamour: The Victorian Barmaid as Cultural Prototype', *Gender and History* 2, 2 (Summer 1990), 165. His analysis of visual representations of the barmaid suggest a similar discomfiture for men: 'the vital role men ascribed to the barmaid in the bidding for, and bestowal of recognition. The considerable emotional investment in the winning of the women's gaze that they signify, suggests strongly the degree of anonymity and competition in the pub crowd that had to be bid against. In consequence men, too, put themselves on display' (p. 163).
6 David Trotter, *Cooking with Mud: The Idea of Mess in Nineteenth-century Art and Fiction* (Oxford University Press, 2000), p. 252.
7 George Gissing, *Thyrza* [1887] (London: Harvester, 1984), p. 37.
8 James describes this distinction as between 'story' and 'discourse', see Simon James, *Unsettled Accounts: Money and Narrative in the Novels of George*

Gissing (London: Anthem, 2003), p. 42; On dialogism see M. M. Bakhtin, 'Discourse in the Novel', in *The Dialogic Imagination* (Austin: University of Texas Press, 1981), pp. 410–411; For a discussion of dialogical speech in Gissing see Fredric Jameson, *The Political Unconscious: Narrative as a Socially Symbolic Act* (London: Methuen, 1981), pp. 202–203.
9 Trotter, *Cooking with Mud*, p. 257.
10 Gissing, *The Nether World*, pp. 5–6.
11 Ibid., p. 6.
12 Patrick Geddes and J. Arthur Thomson, *The Evolution of Sex*, (London: W. Scott, 1889), pp. 87–88.
13 Ibid., p. 125.
14 Ibid., pp. 125–126.
15 Ibid., p. 162. On Freud's take on the relationship between nutrition and desire see Maud Ellmann, *The Hunger Artists: Starving, Writing and Imprisonment* (London: Virago, 1993), pp. 36–39.
16 Olive Schreiner, *Woman and Labour* (London: T. Fisher Unwin, 1911). For an excellent account of Schreiner's relationship to Social Darwinism see Carolyn Burdett, *Olive Schreiner and the Progress of Feminism: Evolution, Gender, Empire* (Basingstoke: Palgrave, 2001), pp. 59–77.
17 Charlotte Perkins Gilman, *Women and Economics* (London: T. Fisher Unwin, 1898), pp. 4–5.
18 In this Gilman followed Thomas Huxley: see his *Evolution and Ethics* [1894] (New York: D. Appleton, 1898).
19 See Stephen Ogden, 'Darwinian Scepticism in George Gissing's *Born in Exile*', in Bouwe Postmus (ed.), *A Garland for Gissing* (Amsterdam: Rodopi, 2001), pp. 171–178.
20 Trotter argues that Clem 'eludes metaphor by the sheer "gusto" with which she attacks her food': *Cooking with Mud*, p. 256.
21 Gissing, *The Nether World*, p. 6.
22 Jane Miller, for example, says that comic moments are 'rare', 'Gloom has always been the quality people have associated with Gissing's novels'. *Seductions: Studies in Reading and Culture* (London: Virago, 1990), p. 96, p. 175, n. 34. John Carey describes a moment of 'broad humour' as unusual: *The Intellectuals and the Masses: Pride and Prejudice among the Literary Intelligentsia 1880–1939* (London: Faber, 1992), p. 95; Fredric Jameson is a rare exception, commenting on the 'electrical dryness' of the later novels' 'wit': *The Political Unconscious*, p. 203.
23 George Gissing, *Demos: A Story of English Socialism* [1886] (Brighton: Harvester, 1982), p. 26.
24 Ellmann, *The Hunger Artists*, p. 36.
25 Trotter, *Cooking with Mud*, p. 253.
26 Mary Douglas, 'Coded Messages', in S. Griffiths and J. Wallace (eds), *Consuming Passions: Food in the Age of Anxiety* (Manchester: Mandolin, 1998), pp. 103–110.
27 Deborah Lupton, *Food, the Body and the Self* (London: Sage, 1996), p. 9.

28 George Gissing, *New Grub Street* [1891] (Harmondsworth, Penguin, 1968), pp. 123–124.
29 The slang term for food and the literary term come from the same root: to 'grub' is to dig either for hack work or for food and of course for the former to get the latter.
30 Gissing, *New Grub Street*, p. 120.
31 Ellmann, *The Hunger Artists*, pp. 18–22. Ellmann writes that in *New Grub Street* Edwin Reardon, 'keeps himself alive by writing, yet also immolates his body with his own prolixity, forfeiting his very substance to the public's greed for three-decker novels' (p. 25).
32 Ibid., p. 22.
33 George Gissing, *Born in Exile*, (London: Nelson, 1910), p. 52.
34 George Gissing, *The Private Papers of Henry Ryecroft* [1903] (Oxford University Press, 1987), p. 29.
35 Gissing, *Thyrza*, p. 383.

9 Smoking and consumption

1 Oscar Wilde, *The Picture of Dorian Gray* [1891] (Harmondsworth: Penguin, 1985), p. 89.
2 Fred Botting, 'The Art of Smoking in an Age of Techno-Moral Consumption', *new formations*, 39 (Winter 1999–2000), 82. According to Richard Klein, the original theorist of smoking's 'futility' was Théodore de Banville. See Richard Klein, *Cigarettes Are Sublime* (Durham: Duke University Press, 1993), p. 22. Klein himself, however, suggests that cigarettes have an expanded utility: 'The Philosopher's example, like most stereotypical representations of the cigarette, systematically discounts its usefulness, even if as [in the case of Sartre], it may have played a determining role in the production of the very philosophical discourse that predicates its inessentiality' (p. 35).
3 Botting, 'The Art of Smoking', p. 84.
4 See Patricia Marks, *Bicycles, Bangs, and Bloomers: The New Woman in the Popular Press* (Lexington: University Press of Kentucky, 1990).
5 See *Punch, Or The London Charivari*, (17 March 1894). Reprinted in Elaine Showalter (ed.), *Daughters of Decadence: Women Writers of the Fin de Siècle* (London: Virago, 1993), pp. 69–73.
6 For a full analysis of *Pilgrimage*'s chronology see George H. Thomson, *A Reader's Guide to Dorothy Richardson's* Pilgrimage (Greensboro, NC: ELT Press, 1996). For Wilde's importance to modernism in Britain and Ireland see Ann L. Ardis, *Modernism and Cultural Conflict: 1880–1922* (Cambridge University Press, 2002), pp. 45–71. She notes 'Wilde's significance for Willa Cather, Katherine Mansfield, and Radcliffe Hall as lesbian writers attempting to find antecedents for their own sexual dissidence . . . and Joyce's interest in Wilde' (pp. 45–46). Wilde's life and work are now considered so important to an historical understanding of English twentieth-century modernity that virtually no cultural study can afford to ignore it.

7 Dorothy Richardson, *Honeycomb*, *Pilgrimage I* (London: Virago, 1979), pp. 434–435.
8 The phrase is Edward Garnett's. See Gloria G. Fromm, *Dorothy Richardson: A Biography* (Urbana: Illinois University Press, 1977), p. 77. It linked her with Conrad's impressionist prose. Conrad's first novel, *Almayer's Folly*, was published in 1895. Richardson recognised him as a profound influence. See *Revolving Lights*, *Pilgrimage* III, (London: Virago, 1979), pp. 275–276.
9 See, for example, Arthur Symons's poem, 'La Mélinite: Moulin Rouge', Wilde's play *Salomé* and Aubrey Beardsley's illustrations for it. Marjorie Garber writes: 'the essence of dances itself, its taboo border-crossing, is not only sensuality, but gender undecidability, and not only gender undecidability, but the paradox of gender identification, the disruptive element that intervenes, transvestisism as a space of possibility, structuring and confounding culture'. *Vested Interests: Cross Dressing and Cultural Anxiety* (New York: Routledge, 1992), p. 324: cited in Tim Armstrong, *Modernism, Technology and the Body: A Cultural Study* (Cambridge University Press, 1998), p. 177.
10 Judith Butler, *Bodies that Matter* (New York: Routledge, 1993), pp. 82–83.
11 Richardson became a chain smoker and was never seen without a cigarette in her hand. She lived to the ripe old age of 84.
12 See, for example, its use about the relationship between Everard and Rhoda in Gissing's *The Odd Women* [1893] (London: Virago, 1980), p. 258.
13 Butler, *Bodies that Matter*, p. 15.
14 Matthew Hilton, *Smoking and British Popular Culture, 1800–2000: Perfect Pleasures* (Manchester University Press, 2000), p. 83. In the USA, rights to the machine were bought by W. Duke Sons and Co.: see Jordan Goodman, *Tobacco in History: The Cultures of Dependence* (London: Routledge, 1993), p. 231.
15 Peter Bird, *The First Food Empire: A History of J. Lyons & Co.* (Chichester: Phillimore, 2000), pp. 6–7. Although this had the effect of depressing prices, it increased sales, so was ultimately in the manufacturer's interest: see Hilton, *Smoking and British Popular Culture*, p. 89.
16 Goodman, *Tobacco in History*, p. 93.
17 On the trials themselves, see Richard Ellmann, *Oscar Wilde* (London: Hamish Hamilton, 1987), pp. 409–449; Ed Cohen, *Talk on the Wilde Side: Towards a Genealogy of a Discourse on Male Sexualities* (London: Routledge, 1993), pp. 126–209; and Matt Cook, *London and the Culture of Homosexuality, 1885–1914* (Cambridge University Press, 2003).
18 On Edward Carpenter's theory of the 'Intermediate Sex', see Edward Carpenter, *Selected Writings Vol. 4* (London: GMP, 1984), pp. 185–244. For further discussion of Miriam's sexual identity see Chapter 16 below.

10 Dietetics and aesthetics

1 'I was cheered this morning by the appearance of two forgotten poems, in *The Queen*, sent ten years ago when Miss B[or R]odye-Smith, who published

my first efforts in the Westminster, was editor.' Letter from Dorothy Richardson to Bryher, 1 January 1933, Box 52, Folder 1921, Beinicke Rare Book and Manuscript Library, Yale University.
2. Dorothy Richardson, 'Review of *In the Days of the Comet*', *The Crank*, 4 (November 1906), 376.
3. Richardson, *Revolving Lights*, *Pilgrimage* III (London: Virago, 1979), p. 257. As an accomplished Germanist, Richardson might have had in mind the word *Stimmung*, which means 'atmosphere', but also mood, morale, opinion, or in a musical context, 'tuning' or 'pitch'.
4. *Queen*, 28 December 1932, 13.
5. I'm grateful to Gillian Hanscombe for pointing out the poem's final double meaning to me.
6. Rita Felski, 'The Invention of Everyday Life', *new formations*, 39 (Winter 1999–2000), 23.
7. Michel de Certeau, Luce Giard, Pierre Mayol, *The Practice of Everyday Life Vol. 2: Living and Cooking* (Minneapolis: University of Minnesota Press, 1998), p. 142.
8. Rose Odle, 'Some Memories of Dorothy M. Richardson and Alan Odle', Talk to the Friday Club, London, 18 November 1957, p. 12, Beinicke Rare Book and Manuscript Library, Yale University.
9. Dorothy Richardson, 'Antheil of New Jersey', *Vanity Fair*, 25 (November 1925), p. 136.
10. On Fletcherism see Tim Armstrong, *Modernism, Technology and the Body: A Cultural Study* (Cambridge University Press, 1998), pp. 42–58.
11. Dorothy Richardson, 'The Reading of "The Jungle"', *Crank*, 4 (September 1906), p. 290.
12. Jo-Ann Wallace, conversation in Kendals department store teashop, Manchester. See her *Edith Ellis: A Cultural Biography* (forthcoming).
13. Dorothy Richardson, Preface to Paul Carson, *Consumption Doomed: A Lecture on the Cure of Tuberculosis*, vol. 4 of *Healthy Life Booklets* (London: C. W. Daniel, 1913), pp. 6–7.
14. Edward Carpenter, *Civilisation: Its Cause and Its Cure* (London: Swan Sonnenschein, 1889), p. 14.
15. Dorothy Richardson, 'The Reality of Feminism', *The Ploughshare*, ns 2 (September 1917), pp. 241–246. *The Tunnel*, *Pilgrimage* II, (London: Virago, 1979), p. 241.
16. See Dorothy Richardson, 'The Queen of Spring', *Focus*, 5 (May 1928), 259–262; and 'Anticipation', *Focus*, 5 (June 1928), 322–325. On electrical treatments see Armstrong, *Modernism, Technology and the Body*, pp. 13–41. Armstrong argues that for modernists 'Even those who wanted to offer the body as the site of authenticity were forced to posit a return to an atavistic substratum which created a temporal discontinuity in their idealizations, a fantasy of primitivism . . . a parade of cures [were] offered for this default: electro-therapy, dietary regimes, eye-therapy, manipulation, hormones, surgery' (p. 3).

17 Under the title of some of the columns there is a disclaimer: 'We do not necessarily endorse these views – ED.'.
18 See Armstrong, *Modernism, Technology and the Body*, p. 9.
19 Dorothy Richardson, 'Comments by a Layman', *Dental Record*, 39 (January 1919), 10–11. The rotting metaphor would of course have had a particular resonance for a dental audience.
20 See Michel Foucault, *The History of Sexuality*, vol. 1, trans. R. Hurley (New York: Pantheon, 1978). For a discussion of Foucault's concept see David Glover, 'Foucault, Sexuality, Liberalism: A Commentary', *new formations*, 55 (Spring 2005), 36–43.
21 See *Dental Record*, 36 (August 1916), 428.
22 Jürgen Habermas, 'The Dialectics of Rationalization', in *Autonomy and Solidarity: Interviews* (London: Verso, 1986), pp. 105–117.
23 Dorothy Richardson, 'Amateur Evidence in Dietetics', *Dental Record*, 36 (June 1916), 300.
24 Ibid.
25 Ibid., p. 301.
26 See Anna Davin, 'Imperialism and Motherhood', *History Workshop*, 5 (Spring 1978), 9–65.
27 Dorothy Richardson, 'Comments by a Layman', *Dental Record*, 39 (February 1919), pp. 57–58.
28 Habermas, 'The Dialectics of Rationalization', p. 106.
29 On Pound's anti-modern modernism see Rebecca Beasley, 'Art as Propaganda for Literary Modernism', *new formations*, 43 (Spring 2001), 117–129.
30 Dorothy Richardson, 'A Spanish Dentist Looks at Spain', *Dental Record*, 38 (1 August 1918), 343–345.
31 Richardson, 'Comments by a Layman', *Dental Record*, 39 (June 1919), 216.
32 Richardson, 'Comments by a Layman', *Dental Record*, 38 (March 1918), 112.
33 Richardson, 'Comments by a Layman', *Dental Record*, 36 (April 1916), 142.
34 Richardson, 'Comments by a Layman', *Dental Record*, 36 (March 1916), 191.
35 Walter Benjamin, *The Arcades Project* (Cambridge, MA: Belknap Press, 1999), [B3, 7], [N3, 2], pp. 69, 463.
36 Dorothy Richardson, 'Cosmic Thinking', Review of Fielding-Hall's *The World Soul*, *Plain Talk*, July 1913, p. 13.
37 Richardson, *Revolving Lights*, *Pilgrimage* III, p. 365.
38 Dorothy Richardson, 'Buns for Tea', *Poetry*, 24 (June 1924), pp. 144–145.

11 Lestrygonians: A Place To Eat

1 See Judith Halberstam, *Female Masculinity* (Durham: Duke University Press, 1998). Quotations from 'Lestrygonians' are from James Joyce, *Ulysses* [1922] (London: The Bodley Head, 1993).

2 John Xiros Cooper argues that a better term for modernist man is the 'Anyman': *Modernism and the Culture of Market Society*, (Cambridge University Press, 2004), p. 165.
3 See Kate Soper, 'Stephen Heroine', in *Troubled Pleasures: Writings on Politics, Gender and Hedonism* (London: Verso, 1995), pp. 246–268, on the gendered limits of Bloom's humanity.
4 Schnitzler's play, *Reigen* in German, dramatises a series of scenes between sexual partners, after which one moves on to a new partner until, to complete the 'round', the final character sleeps with the first. The passing on of infection is implied rather than explicit.
5 'The living body can and should be seen in terms of the interaction of the organs within it, each one having their rhythms but subject to a spatio-temporal whole. Furthermore, this human body is the locus and seat of interaction between the biological, the physiological (nature) and the social (often called the "cultural") and each of these areas, each of these dimensions, has its own specificity, and thus its own space-time: its rhythm. Hence the inevitable shocks (stresses), disorders and disturbances within this whole, whose stability is never absolutely guaranteed.' Henri Lefebvre and Catherine Régulier, quoted in Ben Highmore, *Cityscapes: Cultural Readings in the Material and Symbolic City* (Basingstoke: Palgrave, 2005), p. 147.
6 Bloom's act rehearses the biblical injunction 'Cast thy bread upon the running waters: for after a long time thou shalt find it again', Ecclesiastes 11.1, usually interpreted as the promise that good deed will reap a just reward. In this context, it might be read as: he who feeds shall be fed.
7 Tim Armstrong, *Modernism, Technology and the Body: A Cultural Study* (Cambridge University Press, 1998), p. 65.
8 It is also a reprise of 'he who feeds shall be fed': see note above.
9 See Hansen, 'Room-for-Play': Benjamin's Gamble with Cinema', *October*, 109, 1 (Summer 2004), 44–45.
10 Jürgen Habermas, *Autonomy and Solidarity: Interviews* (London: Verso, 1986), p. 125.

12 Phantasmagoria and the public sphere

1 Dorothy Richardson, *Revolving Lights* [1923], *Pilgrimage* III (London: Virago, 1979), p. 239.
2 George Gissing, *The Nether World* [1889] (Brighton: Harvester, 1974), p. 30.
3 Walter Benjamin, 'Exposé of 1935', *The Arcades Project*, trans. H. Eiland and K. McLaughlin (Cambridge, MA: Belknap Press, 1999), p. 13.
4 Ken Hirschkop, 'The Public Square as Public Sphere', in *Mikhail Bakhtin: An Aesthetic for Democracy* (Oxford University Press, 1999), p. 263.
5 Ibid., p. 267.
6 See Rachel Bowlby, *Just Looking: Consumer Culture in Dreiser, Gissing and Zola* (London: Methuen, 1985), p. 32.
7 Hirschkop, 'The Public Square as Public Sphere', p. 258.

8   The key examples are Raymond Williams, John Goode and Fredric Jameson, all discussed below.
9   Benjamin devotes a whole Convolute to 'Modes of Lighting': Walter Benjamin, *The Arcades Project*, Convolute 'T', pp. 562–570. See also Walter Schivelbusch, *Disenchanted Night: The Industrialisation of Light in the Nineteenth Century*, trans. A. Davies (Oxford: Berg, 1988).
10 Benjamin's Convolute 'R' is titled 'Mirrors', *The Arcades Project*, pp. 537–542.
11 Benjamin described railway stations as 'Dreamhouses of the collective', along with arcades, winter gardens, panoramas, factories, wax museums and casinos: ibid., [L, 1, 3], p. 405.
12 For the fullest study of modernism and mobility see Andrew Thacker, *Moving through Modernity* (Manchester University Press, 2003).
13 See John Xiros Cooper, *Modernism and the Culture of Market Society*, (Cambridge University Press, 2004), p. 87.
14 Dorothy Richardson, *The Tunnel* [1919], *Pilgrimage* II (London: Virago, 1979), p. 74.
15 See Matt Cook, *London and the Culture of Homosexuality, 1885–1914* (Cambridge University Press, 2003), p.23; Peter Bailey, *Popular Culture and Performance in the Victorian City* (Cambridge University Press, 1998), pp. 13–29; Judith R. Walkowitz, *City of Dreadful Delight: Narratives of Sexual Danger in Late-Victorian London* (London: Virago, 1992), particularly chapter 2, 'Contested Terrain: New Social Actors', pp. 41–80.
16 Raymond Williams, *The Politics of Modernism: Against the New Conformists* (London: Verso, 1989), pp. 33–34.
17 See John Carey, *The Intellectuals and the Masses* (London: Faber and Faber, 1992); Andreas Huyssen, *After the Great Divide: Modernism, Mass Culture, Postmodernism* (Bloomington: Indiana University Press, 1986); Michael Tratner, *Modernism and Mass Politics: Joyce, Woolf, Eliot, Yeats* (Stanford: Stanford University Press, 1995); and Ann L. Ardis, *Modernism and Cultural Conflict, 1880–1922* (Cambridge University Press, 2002), pp. 5–6.
18 Their theses have been modified by a number of critics. Cultural historians such as Geoff Eley have argued that the nineteenth-century public sphere was more fragmented than either account suggests. Political theorists like Nancy Fraser have questioned Habermas's gendering of the public/private divide. For the key debates see Craig Calhoun (ed.), *Habermas and the Public Sphere* (Cambridge, MA: MIT Press, 1992).
19 Jürgen Habermas, *The Structural Transformation of the Public Sphere: An Inquiry into a Category of Bourgeois Society* (Cambridge: Polity, 1992); Richard Sennett, *The Fall of Public Man* (New York: Alfred A. Knopf, 1977).
20 Oskar Negt and Alexander Kluge, *Public Sphere and Experience: Towards an Analysis of the Bourgeois and Proletarian Public Sphere* [1972], trans. M. Hansen (Minneapolis: University of Minnesota Press, 1993).
21 Miriam Hansen, 'Foreword', in Negt and Kluge, *Public Sphere and Experience*, p. ix; see also p. 2.

22 Negt and Kluge, *Public Sphere and Experience*, p. 6.
23 Ibid., p. 14.
24 Ibid., p. 18.
25 On the differences between England and France see S. Mennell, *All Manners of Food: Eating and Taste in England and France from the Middle Ages to the Present* (Oxford: Blackwell, 1985).
26 However, in J. Lyons' establishments a 'written code stipulated that "strange ladies", whether alone or in pairs, were not to be admitted, or if by some oversight they had been let in, they were to be secluded by screens from the public gaze': D. J. Richardson, 'J. Lyons & Co. Ltd: Caterers and Food Manufacturers, 1984–1939', in D. Oddy and D. Miller (eds), *The Making of the Modern British Diet* (London: Croom Helm, 1976), p. 166.

13 Teashop dreams

1 L. Nead, *Victorian Babylon: People, Streets and Images in Nineteenth-Century London* (New Haven and London: Yale University Press, 2000), pp. 161–189.
2 The ingredients of the aereated bread can be gleaned from two advertisements in the *Times* classified column on 1 November 1886. The first reads: 'Aerated Bread Company Limited . . . The bread made by the Company's original and recent patents contains all the nourishment of the wheat in the loaf; is perfect as a digestive food and is untouched by hand in its entire manufacture.' The second reads 'Aerated Bread Company's bread is found to give relief to persons suffering acidity of the stomach, flatulence, heartburn, and loss of appetite. It contains all the gluten and digestive properties of the wheat in their natural purity. For sustaining the health of children this bread is most valuable.'
3 A. Service, *London 1900* (St Albans and London: Granada, 1979); R. Thorne, 'Places of Refreshment in the Nineteenth-Century City', in A. King (ed), *Essays in the Social Development of the Built Environment* (London: Routledge, 1980); G. Weightman, *Bright Lights, Big City: London Entertained 1830–1950* (London: Collins and Brown, 1992); and Peter Brooker, *Bohemia in London: The Social Scene of Early Modernism* (Basingstoke: Palgrave Macmillan, 2004), p. 29.
4 Texts which mention the chains include: Bram Stoker, *Dracula* (1897); George Gissing, *The Town Traveller* (1898); H. G. Wells, *Ann Veronica* (1909); Somerset Maugham, *Of Human Bondage* (1915); Berta Ruck, *His Official Fiancée* (1914); Dorothy Richardson, *Pilgrimage* (1915–67); Wyndham Lewis, *Tarr* (1918); Katherine Mansfield, 'Pictures' (1919); T. S. Eliot, 'A Cooking Egg' (1919); Virginia Woolf, *Night and Day* (1919), *Jacob's Room* (1922); and Jean Rhys, *After Leaving Mr Mackenzie* (1930). See Chapter 15.
5 Virgina Woolf, *Night and Day* (London: Grafton, 1978), p. 398.
6 Mary Grover, 'Modernism and the Middle Brow', paper given at the Northern Modernism Seminar, Sheffield Hallam University, May 2003. For

a full account of the importance of eating out in ABCs and elsewhere to the social groups that constituted London's modernist circles see Brooker, *Bohemia in London*; on ABCs see pp. 113–114, 172.
7 O. Negt and A. Kluge, *Public Sphere and Experience: Towards an Analysis of the Bourgeois and Proletarian Public Sphere* [1972], trans. M. Hansen (Minneapolis: University of Minnesota Press, 1993), p. 14.
8 The Aerated Bread Company's depot was on the Camden Road in North West London; Lyons' was in Hammersmith in West London.
9 Information about Lyons & Co. is far more readily available than about the ABCs because the records of the Aerated Bread Company were lost in a flood in Islington, whereas the Lyons archive is in the London Metropolitan Library. Much of the account of Lyons in this chapter is indebted to Peter Bird's history of Lyons, *The First Food Empire: A History of J. Lyons & Co.* (Chichester: Phillimore, 2000).
10 Bill Lancaster, *The Department Store: A Social History* (London and New York: Leicester University Press, 1995).
11 Bird, *The First Food Empire*, pp. 92–93.
12 It was not a strategy that worked well in the new economic environment after the Second World War. A process of gradual decline culminated in Lyons becoming the food division of Allied Breweries in 1978. The last teashop closed in 1981.
13 Bird, *The First Food Empire*, p. 8.
14 Ibid., p. 15.
15 Popular orientalism was a common feature of the new phantasmagoric consumer culture creating what Judith Walkowitz calls 'imaginary landscapes': 'On the one hand, these displays linked the commercial power of empire to the purveryance of Oriental luxuries in the metropolis. On the other hand, they served as a material backdrop for a new world of female shopping that could be identified as a distinctly un-English practice associated with unrestrained licence and sensuous pleasures of the East.' Judith Walkowitz, 'Going Public: Shopping, Street Harassment, and Streetwalking in Late Victorian London', *Representations*, 62 (Spring 1998), 4.
16 Montague Gluckstein, 'The Development of an Ideal: How the World's Greatest Catering Service Grew from a Teashop', *Daily Mail*, 5 October 1921, p. II.
17 Jean Rhys, *After Leaving Mr Mackenzie* (Harmondsworth: Penguin, 1988), p. 50. Julia has probably entered the Maison Lyons restaurant in Oxford Street, which, like the Cornerhouses, was a much bigger affair than the teashops, as it is described as having a band: 'A band filled the air with military music, played at the top of its voice. Grandiose . . .' (p. 49). But the teashops anticipated the grandiosity of these later creations.
18 Richardson, *The Tunnel, Pilgrimage II* (London: Virago, 1979), p. 150.
19 However, Peter Bailey's work on the London pub suggest that the teashops also made available to 'respectable' women some of the glamour of the Victorian gin palace, where 'the bar counter with its newly sumptuous

fittings was the visual as well as the transactional focus of the pub-gin palace and provided a framing effect that gave it the dramatic properties of a stage, thus heightening the presence of its attendants as social actors and objects of display'. 'Parasexuality and Glamour: The Victorian Barmaid as Cultural Prototype', *Gender and History*, 2, 2 (Summer 1990), 151.
20. Benjamin, *The Arcades Project*, (Cambridge, MA: Belknap Press, 1999), [R1, 3], pp. 537–538.
21. Henri Lefebvre, *Writings on Cities*, (Oxford: Blackwell, 1999), p. 113.
22. Ben Highmore argues that the 'insistence on plural rhythms is crucial to the rhythmanalytical project. It is only when two different rhythms intersect that a rhythm can be recognized at all': Ben Highmore, *Cityscapes: Cultural Readings in the Material and Symbolic City* (Basingstoke: Palgrave Macmillan, 2005), p. 147.
23. Benjamin, *The Arcades Project*, [K1a, 7], p. 391.
24. In other words, this is another example of what Miriam Hansen calls vernacular modernism. See *Modernism/Modernity*, 6, 2 (1999), 59–77, and the introduction to this book.
25. Janet Wolff, 'The Invisible Flâneuse: Women and the Literature of Modernity', *Theory Culture and Society*, special issue, 'The Fate of Modernity', 2, 3 (1985), 37–46; Griselda Pollock, 'Modernity and the Spaces of Femininity', in *Vision and Difference: Femininity, Feminism and the Histories of Art* (London: Routledge, 1988).
26. Elizabeth Wilson, *The Sphinx in the City* (London: Virago, 1991). See also Judith Walkowitz, *City of Dreadful Delight* (London: Virago, 1992) and 'Going Public', 4.
27. Nead, *Victorian Babylon*, p. 143.
28. E. D. Rappaport, *Shopping for Pleasure: Women in the Making of London's West End* (Princeton University Press, 2000), p. 12.
29. Julian Salmon, Address to the 'Twenty Club', 1 October 1957, 'J. Lyons and Co. Ltd.', London Metropolitan Archive, File Acc3527/227.
30. J. Lyons & Company document, 'Development and Growth of the Business', amended June 1971, p. 1, London Metropolitan Archive, File Acc3527/227.
31. C. Whitehorn, 'Days of Nippies and Soda Fountains', *Baking Industries Journal*, March 1978, pp. 8–9, J. Lyons & Co. Archive, London Metropolitan Library, File Acc3527/227.
32. Rappaport, *Shopping for Pleasure*, p. 220.
33. Walter Benjamin, *The Arcades Project*, [N3a, 3] pp. 463–464. See also Peter Buse, Ken Hirschkop, Scott McCracken, Bertrand Taithe, 'Awakening', in *The Arcades Project: An Unguided Tour* (Manchester University Press, 2006).
34. See Judith Walkowitz, 'Going Public', p. 4.
35. A. Forbes, 'A Woman's Point of View', *Daily Mail*, 5 October 1921, p. II.
36. Benjamin, *The Arcades Project*, [C3, 3], p. 88.
37. Thomas Richards, *The Commodity Culture of Victorian England: Advertising and Spectacle, 1851–1914* (London, Verso, 1991), p. 28.

14 Gissing and eating out

1. George Gissing, *The Town Traveller* (Brighton: Harvester, 1981), p. 55.
2. Habermas, *The Structural Transformation of the Public Sphere: An Inquiry into a Category of Bourgeois Society* (Cambridge: Polity, 1992), p. 175.
3. David Glover, ' "This spectacle of a world's wonder": Commercial Culture and Urban Space in Gissing's In the Year of the Jubilee', in Bouwe Postmus (ed), *A Garland for Gissing* (Amsterdam: Rodopi, 2001), pp. 137–151.
4. See Chapter 1.
5. Pierre Coustillas (ed), *London and the Life of Literature in Late Victorian England: The Diary of George Gissing, Novelist* (Brighton: Harvester, 1978). See for example the entry for 3 December 1888, 'Strange to see everywhere about the streets – on public proclamations, offices, even dust-carts, the letters "S.P.Q.R." '(p. 87); or for 11 December. Or, on the same trip: 'An interesting feature of the by-streets are the splendid teams of oxen bringing in loads of straw etc. from the country. These fine beasts, with their immense horns, always make me think of the antique. Such animals Virgil saw, and Homer, I suppose' (p. 93).
6. On porosity and Benjamin see Graeme Gilloch, *Myth and Metropolis: Walter Benjamin and the City* (Cambridge: Polity, 1997), pp. 25–26.
7. The two passages are, from Gissing's diary: 'Let me see if I can put down some of the points which seem most characteristic of Naples to one who has just arrived. The amount of buying and selling, especially in poor streets; the fanciful harness of horses; the multitudes of donkeys; the hard and excellent paving, squares placed diamond-wise; the enormous houses, vast doorways, great rooms, thick walls; the madonna faces among the lower classes; the elegant appearance of officers; the abundances of clerics in the street and their leisurely walk, – including monks of medieval appearance; the gradoni; the soft note of the street-organs; the saints with lamps before them; the long musical cry of the sellers going about the streets at night.' Coustillas (ed.), *The Diary of George Gissing*, 31 October 1888, p. 61. And from Benjamin: 'As porous as this stone is the architecture. Building and action interpenetrate in the courtyards, arcades and stairways. In everything they preserve the scope to become a theatre of new, unforeseen constellations. The stamp of the definitive is avoided. No situation appears intended forever, no figure asserts its "thus and not otherwise". This is how architecture, the most binding part of the communal rhythm, comes into being here: civilized private, and ordered only in the great hotel and warehouse buildings on the quays; anarchical, embroiled, village-like in the centre, into which large networks of streets were hacked only forty years ago. And only in these streets is the house, in the Nordic sense, the cell of the city's architecture. In contrast, within the tenement blocks, it seems held together at the corners, as if by iron clamps, by the murals of the Madonna.' Walter Benjamin, 'Naples', in M. Bullock and M. W. Jennings (eds), *Selected Writings Vol. 1: 1913–1926* (Cambridge, MA: Belknap Press, 1996), p. 416.

8 Thomas Richards has described how Victorian advertising took its cue from the Great Exhibition of 1851. See *The Commodity Culture of Victorian England: Advertising and Spectacle, 1851–1914* (London: Verso, 1991), pp. 21–72.
9 *The Arcades Project*, [G5, 2], [G5a, 1], p. 182.
10 Ibid., [G4a, 1] p. 180.
11 Gissing, *The Nether World*, p. 108.
12 See Buse et al., *Benjamin's Arcades Project* (Manchester University Press, 2006), 'Empathy'.
13 Gissing, *The Nether World*, p. 112.
14 Ibid.
15 Simon James, *Unsettled Accounts: Money and Narrative in the Novels of George Gissing* (London: Anthem, 2003), p. 42. See Chapter 8, note 8.
16 George Gissing, *Demos: A Story of English Socialism* (Brighton: Harvester, 1972), p. 34.
17 Ibid., pp. 37–38.
18 Miriam Hansen, 'Foreword', in Oskar Negt and Alexander Kluge, *Public Sphere and Experience: Towards an Analysis of the Bourgeois and Proletarian Public Sphere* [1972], trans. M. Hansen (Minneapolis: University of Minnesota Press, 1993), p. xxi.
19 Peter Bailey writes that the 'The barmaid and the pub were . . . part of a larger nexus of people and institutions that stood athwart the public/private line and provided the social space in which a more democratised, heterosocial world of sex and socialility was being constituted, a world that is still inadequately mapped by historians.' 'Parasexuality and Glamour: The Victorian Barmaid as Cultural Prototype', *Gender and History*, 2, 2 (Summer 1990), 147.
20 See, for example, Joanne Finkelstein, *Dining Out: A Sociology of Modern Manners* (Cambridge: Polity, 1989).
21 Lydia Martens and Alan Warde, 'The Meaning of Eating Out in a Northern City', in P. Caplan (ed.), *Food, Health and Identity* (London: Routledge, 1997), p. 147.
22 Ibid.
23 Richard Sennett, *The Fall of Public Man* (New York: Alfred A. Knopf, 1977), p. 215.
24 Ibid, p. 17.
25 Gissing, *The Town Traveller*, p. 18.
26 Ibid., p. 16.
27 George Gissing, *The Odd Women* [1893] (London: Virago, 1980) p. 282.
28 George Gissing, *In the Year of the Jubilee* [1894] (London: Hogarth, 1987), p. 113; Arlene Young, 'Mapping the Citizen: Characterisation and the City in *The Odd Women*, *In the Year of the Jubilee*, and *Eve's Ransom*'. Second International Gissing Conference, 'Gissing and the City', London, July 2003.
29 Rachel Bowlby, *Just Looking: Consumer Culture in Dreiser, Gissing and Zola* (London: Methuen, 1985), p. 32.
30 George Gissing, *Eve's Ransom* (New York: Dover, 1980), p. 13.

31 Sennett, *The Fall of Public Man*, p. 215.
32 Maud Ellmann, *The Hunger Artists: Starving, Writing and Imprisonment* (London: Virago, 1993).

15 Modernism's ABC

1 Richard Aldington, *A Life for Life's Sake: A Book of Reminiscences* [1941] (London: Cassell, 1968), p. 122.
2 Ibid.
3 P. Hutchins, *Ezra Pound's Kensington: An Exploration 1885–1913* (London: Faber and Faber, 1965), p. 107.
4 Berta Ruck, *His Official Fiancée* [1914], (London: Hurst, Blackett, 1974), p. 93.
5 T. S. Eliot, *Collected Poems 1909–1962* (London: Faber, 1974), p. 47.
6 Virgina Woolf, *Jacob's Room* (New York: Harcourt, Brace and World, 1950), p. 78.
7 Florinda in *Jacob's Room* fights back: she 'detected glass in the sugar bowl; accused the waitress of wishing to poison her; declared that young men stared at her'. Ibid.
8 Wyndham Lewis, *Tarr: The 1918 Version*, ed. P. Keefe (Santa Rosa: Black Sparrow Press, 1990), p. 22.
9 Katherine Mansfield, 'Pictures', in A. Alpers (ed), *The Stories of Katherine Mansfield* (Oxford University Press, 1984), p. 326.
10 Woolf, *Jacob's Room*, p. 119.
11 See also the calls of the waitresses in *Jacob's Room*: 'Hot milk and scone for one. Pot of tea. Roll and butter'. Ibid.
12 The waitress suggests a strong link between the culture of the ABC and that of musical comedy as described by Peter Bailey: 'In musical comedy the bidding and dealing in sexual favours echo the speculative transactions of the market and the risk and rewards of the business deal. Thus sex itself is a resource or commodity like the nitrates, the oil, soap or pork that generated the spectacular new wealth of the era.' Or one might add the food products served in teashops. See *Popular Culture and Performance in the Victorian City* (Cambridge University Press, 1998), p. 188.
13 Cited in Walkowitz, 'Going Public: Shopping, Street Harassment, and Streetwalking in Late Victorian London', *Representations*, 62 (Spring 1998), 18.
14 As Philip Holden has suggested to me, the distribution of this network was probably connected to the London transport system. Literary evidence of this can be found in the appearance of an ABC in Bram Stoker's *Dracula*. Searching for Dracula in London, Jonathan Harker pops into an ABC to get a cup of tea before catching the train for Purfleet. The vampire pervades the city like the systems of modernity. It is interesting that it is Jonathan Harker who makes use of the teashop. He is the most emasculated of the team of men who try to defeat Count Dracula, having experienced a terrifying

imprisonment in the Count's castle: Bram Stoker, *Dracula* [1897](Oxford University Press, 1983), p. 266.
15 Sigmund Freud, *On Sexuality* (Harmondsworth: Penguin, 1977), pp. 243–260.
16 Dorothy Richardson, *The Tunnel, Pilgrimage* III (London: Virago, 1979), p. 136; See also *Deadlock, Pilgrimage* II, pp. 106–107.
17 H. G. Wells, *Ann Veronica* [1909] (London: Virago, 1980), p. 82. On male pests see Walkowitz, 'Going Public'. To a greater or lesser extent, Sidney Kirkwood, Hilliard, Bloom and Philip are all male pests.
18 James Joyce, *Ulysses* (London: Bodley Head, 1993) p. 58.
19 See Fredric Jameson, '*Ulysses* in History', W. J. McCormack and A. Stead (eds), *James Joyce and Modern Literature* (London: Routledge & Kegan Paul, 1982), pp. 126–141.
20 See Don Gifford and Robert J. Seidman, *Ulysses Annotated Notes for James Joyce's Ulysses* (Berkeley University of California Press, 1992), p. 280.
21 Walter Benjamin, *The Arcades Project*, (Cambridge, MA: Belknap Press, 1999), [O2a, 1], p. 494.
22 Ezra Pound, *Collected Shorter Poems* (London: Faber and Faber, 1968), p. 127.
23 Ibid., [N3a, 3], pp. 463–464.
24 Both lines were short substitutions for cancelled lines. See Peter Brooker, *A Student's Guide to the Selected Poems of Ezra Pound* (London: Faber and Faber, 1979), pp. 106–107.
25 The story was first published in *New Age*, 4 October 1917, and then revised for *Bliss and Other Stories*, published in 1920: A. Alper, 'Commentary', *The Stories of Katherine Mansfield* (Oxford University Press, 1984), p. 558.
26 Ibid., p. 271.
27 Judith Walkowitz, 'Going Public', pp. 3–4; Andrew Thacker, ' "Mad After Foreign Notions": Ezra Pound, Imagism and the Geography of the Orient', in P. Brooker and A. Thacker (eds), *The Geographies of Modernism: Literatures, Cultures, Spaces* (London: Routledge, 2005), pp. 31–42.
28 According to Antony Alpers the story was based on an actual incident with a former lover: *The Life of Katherine Mansfield* (New York: Viking, 1980), pp. 122–123.

16 Miriam, teashops and the industrialised public sphere

1 Letter to Percy Beaumont Wadsworth (Summer 1921), in Gloria G. Fromm (ed.), *Windows on Modernism: Selected Letters of Dorothy Richardson* (Athens: University of Georgia Press, 1995), p. 51. In fact, this experiment in broadening the audience of what had been and later continued to be the Lyons staff magazine seems to have been short-lived.
2 See Chapter 12.
3 Oskar Negt and Alexander Kluge, *Public Sphere and Experience: Towards an Analysis of the Bourgeois and Proletarian Public Sphere* [1972] (Minneapolis: University of Minnesota Press, 1993), pp. 12–13.

4 Richardson, 'Continuous Performance', in J. Donald, A. Friedberg and L. Marcus (eds), *Close Up 1927–1933: Cinema and Modernism* (London: Cassell, 1998), p. 160; see also Laura Marcus's introduction to this section on Richardson's theory of the cinema audience as a new public sphere, pp. 150–159.
5 Miriam Hansen, 'Early Silent Cinema: Whose Public Sphere?', *New German Critique*, 29 (1983), 156.
6 Dorothy Richardson, *Interim* (1919), *Pilgrimage* II (London: Virago, 1979), p. 336.
7 Richardson, *Deadlock* (1921), *Pilgrimage* III, p. 81.
8 Dorothy Richardson, *The Tunnel*, *Pilgrimage* II, p. 74.
9 Benjamin, *The Arcades Project*, trans. H. Eiland and K. McLaughlin (Cambridge, MA: Belknap Press, 1999), [C3, 3], p. 88.
10 Nancy Fraser, *Unruly Practices: Power, Discourse and Gender in Contemporary Social Theory* (Cambridge: Polity Press, 1989), p. 124.
11 Rachel Bowlby, *Just Looking: Consumer Culture in Dreiser, Gissing and Zola* (London: Methuen, 1985), pp. 23–30.
12 See Regenia Gagnier, 'Production, Reproduction, and Pleasure in Victorian Aesthetic', chapter 4 in her *The Insatiability of Human Wants* (University of Chicago Press, 2000), pp. 115–145.
13 Elizabeth Grosz, *Volatile Bodies: Towards a Corporeal Feminism* (Bloomington and Indianapolis: Indiana University Press, 1994), p. 22.
14 Judith Butler, *Bodies that Matter* (London: Routledge, 1993), p. 7.
15 Martha Vicinus, *Independent Women: Work and Community for Single Women, 1850–1920* (London: Virago, 1985), pp. 25–30.
16 M. S. Reeves, *Round about a Pound a Week* (London: G. Bell and Sons, 1913).
17 S. Mennell, *All Manners of Food: Eating and Taste in England and France from the Middle Ages to the Present* (Oxford: Blackwell, 1985), p. 34.
18 'the agency denoted by the performativity of "sex" will be directly counter to any notion of the voluntarist subject who exists quite apart from the regulatory norms which she/he opposes.' Butler, *Bodies that Matter*, p. 15.
19 Deborah Lupton, *Food, the Body and the Self* (London: Sage, 1996), p. 22.
20 ' "I don't know the names of the translations," announced Miriam conceitedly. / A long loud yawn resounded through the door.' Richardson, *The Tunnel*, *Pilgrimage* II, p. 62.
21 Susie Orbach, *Fat Is a Feminist Issue* (London: Arrow, 1988).
22 Judith Walkowitz, *Prostitution and Victorian Society: Women, Class and the State* (Cambridge University Press, 1980).
23 Walkowitz, 'Going Public: Shopping, Street Harassment, and Streetwalking in Late Victorian London', *Representations*, 62 (Spring 1998), 4.
24 See Kevin Lynch, *The Image of the City* (Cambridge, MA: MIT Press, 1960).
25 Butler, *Bodies that Matter*, pp. 83, 89.
26 Franco Moretti, *Atlas of the European Novel 1800–1900* (London: Verso, 1998) p. 86.

27 George Gissing, *Demos: A Story of English Socialism* [1886] (Brighton: Harvester, 1982), p. 26. And see James Joyce, *Portrait of the Artist as a Young Man* (New York: Signet, 1991), p. 108, discussed in Chapter 2.
28 Richardson, *Revolving Lights* (1923), *Pilgrimage* III (London: Virago, 1979), p. 250.
29 Edward Carpenter, 'Intermediate Sex', *Selected Writings Vol. 1* (London: GMP, 1984), pp. 185–244. On Richardson and same-sex desire see Joanne Winning, *The Pilgrimage of Dorothy Richardson* (Madison: University of Wisconsin Press, 2000) and Jane Garrity, *Step-daughters of England: British Women Modernists and the National Imaginary* (Manchester University Press, 2003).
30 Laura Doan, *Fashioning Sapphism*, p. xiv.
31 Doan, *Fashioning Sapphism*, p. 36.
32 Richardson, *Revolving Lights*, *Pilgrimage* III, p. 274.
33 Ibid., pp. 275–276.
34 Ibid., p. 277. For a brilliant reading of the whole walk in relation to Baudelaire's poem see Deborah Parsons, *Streetwalking the Metropolis: Women, the City and Modernity* (Oxford University Press, 2000), pp. 72–81.
35 Richardson, *Revolving Lights*, *Pilgrimage* III, p. 278.
36 Richardson, *March Moonlight* (1967), *Pilgrimage* IV, p. 615.

17 Kafka, masculinity and the public sphere

1 Franz Kafka, 'The Judgement' (1913), *The Complete Stories* (New York: Schocken, 1971), p. 88 (translation slightly altered); 'Das Urteil', *Sämtliche Erzählungen* (Frankfurt: Fischer, 1970), p. 32.
2 Judith Butler, 'Imitation and Gender Insubordination', in D. Fuss (ed.), *Inside/Out: Lesbian Theories, Gay Theories*, (London: Routledge, 1991).
3 Christoph Stölzl, 'Treffpunkte', in Hartmut Binder (ed.), *Kafka-Handbuch*, vol. 1 (Stuttgart: Alfred Kröner, 1979), pp. 81–83.
4 See Mark Anderson, *Kafka's Clothes: Ornament and Aestheticism in the Habsburg Fin de Siècle* (Oxford: Clarendon, 1992).
5 Ibid., p. 89.
6 Kafka, *The Complete Stories*, p. 77, *Sämtliche Erzählungen*, p. 23.
7 Ibid., p. 183.
8 Kafka, 'Letter to His Father', pp. 177, 205. Franz Kafka, *Brief an den Vater: mit einem unbekannten Bericht über Kafkas Vater als Lehrherr und anderen Materialien*, herausgegeben von Hans-Gerd Koch, mit einem Nachwort von Alena Wagnerova (Berlin: Klaus Wagenbach, 2004), pp. 14, 40.
9 'Das Urteil', p. 23. My translation.
10 Ibid.
11 'The Judgement', p. 78; 'Das Urteil', p. 24.
12 'The Judgement', p. 79; 'Das Urteil', p. 25.
13 Ibid., p. 80.

14 Ibid.
15 Ibid., pp. 80–81 (translation slightly altered).
16 Christoph Stölzl, 'Die Presse', in Hartmut Binder (ed.), *Kafka-Handbuch*, vol. 1, p. 78. The two newspapers appear suggestively in Kafka's diary entries for 26–28 February 1912, a few months before he wrote 'The Judgement': Franz Kafka, *Franz Kafka, 1910–1923: The Diaries*, ed. M. Brod (New York: Schocken, 1988), pp. 185–189.
17 Kafka, *The Complete Stories*, p. 81.
18 Ibid., p. 82.
19 Ibid.
20 T. W. Adorno, *Negative Dialectics* (London: Routledge, 1990), p. 163.
21 Walter Benjamin concluded that 'There is nothing more memorable than the fervour with which Kafka emphasized his failure': 'Some Reflections on Kafka', *Illuminations*, p. 145. See also letter to Gershom Scholem, 12 June 1938, in *Walter Benjamin Selected Writings Vol. 3: 1935–1938* (Cambridge, MA: Belknap Press, 2002), p. 327.
22 T. W. Adorno, 'Notes on Kafka', *Prisms* (Cambridge, MA: MIT Press, 1983), p. 246.

Bibliography

Adams, J. E. *Dandies and Desert Saints: Styles of Victorian Masculinity* (Ithaca and London: Cornell University Press, 1995)
Adorno, T. W. *Negative Dialectics*, trans. E. B. Ashton (London: Routledge & Kegan Paul, 1990)
Adorno, T. W. 'Reconciliation under Duress', in E Block, et al., *Aesthetics and Politics: Debates between Bloch, Lukács, Brecht, Benjamin, Adorno* (London: Verso, 1980)
Adorno, T. W. 'Notes on Kafka', *Prisms* (Cambridge, MA: MIT Press, 1983)
Adorno, T. W. and Horkheimer, M. *Dialectic of the Enlightenment* (Stanford University Press, 2002)
Alderson, D. *Mansex Fine: Religion, Manliness and Imperialism in Nineteenth-century British Culture* (Manchester University Press, 1998)
Aldington, R. *A Life for Life's Sake: A Book of Reminiscences* [1941] (London: Cassell, 1968)
Anderson, M. *Kafka's Clothes: Ornament and Aestheticism in the Habsburg* Fin de Siècle (Oxford: Clarendon, 1992)
Anderson, P. 'Modernity and Revolution', *New Left Review*, 144 (March–April 1984), 96–113
Anderson, P. 'Renewals', *New Left Review*, 1 (January–February 2000), 5–24
Ardis, A. *New Women, New Novels Feminism and Early Modernism* (New Brunswick: Rutgers University Press, 1990)
Ardis, A. *Modernism and Cultural Conflict, 1880–1922* (Cambridge University Press, 2002)
Arendt, H. 'Walter Benjamin, 1892–1940', Introduction to W. Benjamin, *Illuminations: Essays and Reflections* (New York: Schocken, 1968)
Armstrong, T. *Modernism, Technology and the Body: A Cultural Study* (Cambridge University Press, 1998)
Bailey, P. 'Parasexuality and Glamour: The Victorian Barmaid as Cultural Prototype', *Gender and History*, 2, 2 (Summer 1990), 148–172
Bailey, P. *Popular Culture and Performance in the Victorian City* (Cambridge University Press, 1998)
Bakhtin, M. *The Dialogic Imagination*, ed. M. Holquist, trans. C. Emerson and M. Holquist (Austin: University of Texas Press, 1981)

Barthes R. *Sarassine, S/Z* (Paris: Editions du Seuil, 1970)
Beasley, R. 'Art as Propaganda for Literary Modernism', *new formations*, 43 (Spring 2001), 117–129
Benjamin, A. 'Tradition and Experience: Walter Benjamin's 'On Some Motifs in Baudelaire', in A. Benjamin (ed.), *The Problems of Modernity: Adorno and Benjamin* (London: Routledge, 1989)
Benjamin, J. *The Bonds of Love: Psychoanalysis, Feminism and the Problem of Domination* (New York: Pantheon, 1988)
Benjamin, W. 'Some Reflections on Kafka', *Illuminations* (New York: Schocken, 1969)
Benjamin, W. *Gesammelte Schriften*, eds, R. Tiedemann and H. Schweppenhäuser, (Frankfurt: Suhrkamp, 1974)
Benjamin, W. *The Origin of German Tragic Drama*, trans. John Osborne (London: New Left Books, 1977)
Benjamin, W. *Selected Writings Vol. 1–4: 1913–1940*, eds, M. Bullock, H. Eiland and M. W. Jennings (Cambridge, MA: Belknap Press, 1996–2003)
Benjamin, W. *The Arcades Project*, trans. H. Eiland and K. McLaughlin (Cambridge, MA: Belknap Press, 1999)
Bennett, A. *The Author's Craft*, ed. S. Hynes (Lincoln: University of Nebraska Press, 1968)
Bewes, T. and Gilbert, J. 'Politics after Defeat', Introduction to T. Bewes and J. Gilbert (eds), *Cultural Capitalism* (London: Lawrence and Wishart, 2000)
Bird, P. *The First Food Empire: A History of J. Lyons & Co.* (Chichester: Phillimore, 2000)
Bland, L. *Banishing the Beast: English Feminism and Sexual Morality, 1885–1914* (London: Penguin, 1995)
Bluemel, K. *Experimenting on the Borders of Modernism: Dorothy Richardson's Pilgrimage* (Athens: University of George Press, 1997)
Boa, E. *Kafka: Gender, Class and Race in the Letters and Fictions* (Oxford: Clarendon, 1996)
Boone, J. A. *Libidinal Currents: Sexuality and the Shaping of Modernism* (The Univesity of Chicago Press, 1998)
Booth, C. *Inquiry into the Life and Labour of the People in London* (New York: Augustus M. Kelly, 1969).
Botting, F. 'The Act of Smoking in an Age of Techno-Moral Consumption', *new formations*, 39 (Winter 1999–2000), 80–99
Boumelha, P. *Thomas Hardy and Women: Sexual Ideology and Narrative Form* (Brighton: Harvester, 1982)
Bourdieu, P. *Masculine Domination*, trans. Richard Nice (Cambridge: Polity, 2001)
Bowlby, R. *Just Looking: Consumer Culture in Dreiser, Gissing and Zola* (London: Methuen, 1985)
Breward, C. *The Hidden Consumer: Masculinities, Fashion and City Life 1860–1914* (Manchester University Press, 1999)
Brooker, P. *A Student's Guide to the Selected Poems of Ezra Pound* (London: Faber and Faber, 1979)

Brooker, P. *Bohemia in London: The Social Scene of Early Modernism* (Basingstoke: Palgrave Macmillan, 2004)
Brooker, P. and Thacker, A. (eds), *The Geographies of Modernism: Literatures, Cultures, Spaces* (London: Routledge, 2005)
Buck-Morss, S. *Dialectics of Seeing: Walter Benjamin and the Arcades Project* (Cambridge, MA: MIT Press, 1989)
Budgen, F. *James Joyce and the Making of Ulysses* (London: Grayson and Grayson, 1934)
Burdett, C. *Olive Schreiner and the Progress of Feminism: Evolution, Gender, Empire* (Basingstoke: Palgrave, 2001)
Bürger, C. and Bürger, P. *Prosa der Moderne* (Frankfurt: Suhrkamp, 1988)
Buse, P. and Stott, A. *Ghosts: Deconstruction, Psychoanalysis, History* (London: Palgrave, 1999)
Buse, P., Hirschkop, K., McCracken, S. and Taithe, B. *Benjamin's Arcades: An Unguided Tour* (Manchester University Press, 2006)
Butler, J. 'Imitation and Gender Insubordination', in D. Fuss (ed.), *Inside/Out: Lesbian Theories, Gay Theories*, (London: Routledge, 1991)
Butler, J. *Gender Trouble: Feminism and the Subversion of Identity* (New York: Routledge, 1990)
Butler, J. *Bodies that Matter: On the Discursive Limits of 'Sex'* (London: Routledge, 1993)
Butler, J. 'Merely Cultural', *New Left Review*, 227 (1998), 33–44
Calhoun, C. (ed.), *Habermas and the Public Sphere* (Cambridge, MA: MIT Press, 1992)
Carey, J. *The Intellectuals and the Masses: Pride and Prejudice among the Literary Intelligentsia 1880–1939* (London: Faber, 1992)
Carpenter, E. *Civilisation: Its Cause and Its Cure* (London: Swan Sonnenschein, 1889)
Carpenter, E. *Selected Writings Vol. 1*, ed. N. Greig (London: GMP, 1984)
Cohen, E. *Talk on the Wilde Side: Towards a Genealogy of a Discourse on Male Sexualities* (London: Routledge, 1993)
Cohen, W. A. *Sex Scandal: The Private Parts of Victorian Fiction* (Durham: Duke University Press, 1996)
Connell, R. W. *Masculinities* (Cambridge: Polity, 1995)
Conor, L. *The Spectacular Modern Woman: Feminine Visibility in the 1920s* (Bloomington: Indiana University Press, 2004)
Cook, M. *London and the Culture of Homosexuality, 1885–1914* (Cambridge University Press, 2003)
Cooper, J. X. *Modernism and the Culture of Market Society* (Cambridge University Press, 2004)
Cunningham, A. R. 'The "New Women Fiction" of the 1890s', *Victorian Studies*, 17, 1 (September, 1973), 177–186
Cunningham, G. *The New Woman and the Victorian Novel* (New York: Barnes and Noble, 1978)

Davidoff, L. and Hall, C. *Family Fortunes: Men and Women of the English Middle Class 1780–1850* (London: Hutchinson, 1987)
Davin, A. 'Imperialism and Motherhood', *History Workshop*, 5 (Spring 1978), 9–65
De Certeau, M., Giard, L. and Mayol, P. *The Practice of Everyday Life Vol. 2: Living and Cooking* (Minneapolis: University of Minnesota Press, 1998)
Delany, P. *Literature, Money and the Market: From Trollope to Amis* (Basingstoke: Palgrave, 2002)
Derrida, J. *Spectres of Marx* (London: Routledge, 1994)
Dettmar, K. and Watts, S. (eds), *Marketing Modernisms: Self-Promotion, Canonization, Rereading* (Ann Arbor: University of Michigan Press, 1996)
Dews, P. *The Logics of Disintegration: Post-structuralist Thought and the Claims of Critical Theory* (London: Verso, 1987)
Doan, L. *Fashioning Sapphism: The Origins of a Modern English Lesbian Culture* (New York: Columbia University Press, 2001)
Dollimore, J. *Sexual Dissidence: Augustine to Wilde, Freud to Foucault* (Oxford University Press, 1991)
Dollimore, J. and Sinfield, A. (eds), *Political Shakespeare: New Essays in Cultural Materialism* (Manchester University Press, 1985)
Douglas, M. 'Coded Messages', in S. Griffiths and J. Wallace (eds), *Consuming Passions: Food in the Age of Anxiety* (Manchester: Mandolin, 1998), 103–110
Douglas, M. *Food in the Social Order: Studies of Food and Festivities in Three American Communities* (New York: Russell Sage Foundation, 1984)
Dowling L. 'The Decadent and the New Woman in the 1890s', *Nineteenth Century Fiction*, 33, 4 (March 1979), 177–186
Eagleton, T. 'Edible Ecriture', in S. Griffiths and J. Wallace (eds), *Consuming Passions: Food in the Age of Anxiety*, (Manchester: Mandolin, 1998), 203–208.
Egerton, G. *Keynotes* [1893] (London: Virago, 1983)
Egerton, G. *The Wheel of God* (London: Grant Richards, 1898)
Eliot, T. S. *Collected Poems 1909–1962* (London: Faber, 1974)
Elliot B. 'New and Not so "New Women" on the London Stage: Audrey Beardsley's Yellow Book Images of Mrs Patrick Campbell and Réjane', *Victorian Studies*, 31 (Autumn 1987), 33–57
Ellmann, M. *The Hunger Artists: Starving, Writing and Imprisonment* (London: Virago, 1993)
Ellmann, R. *Oscar Wilde* (London: Hamish Hamilton, 1987)
Felski, R. *Beyond Feminist Aesthetics: Feminist Literature and Social Change* (Cambridge, MA: Harvard University Press, 1989)
Felski, R. *The Gender of Modernity* (Cambridge, MA: Harvard University Press, 1995)
Felski, R. 'The Invention of Everyday Life', *new formations*, 39 (Winter 1999–2000), 13–31
Felski, R. 'Modernist Studies and Cultural Studies: Reflections on Method', *Modernism/modernity*, 10, 3 (September 2003), 501–517

Finkelstein, J. *Dining Out: a sociology of modern manners* (Cambridge: Polity, 1989)
First, R. and Scott, A. *Olive Schreiner* (New York: Schocken, 1980)
Forbes, A. 'A Woman's Point of View', *Daily Mail*, 5 October 1921, p. II.
Foucault, M. *The History of Sexuality Vol. 1*, trans. R. Hurley (New York: Pantheon, 1978)
Fraser, N. *Unruly Practices: Power, Discourse and Gender in Contemporary Social Theory* (Cambridge: Polity Press, 1989)
Fraser, N. 'Heterosexism, Misrecognition and Capitalism: A Response to Judith Butler', *New Left Review*, 227 (1998), 140–149
Freud, S. *On Sexuality* (Harmondsworth: Penguin, 1977)
Fromm, G. G. *Dorothy Richardson: A Biography* (Urbana: Illinois University Press, 1977)
Gagnier, R. *Subjectivities: A History of Self-representation in Britain, 1832–1920* (Oxford University Press, 1991)
Gagnier, R. *The Insatiability of Human Wants: Economic and Aesthetics in Market Society* (Chicago: University of Chicago Press, 2000)
Gallop, J. *The Daughter's Seduction: Feminism and Psychoanalysis* (Ithaca: Cornell University Press, 1982)
Garber, M. *Vested Interests: Cross Dressing and Cultural Anxiety* (New York: Routledge, 1992)
Garrity, J. *Step-daughters of England: British Women Modernists and the National Imaginary* (Manchester University Press, 2003)
Geddes, P. and Thomson, J. A. *The Evolution of Sex*, (London: W. Scott, 1889)
Gilbert, S. and Gubar, S. *No Man's Land: The Place of the Woman Writer in the Twentieth Century*, 3 vols (New Haven: Yale University Press, 1988–94)
Gilloch, G. ' "The Return of the Flaneur": The Afterlife of an Allegory', *new formations*, 38 (Summer 1999), 101–109
Gilloch, G. *Myth and Metropolis: Walter Benjamin and the City* (Cambridge: Polity, 1997)
Gilman, C. P. *Women and Economics* (London: T. Fisher Unwin, 1898)
Gissing, G. *Demos: A Story of English Socialism* [1886] (Brighton: Harvester, 1982)
Gissing, G. *Thyrza* [1887] (London: Harvester, 1984)
Gissing, G. *The Nether World* [1889] (Brighton: Harvester, 1974)
Gissing, G. *New Grub Street* [1891] (Harmondsworth, Penguin, 1968)
Gissing, G. *Born in Exile* [1892] (London: Nelson, 1910)
Gissing, G. *The Odd Women* [1893] (London: Virago, 1980)
Gissing, G. *In the Year of the Jubilee* [1894] (London: Hogarth, 1987)
Gissing, G. *Eve's Ransom* [1895] (New York: Dover, 1980)
Gissing, G. *The Town Traveller* [1898] (Brighton: Harvester, 1981)
Gissing, G. *The Immortal Dickens* [1898–1900] (London: Cecil Palmer, 1925)
Gissing, G. *The Private Papers of Henry Ryecroft* [1903] (Oxford University Press, 1987)
Gissing, G. *London and the Life of Literature in Late Victorian England: The Diary of George Gissing, Novelist*, ed. P. Coustillas (Brighton: Harvester, 1978)

Glover, D. ' "This spectacle of a world's wonder": Commercial Culture and Urban Space in Gissing's In the Year of the Jubilee', in B. Postmus (ed.), *A Garland for Gissing* (Amsterdam: Rodopi, 2001), 137–151
Glover, D. 'Foucault, Sexuality, Liberalism: A Commentary', *new formations*, 55 (Spring 2005), 36–43.
Glover, D. and Kaplan, C. *Genders* (London: Routledge, 2000)
Gluckstein, M. 'The Development of an Ideal: How the World's Greatest Catering Service Grew from a Teashop', *Daily Mail*, 5 October 1921, p. II
Goode, J. *George Gissing, Ideology and Fiction* (London: Vision, 1978)
Goodman, J. *Tobacco in History: The Cultures of Dependence* (London: Routledge, 1993)
Gramsci, A. *Prison Notebooks* (London: Lawrence and Wishart, 1971)
Grand, S. *The Heavenly Twins* (London: Heinemann, 1893)
Grosz, E. *Volatile Bodies: Towards a Corporeal Feminism* (Bloomington and Indianapolis: Indiana University Press, 1994)
Grover, M. 'Modernism and the Middle Brow', paper given at the Northern Modernism Seminar, Sheffield Hallam University, May 2003.
Habermas, J. *The Structural Transformation of the Public Sphere: An Inquiry into a Category of Bourgeois Society*, (Cambridge: Polity, 1992)
Habermas, J. *The Theory of Communicative Action*, trans. T. McCarthy (Cambridge, MA: MIT Press, 1984)
Habermas, J. *Autonomy and Solidarity: Interviews*, ed. P. Dews (London: Verso, 1986)
Halberstam, J. *Female Masculinity* (Durham: Duke University Press, 1998)
Hall, D. E. (ed.), *Muscular Christianity* (Cambridge University Press, 1994)
Hanscombe, G. *The Art of Life: Dorothy Richardson and the Development of Feminist Consciousness* (London: Peter Owen, 1982)
Hansen, M. 'Early Silent Cinema: Whose Public Sphere?', *New German Critique*, 29 (1983), 147–184.
Hansen, M. 'Benjamin, Cinema and Experience: "The Blue Flower in the Land of Technology" ', *New German Critique*, 40 (Winter, 1987), 179–224
Hansen, M. 'Foreword', in O. Negt and A. Kluge, *Public Sphere and Experience: Towards an Analysis of the Bourgeois and Proletarian Public Sphere* [1972], trans. M. Hansen (Minneapolis: University of Minnesota Press, 1993)
Hansen, M. 'The Mass Production of the Senses: Classical Cinema as Vernacular Modernism', *Modernism/Modernity*, 6, 2 (1999), 59–77
Hansen, M. B. 'Benjamin and Cinema: Not a One-Way Street', *Critical Inquiry*, 25, 2 (Winter 1999), 306–343
Hansen, M. ' "Room-for-Play": Benjamin's Gamble with Cinema', *October*, 109, 1 (Summer 2004), 3–45
Harris, W. V. 'Egerton: Forgotten Realist', *Victorian Newsletter*, 33 (Spring 1968), 31–55
Harris, W. V. 'John Lane's Keynotes Series and the Fiction of the 1890s', *PMLA*, 83 (October 1968), 1407–1413

Heilmann, A. *New Woman Fiction: Women Writing First-wave Feminism* (London: Macmillan, 2000)
Heilmann, A. *Feminist Forerunners: New Womanism and Feminism in the Early Twentieth Century* (London: Rivers Oram, 2003)
Heilmann, A. *New Woman Strategies: Sarah Grand, Olive Schreiner, Mona Caird* (Manchester University Press, 2004)
Highmore, B. *Cityscapes: Cultural Readings in the Material and Symbolic City* (Basingstoke: Palgrave Macmillan, 2005)
Hilton, M. *Smoking and British Popular Culture, 1800–2000: Perfect Pleasures* (Manchester University Press, 2000)
Hirschkop, K. *Mikhail Bakhtin: An Aesthetic for Democracy* (Oxford University Press, 1999)
Hobsbawm, E. J. *The Age of Empire* (London: Weidenfeld and Nicolson, 1987)
Hutchins, P. *Ezra Pound's Kensington: An Exploration 1885–1913* (London: Faber and Faber, 1965)
Huxley, T. *Evolution and Ethics* [1894] (New York: D. Appleton, 1898)
Huyssen, A. *After the Great Divide: Modernism, Mass Culture, Postmodernism* (Bloomington: Indiana University Press, 1986)
James, S. *Unsettled Accounts: Money and Narrative in the Novels of George Gissing* (London: Anthem, 2003)
Jameson, F. *The Political Unconscious: Narrative as a Socially Symbolic Act* (London: Methuen, 1981)
Jameson, F. 'Ulysses in History', in W. J. McCormack and A. Stead (eds), *James Joyce and Modern Literature* (London: Routledge & Kegan Paul, 1982), pp. 126–141
Joyce, J. *A Portrait of the Artist as a Young Man* [1916] (New York: Signet, 1991)
Joyce, J. *Ulysses* [1922] (London: The Bodley Head, 1993)
Kafka, F. *Sämtliche Erzählungen* (Frankfurt: Fischer, 1970)
Kafka, F. *The Complete Stories* (New York: Schocken, 1971)
Kafka, F. *The Trial* [1925] (Harmondsworth: Penguin, 1984)
Kafka, F. *Franz Kafka, 1910–1923: The Diaries*, ed. M. Brod (New York: Schocken, 1988)
Kafka, F. *Collected Stories* (New York: Alfred A. Knopf, 1993)
Kafka, F. 'Letter to His Father', in H. Kiesel (ed.), *Kafka's The Metamorphosis and Other Writings* (New York, London: Continuum, 2002)
Kafka, F. *Brief an den Vater: mit einem unbekannten Bericht über Kafkas Vater als Lehrherr und anderen Materialien*, herausgegeben von Hans-Gerd Koch, mit einem Nachwort von Alena Wagnerova (Berlin: Klaus Wagenbach, 2004)
Katz, T. *Impressionist Subjects: Gender, Interiority, and Modernist Fiction in England* (Urbana: University of Illinois Press, 2000)
Kimmel, M. S., Hearn, J. and Connell, R. W. *Handbook of Studies on Men and Masculinities* (London: Sage, 2005)
Klein, R. *Cigarettes Are Sublime* (Durham: Duke University Press, 1993)
Knights, B. *Writing Masculinities*, (Basingstoke: Palgrave, 1999)

Kristeva, J. *Powers of Horror: An Essay on Abjection* (New York: Columbia University Press, 1982)
Lacan, J. *Ecrits: A Selection*, trans. A. Sheridan (New York: Norton, 1977)
Lancaster, B. *The Department Store: A Social History* (London and New York: Leicester University Press, 1995)
Lane, C. *The Burdens of Intimacy: Psychoanalysis and Victorian Masculinity* (University of Chicago Press, 1999)
Ledger, S. *The New Woman: Fiction and Feminism at the Fin de Siècle* (Manchester University Press, 1997)
Ledger, S. and McCracken, S. *The Cultural Politics of the Fin de Siècle* (Cambridge University Press, 1995)
Lefebvre, H. *Writings on Cities* (Oxford: Blackwell, 1999)
Leslie, E. 'Stars, Phosphor and Chemical Colours: Extraterrestiality in *The Arcades*', *new formations*, 54 (Winter 2004/5), 13–27
Lévi-Strauss, C. *The Raw and the Cooked*, trans. J. and D. Weightman (New York: Harper & Row, 1969)
Lewis, W. *Tarr: The 1918 Version*, ed. P. Keefe (Santa Rosa: Black Sparrow Press, 1990)
Liddington, J. and Norris, J. *One Hand Tied Behind Us: The Rise of the Women's Suffrage Movement* (London: Virago, 1978)
Lovell, T. *Consuming Fiction* (London: Verso, 1987)
Lukács, G. *The Theory of the Novel* [1916] (London: Merlin, Press, 1978)
Lukács, G. *Studies in European Realism*, (New York: Grosset and Dunlap, 1964)
Lupton, D. *Food, the Body and the Self* (London: Sage, 1996)
Lynch, K. *The Image of the City* (Cambridge, MA: MIT Press, 1960)
Mansfield, K. *The Stories of Katherine Mansfield*, ed. A. Alpers (Oxford University Press, 1984)
Marcus, L. (ed.), *Mass-Observation as Poetics and Science*, special issue of *new formations*, 44 (Autumn 2001)
Marcus, L. 'Introduction' to 'Continuous Performance: Dorothy Richardson', Part 4 of J. Donald, A. Friedberg and L. Marcus (eds), *Close Up 1927–1933: Cinema and Modernism* (London: Cassell, 1998), 150–159
Marcus, S. *The Other Victorians: A Study of Sexuality and Pornography in Mid-nineteenth-century England* (New York: Basic Books, 1966)
Marks, P. *Bicycles, Bangs and Bloomers: The New Woman in the Popular Press* (Lexington: University Press of Kentucky, 1990)
Martens, L. and Warde, A. 'The Meaning of Eating Out in a Northern City', in P. Caplan (ed.), *Food, Health and Identity* (London: Routledge, 1997)
Marx, K. 'Theses on Feuerback', in *Karl Marx: Early Writings* (Harmondsworth: Penguin, 1975)
McCracken, S. 'A Hard and Absolute Condition of Existence: Reading Masculinity in Lord Jim', *The Conradian*, 17, 2 (Spring 1993), 17–38
McCracken, S. 'Postmodernism a *Chance* to Reread?', in S. Ledger and S. McCracken (eds), *Cultural Politics at the Fin de Siècle* (Cambridge University Press, 1995), 267–289

McCracken, S. 'A Novel from/on the Margins: George Egerton's *Wheel of God*', in T. Foley, L. Pilkington, S. Ryder and E. Tilley (eds), *Gender and Colonialism* (Galway: Galway University Press, 1995), 145–163
McCracken, S. 'Embodying the New Woman: Dorothy Richardson, Work and the London Café', in A. Horner and A. Keane (eds), *Body Matters: Feminism, Texuality, Corporeality* (Manchester University Press, 2000)
McCracken, S. 'Stages of Sand and Blood: The Performance of Gendered Subjectivity in Olive Schreiner Colonial Allegories', in A. Jenkins and J. John (eds), *Rereading Victorian Fiction* (Basingstoke: Macmillan, 2000), 145–158
McCracken, S. 'The Completion of Old Work: Walter Benjamin and the Everyday', *Cultural Critique*, 52 (Fall 2002), 145–166
McCracken, S. 'Between Real Worlds and Dream Worlds: Gissing's London', in John Spiers (ed.), *Gissing and the City* (Basingstoke: Palgrave Macmillan, 2005)
McDonald, G. 'Product Placement: Literary Modernism and Crisco', *Modernist Cultures* (forthcoming 2006)
McGee, D.E. *Writing the Meal: Dinner in the Fiction of Early Twentieth-century Women Writers* (University of Toronto Press, 2001)
Mennell, S. *All Manners of Food: Eating and Taste in England and France from the Middle Ages to the Present* (Oxford: Blackwell, 1985)
Merck, M. 'Editorial', *Cultures and Economies*, special issue of *new formations*, 52 (Spring 2004), 7–9
Merck, M. 'Sexuality, Subjectivity and ... Economics?', *Cultures and Economies*, special issue of *new formations*, 52 (Spring 2004), 82–93
Middleton, P. *The Inward Gaze: Masculinity and Subjectivity in Modern Culture* (London: Routledge, 1992)
Miles, R. 'George Egerton, 'Bitextuality and Cultural Representation in the 1890s', *Women's Writing*, 3, 3 (1996)
Miller, J. *Seductions: Studies in Reading and Culture* (London: Virago, 1990)
Mitchell, J. and Rose, J. (eds), *Feminine Sexuality: Jacques Lacan and the Ecole Freudienne* (London: Macmillan, 1982)
Moi, T. *What Is a Woman?* (Oxford University Press, 1999)
Moretti, F. *Signs Taken for Wonders* (London: Verso, 1983)
Moretti, F. *The Way of the World: The Bildungsroman in European Culture* (London: Verso, 1987)
Moretti, F. 'The Spell of Indecision', *New Left Review*, 164 (July/August, 1987), 27–33
Moretti, F. *Atlas of the European Novel 1800–1900* (London: Verso, 1998)
Mosse, G. L. *The Image of Man: The Creation of Modern Masculinity* (Oxford University Press, 1996)
Nead, L. *Victorian Babylon: People, Streets and Images in Nineteenth-Century London* (New Haven and London: Yale University Press, 2000)
Negt, O. and Kluge, A. *Public Sphere and Experience: Towards an Analysis of the Bourgeois and Proletarian Public Sphere* [1972], trans. M. Hansen (Minneapolis: University of Minnesota Press, 1993)

Nicholls, P. *Modernisms: A Literary Guide* (Basingstoke: Macmillan, 1995)
North, M. *Reading 1922: A Return to the Scene of the Modern* (New York: Oxford University Press, 1999)
Ogden, S. 'Darwinian Scepticism in George Gissing's *Born in Exile*', in B. Postmus (ed.), *A Garland for Gissing* (Amsterdam: Rodopi, 2001), 171–178
Orbach, S. *Fat Is a Feminist Issue* (London: Arrow, 1988)
Orwell, G. *Nineteen Eighty-four* (Harmondsworth: Penguin, 1983)
Parsons, D. *Streetwalking the Metropolis: Women, the City and Modernity* (Oxford University Press, 2000)
Pawel, E. *The Nightmare of Reason: A Life of Franz Kafka* (New York: Farrar, Straus, Giroux, 1984)
Pollock, G. 'Modernity and the Spaces of Femininity', in *Vision and Difference: Femininity, Feminism and the Histories of Art* (London: Routledge, 1988)
Pound, E. *Collected Shorter Poems* (London: Faber and Faber, 1968)
Probyn, E. *Carnal Appetites: FoodSexIdentities* (London: Routledge, 2000)
Proust, M. *In Search of Lost Time Vol. II: Within a Budding Grove*, trans. C. K. Scott Moncrieff, T. Kilmartin, D. J. Enright (London: Vintage, 2002)
Pykett, L. *The Improper Feminine: The Sensation Novel and the New Woman Writing* (London: Routledge, 1992)
Pykett, L. *Engendering Fictions: The English Novel in the Early Twentieth Century* (London: Edward Arnold, 1995)
Radford, J. *Dorothy Richardson* (Hemel Hempstead: Harvester Wheatsheaf, 1991)
Rainey, L. *Institutions of Modernism: Literary Elites and Public Culture* (New Haven: Yale University Press, 1998)
Rappaport, E. D. *Shopping for Pleasure: Women in the Making of London's West End* (Princeton University Press, 2000)
Reeves, M. S. *Round about a Pound a Week* (London: G. Bell and Sons, 1913)
Richards, T. *The Commodity Culture of Victorian England: Advertising and Spectacle, 1851–1914*, (London, Verso, 1991)
Richardson, D. 'The Reading of "The Jungle"', *Crank*, 4 (September 1906), 290–293
Richardson, D. 'Review of *In the Days of the Comet*', *The Crank*, 4 (November 1906), 372–376
Richardson, D. 'Cosmic Thinking', Review of Fielding-Hall's *The World Soul*, *Plain Talk*, July 1913, p. 13
Richardson, D. 'Preface' to Paul Carson, *Consumption Doomed: A Lecture on the Cure of Tuberculosis, Vol. VII of Healthy Life Booklets* (London: C. W. Daniel, 1913)
Richardson, D. *Pilgrimage Vols I–IV* [1915–67] (London: Virago, 1979)
Richardson, D. 'Comments by a Layman', *Dental Record*, 35–39 (November 1915–June 1919)
Richardson, D. 'Amateur Evidence in Dietetics', *Dental Record*, 36 (June 1916), 300–303

Richardson, D. 'The Reality of Feminism', *The Ploughshare*, ns 2 (September 1917), 241–246
Richardson, D. 'Spanish Dentist Looks at Spain', *Dental Record*, 38 (1 August 1918), 343–345
Richardson, D. 'Antheil of New Jersey', *Vanity Fair*, 25 (November 1925), 136–138
Richardson, D. 'Anticipation', *Focus*, 5 (June 1928), 322–325
Richardson, D. 'Buns for Tea', *Poetry*, 24 (June 1924), 144–145
Richardson, D. 'The Queen of Spring', *Focus*, 5 (May 1928), 259–262
Richardson, D. 'Afternoon Tea', *Queen*, 28 December 1932, 13
Richardson, D. *Windows on Modernism: Selected Letters of Dorothy Richardson*, ed. G. G. Fromm (Athens: University of Georgia Press, 1995)
Richardson, D. 'Continuous Performance', in J. Donald, A. Friedberg and L. Marcus (eds), *Close Up 1927–1933: Cinema and Modernism* (London: Cassell, 1998)
Richardson, D. J. 'J. Lyons & Co. Ltd: Caterers and Food Manufacturers, 1984–1939', in D. Oddy and D. Miller (eds), *The Making of the Modern British Diet* (London: Croom Helm, 1976)
Roberts, A. M. *Conrad and Masculinity* (Basingstoke: Macmillan, 2000)
Ruck, B. *His Official Fiancée* [1914] (London: Hurst, Blackett, 1974)
Ryle M. and Soper, K. *To Relish the Sublime: Cultural Self-realization in Postmodern Times* (London: Verso, 2002)
Ryle, M. and Taylor, J. B. *George Gissing, 1903–2003: Voices of the Unclassed* (London: Ashgate, 2005)
Salmon, J. 'Address to the "Twenty Club", 1 Oct 1957: J. Lyons and Co. Ltd.', London Metropolitan Archive, File Acc3527/227
Schivelbusch, W. *Disenchanted Night: The Industrialisation of Light in the Nineteenth Century*, trans. A. Davies (Oxford: Berg, 1988)
Schreiner, O. *Story of an African Farm* [1883] (Harmondsworth, Penguin, 1971)
Schreiner, O. *Dreams* (London: T. Fisher Unwin, 1890)
Schreiner, O. *Woman and Labour* (London: T. Fisher Unwin, 1911)
Scott, B. K. *Refiguring Modernism* (Bloomington: Indiana University Press, 1995)
Sedgwick, E. K. *Between Men: English Literature and Homosocial Desire* (New York: Columbia University Press, 1985)
Sedgwick, E. K. *The Epistemology of the Closet* (Berkeley: University of California Press, 1990)
Sennett, R. *The Fall of Public Man* (New York: Alfred A. Knopf, 1977)
Service, A. *London 1900* (St Albans and London: Granada, 1979)
Shapiro, S. 'Marx to the Rescue', *new formations*, 53 (Summer 2004), 77–90
Showalter, E. *Sexual Anarchy: Gender and Culture at the Fin de Siècle* (New York: Viking, 1990)
Silverman, K. *Male Subjectivity at the Margins* (New York: Routledge, 1992)
Sinfield, A. *The Wilde Century: Effeminacy, Oscar Wilde, and the Queer Moment* (New York: Columbia University Press, 1994)

Singer, B. *Melodrama and Modernity: Early Sensational Cinema and its Contexts* (New York: Columbia University Press, 2001)
Soper, K. 'Stephen Heroine', in *Troubled Pleasures: Writings on Politics, Gender and Hedonism* (London: Verso, 1995), 246–268
Stoker, B. *Dracula* [1897] (Oxford University Press, 1983)
Stölzl, C. 'Die Presse', in Hartmut Binder (ed.), *Kafka-Handbuch*, vol. 1 (Stuttgart: Alfred Kröner, 1979)
Stölzl, C. 'Treffpunkte', in Hartmut Binder (ed.), *Kafka-Handbuch*, vol. 1 (Stuttgart: Alfred Kröner, 1979)
Stötzl, C. *Kafkas Böses Böhmen: Zur Sozialgeschichte eines Prager Juden* (Berlin: Ullstein, 1989)
Sussman, H. *Victorian Masculinities: Manhood and Masculine Poetics in Early Victorian Literature and Art* (Cambridge University Press, 1995)
Sutherland, J. Review, W. A. Cohen, *Sex Scandal*, Times Literary Supplement, 3 January 1997
Symons, A. 'La Mélinite: Moulin Rouge', in R. K. R. Thornton and M. Thain, *Poetry of the 1890s* (Harmondsworth: Penguin, 1997), 104–5
Thacker, A. *Moving Through Modernity* (Manchester University Press, 2003)
Thomson, G. H. *A Reader's Guide to Dorothy Richardson's* Piligrimage (Greensboro, NC: ELT Press, 1996)
Thorne, R. 'Places of Refreshment in the Nineteenth-Century City', in A. King (ed.), *Essays in the Social Development of the Built Environment* (London: Routledge, 1980)
Tickner, L. *The Spectacle of Women: Imagery of the Suffrage Campaign 1907–14* (London: Chatto & Windus, 1987)
Tratner, M. *Modernism and Mass Politics: Joyce, Woolf, Eliot, Yeats* (Stanford University Press, 1995)
Trotter, D. *Cooking with Mud: The Idea of Mess in Nineteenth-century Art and Fiction* (Oxford University Press, 2000)
Valente, J. (ed.), *Quare Joyce* (Ann Arbor: University of Michigan Press, 2000)
Vicinus, M. *Independent Women: Work and Community for Single Women, 1850–1920* (London: Virago, 1985)
Walkowitz, J. 'Going Public: Shopping, Street Harassment, and Streetwalking in Late Victorian London', *Representations*, 62 (Spring 1998), 1–30
Walkowitz, J. *Prostitution and Victorian Society: Women, Class and the State* (Cambridge University Press, 1980)
Walkowitz, J. *City of Dreadful Delight: Narratives of Sexual Danger in Late-Victorian London* (London: Virago, 1992)
Watts, C. *Dorothy Richardson* (London: Northcote House, 1995)
Watts, S. 'The Construction of the Artist as a Young Man: Masculinity in Joyce's *A Portrait*', unpublished paper, 1985.
Weightman, G. *Bright Lights, Big City: London Entertained 1830–1950* (London: Collins and Brown, 1992)
Wells, H.G. *Ann Veronica* [1909] (London: Virago, 1980)

Whitehorn, C. 'Days of Nippies and Soda Fountains', *Baking Industries Journal* (March 1978), J. Lyons & Co Archive, London Metropolitan Library, File Acc3527/227.
Wilde, O. *The Picture of Dorian Gray* [1891] (Harmondsworth: Penguin, 1985)
Wilde, O. *Salomé*, in *Wilde: The Complete Plays* (London: Methuen, 1998), 379–414
Williams, R. *Culture and Society* (Harmondsworth: Penguin, 1963)
Williams, R. *Marxism and Literature* (Oxford University Press, 1977)
Williams, R. *The Politics of Modernism: Against the New Conformists*, ed. T. Pinkney (London: Verso, 1989)
Wilson, E. *The Sphinx in the City* (London: Virago, 1991)
Winning, J. *The Pilgrimage of Dorothy Richardson* (London, Madison: University of Wisconsin Press, 2000)
Wolff, J. 'The Invisible Flâneuse: Women and the Literature of Modernity', *Theory Culture and Society*, special issue, 'The Fate of Modernity', 2, 3 (1985), 37–46
Woolf, V. *Night and Day* [1919] (London: Grafton, 1978)
Woolf, V. *Jacob's Room* [1922] (New York: Harcourt, Brace and World, 1950)
Young, A. 'Mapping the Citizen: Characterisation and the City in *The Odd Women*, *In the Year of the Jubilee*, and *Eve's Ransom*'. Second International Gissing Conference, 'Gissing and the City', London, July 2003

Index

Note: 'n.' after a page number indicates the number of a note on that page

ABC *see* Aereated Bread Company (ABC)
Adorno, T. W. 16, 38, 40–1, 141, 148, 149, 162n.20
aereated bread 140, 142, 174n.2
Aereated Bread Company (ABC) 93, 95, 96, 174n.2, 175n.8, 179n.12, 179n.14
  see also teashops
Aldington, Richard 120
Allison, Adrian 71–2
Althusser, Louis 15, 16
Anderson, Mark 36, 37, 146
Anderson, Perry ix
Antheil, George 71
Ardis, Ann 14, 160n.1, 168n.6.
Armstrong, Tim 83, 165n.12, 169n.9, 170n.16
awakening 52, 101, 104, 128, 134, 141, 176n.33

Bailey, Peter 152n.6, 158n.16, 166n.5, 175n.19, 178n.19, 179n.12
Bakhtin, Mikhail 55, 90
Balzac, Honoré de 19, 26, 73
Baudelaire, Charles 9, 28, 29, 30, 31–2, 34, 36, 40–1, 44, 45, 77, 144
Beardsley, Aubrey 22, 145, 169n.9
Beauvoir, Simone de vii, 7, 33

Beckett, Samuel 19
Benjamin, Jessica 6
Benjamin, Walter viii, xi, 4, 9, 10, 13, 14, 15, 18, 28, 31–4, 36, 37, 38, 42, 43, 44, 50–2, 76, 82, 83, 98, 99, 104, 106, 116, 122, 126–7, 128, 134, 138, 148, 177n.7, 183n.21
  The Arcades Project 30, 31, 32, 52, 70, 77, 89, 90, 98, 101
  'Berlin Chronicle' 32–4
Bennett, Arnold 5, 95
Bergson, Henri 77
Berlin 32, 34
Berman, Marshal ix
Bewes, Timothy 152n.13
biopolitics 74–5, 137
Bird, Peter 154n.20, 175n.9
Boa, Elizabeth 36
Bonsack machine *see* cigarettes
Booth, Charles 17
Botting, Fred 61, 160n.18, 168n.2
Bourdieu, Pierre 30
Brecht, Bertolt 38–9
Bürger, Peter 35–6
Buse, Peter 155n.38, 160n.4
Butler, Judith 27, 63, 65, 135, 140, 145, 159n.8, 181n.18

Carey, John ix, 167n.22
Carpenter, Edward 21, 73, 74, 143

Carton, Paul 72
Certeau, Michel de 71
cigarettes 27–9, 61–6, 129, 130, 139, 159n.15, 168n.2, 169n.11
  Bonsack machine 27, 65
Cocteau, Jean 29
Conor, Liz 166n.4
Conrad, Joseph 21, 143
Cook, Matt 155n.34
Cooper, John Xiros x, 154n.27, 172n.2.
Crystal Palace *see* exhibitions
Cubism 99
cultural materialism vii, 4–5, 14

Darwin, Charles 26
Darwinism 59, 118,
Delaunay, Robert 99
Dews, Peter 6
Dickens, Charles 14, 16, 19, 53, 155n.2
Doan, Laura 143, 162n.12
Doolittle, Hilda 120
Douglas, Mary 53, 58
dreaming 18, 52, 89, 90, 101, 103–4, 124–5, 127–8, 129, 130, 133–4, 138

Eagleton, Terry 53
effeminacy 154n.34
Egerton, George (Maria Chavelita Dunne) 22, 23, 25, 61
Eley, Geoff 173n.18
Eliot, T. S. ix, 3, 75, 95, 120–1
Ellmann, Maud 58, 59, 167n.15, 168n.31
embodiment vii, 6–9, 50–3, 135
Erfahrung 9, 13, 31, 52
Erlebnis 9, 13, 31, 50, 77, 155n.38
everyday viii, ix, xi, 3, 9, 49–53, 58, 58, 61, 68–71, 76–9, 97, 104, 125, 127
exhibitions 54, 97–9, 104, 106, 118
  Crystal Palace 106–8

exhibitive space 107, 108, 119, 129
great exhibitions ix, 93, 107, 178n.8
International Health Exhibition, Kensington 114–15
Japan-British Exhibition, White City 129
Newcastle Jubilee Exhibition 97–8, 107, 129

Fabianism x, 73–5, 135
Felski, Rita 4, 70–1, 153n.19
feminism 23–4, 57, 73, 137
feminist criticism vii, 15
Fletcher, Horace 71
Forbes, Angela 102
Franklin, Aretha 145
Fraser, Nancy 134, 173n.18
Freud, Sigmund vii, 9, 26, 124, 165n.13, 167n.15

Gagnier, Regenia 154n.33, 181n.12
Garnett, Edward 169n.8
Geddes, Patrick 56–7, 115, 118
Gideon, Siegfried ix
Gilbert, Jeremy 152n.13
Gilbert, W. S. 112
Gilman, Charlotte Perkins 57, 73, 115
Gissing, George viii, x–xi, 13–20, 21, 177n.5, 7, 24, 38, 43, 53, 54–60, 93, 95, 97, 105–19, 141, 149
  Born in Exile 59, 111–12
  Demos: a Story of English Socialism 19, 43, 108
  Eve's Ransom 112–19, 136
  In the Year of the Jubilee 18, 97, 105, 112, 113
  The Nether World 1–3, 6, 18, 21, 49, 54, 55–6, 58, 81, 89–90, 106, 108
  New Grub Street 58–60, 112, 114
  The Odd Women 58, 113, 169n.12

The Private Papers of Henry Ryecroft 18, 59
Thyrza 55, 58, 60, 116
The Town Traveller 105, 111, 112, 122
Glover, David 105, 153n.11
Gluckstein, Montague 16
Goode, John 15–18, 19, 156n.14
Goodman, Jordan 169n.14
Gramsci, Antonio 15, 17
Grand, Sarah 23, 24, 26
Grosz, Elisabeth 135

Habermas, Jürgen 54, 74, 75, 86, 91–2, 105, 109, 110, 111, 134, 166n.1
Haggard, Rider 21
Halberstam, Judith 20, 80
Hanscombe, Gillian E. 170n.5
Hansen, Miriam 50, 51, 52, 55, 63, 83, 92, 133, 153n.12, 161n.18, 165n.13, 176n.24
Heilmann, Ann 14
Highmore, Ben 176n.22
Hilton, Matthew 159n.11, 169n.14–15
Hirschkop, Ken 89, 90, 153n.16, 155n.38
Hobsbawm, Eric ix
Holden, Philip 179n.14
homosexuality 8, 155n34
homosociality 8, 21
Huysman, Joris-Karl 42
Huyssen, Andreas ix

intersubjectivity vii, 3, 4, 6–8, 10, 19, 45, 86, 104, 109, 114, 118, 127, 129, 130, 139, 153n.16

James, Simon 55, 166n.8.
Jameson, Fredric 15, 16, 18–19, 155n.35, 167n.22
Joyce, James viii, ix, xi, 4, 6, 14, 30, 33, 149

A Portrait of the Artist as a Young Man 29, 30, 40–8
Ulysses 40, 41, 42, 44–5, 50, 52, 80–6, 93, 125–7, 163n.23, 24

Kafka, Franz x, 6, 13, 18–19, 30–1, 35–9, 41, 42, 50, 93
'The Cares of a Family Man' 36
'The Judgement' 18, 31–2, 145–50
'Letter to His Father' 35–7, 49–50, 146–7, 164n.6
The Trial 18, 36, 37–9, 49, 53 125
Der Verschollene (Amerika) 38, 162n.19
Kafka, Hermann 37, 49–50, 146
Kaplan, Cora 153n.11
Klein, Richard 28–9, 159n.15, 168n.2
Kluge, Alexander 91–3, 96, 109, 132, 149
Knights, Ben 161n.20

Lane, Christopher viii, 151n.1
law of the father vii, 7, 43, 148
Lawrence, D. H. 30
Ledger, Sally 14, 23, 24
Lefebvre, Henri 99, 127, 172n.5
lesbian and gay studies vii
lesbian identity 143
lesbian sexuality 159n.8
Lévi-Strauss, Claude 53
Lewis, Wyndham 30, 122
life world 54, 74, 75, 166n.1.
Lukács, Georg 15, 17, 18, 19, 156n.14
Lupton, Deborah 53
Lynch, Kevin 140
Lyons & Co. vii, 93, 96–104, 107, 111, 114, 122, 125, 128
newspaper 132, 180n.1
Salmon and Gluckstein 65, 66, 96, 97
see also teashops
Lyons, Joseph 97

Mansfield, Katherine 95
  'A Dill Pickle' 128–131
  'Pictures' 122–3
Martens, Lydia 109–10
Marx, Karl xi, 89, 90
Marxism 15,107
Maugham, Somerset 3, 5, 95, 121–4
Mennell, Stephen 135, 174n.25
Miles, Rosie 23
Miller, Jane 167n.22
Moi, Toril 7–8, 33
Moore, George 24, 76
Moretti, Franco ix, 140
Morris, William 74
Morrison, Arthur 24, 141
muffins 5, 97, 127–8

Naples viii, 106, 177n.7
Nead, Lynda 100, 101
Negt, Oskar 91–3, 96, 109, 132, 149
New Woman 1–2, 20, 27, 45, 49, 55, 60, 61, 64–6, 76, 80, 121, 131, 133–5, 138
New Woman fiction 13–14, 20, 21–5

Odle, Alan 71, 72
Oedipus complex vii, 6, 9–10
Orientalism 129, 175n.15
Orwell, George 14–15, 156n.11
Owen, Meirion 154n.21

Paris 33, 52, 93, 98, 106, 110, 112, 113, 114, 116, 119, 120
Parsons, Deborah 163n.16, 182n.34
phantasmagoria 89–93, 98, 99,112–13, 125, 129, 175n.15, 175n.15.
  phantasmagoric space 106–8
Plekhanov, Georgi 106–7, 108
Pound, Ezra 5, 75, 95, 120, 127–8, 129, 130
Prague 4–5, 35, 37, 39, 145–6
Proust, Marcel 51, 101, 164n.11
Psychoanalysis vii, 148

queer theory vii, 34, 145

realism 13–18, 23–4, 26, 30, 55, 61, 90, 94, 99, 108, 128, 141, 155n.2
Rhys, Jean 95, 98, 175n.17
Richards, Thomas 104, 178n.8
Richardson, Dorothy viii, x, xi, 3, 14, 20, 21–9, 30, 45, 49, 50, 60, 61–79, 91, 93, 95, 98, 113, 124, 131, 132–44, 149, 181n.20
  Backwater 27– 9, 42, 62, 63, 69, 139–40
  Honeycomb 62–6, 73, 124, 139, 142
  Pointed Roofs 26–7, 29, 138
  Revolving Lights 4, 68–71, 74, 77, 134, 137, 142–4
  The Tunnel 133–8, 140–2
Ruck, Bertha 95, 120, 121

Salmon and Gluckstein *see* Lyons & Co.
Salmon, Julian 100
same-sex desire 8
Sartre, Jean Paul 33, 259n.15, 168n.2
Schnitzler, Arthur 82, 172n.4
Schreiner, Olive 22, 23, 24, 25, 57, 73, 115
Sedgwick, Eve Kosofsky 8, 154n.33
Sennett, Richard 91, 110, 116
Shaw, Bernard 74
Sinclair, Upton 71–2
Sinfield, Alan 154n.34
Social Darwinism 55, 57, 59, 113, 115, 118, 167n.16
Spielraum (room for play) 52, 55, 60, 63, 65, 66, 83–5, 165n.20
Spiers and Pond 93, 112, 114
Stoker, Bram 95
Stölzl, Christoph 148
Stott, Andrew 160n.4
Surrealism 50–1, 52, 159n.16
Symons, Arthur 169n.9

systems-world xi, 54, 74, 125, 137, 166n.1.

Taithe, Bertrand 155n.38
teashops vii, 3–5, 8, 9, 10, 85, 93, 95–144
  ABC teashops vii, 3, 4, 5, 93, 95, 98, 104, 111, 120–4, 125, 133, 134, 138–42, 174n.6, 175n.9
  distribution of 102
  Lyons' teashops vii, 3, 95, 101–4, 120–1, 124, 132, 143, 144, 153n.20, 174n.26, 175n.8, 9, 12, 17, 180n.1
Thomson, Arthur 56–7, 115, 118
Tratner, Michael ix
Trotter, David 54, 55, 167n.20

Vorticism 120

waitresses 3, 5, 97, 112, 121–3, 127–8, 154n.20, 179n.7, 179n.11, 179n.12
'Nippies' 97, 121
Walkowitz, Judith 102, 123, 175n.15
Wallace, Jo-Ann 72–3
Warde, Alan 109–10
Webb, Beatrice 74
Webb, Sidney 74
Wells, H.G. 61, 68–9, 74, 75, 95, 124
Wilde, Oscar 21, 27, 42, 61, 62, 63, 66, 73, 142, 145, 163n.8, 169n.9
Williams, Raymond ix, 4, 6, 14–15, 17, 19, 91–2, 151n.3, 155n.2
Wilson, Elizabeth 100
Woolf, Virginia ix, 3, 5, 95, 96, 121, 123, 179n.7

Zola, Emile 136

EU authorised representative for GPSR:
Easy Access System Europe, Mustamäe tee 50,
10621 Tallinn, Estonia
gpsr.requests@easproject.com